W9-BRI-950

THE
WEDDING CAKE
BOOK

THE WEDDING CAKE BOOK

DEDE WILSON

MACMILLAN · USA

For Harry, for everything

MACMILLAN
A Simon & Schuster Macmillan Company
1633 Broadway
New York, NY 10019-6785

Copyright © 1997 by Dede Wilson

Photography copyright © 1997 by Dennis Gottlieb

All rights reserved. No part of this book may be reproduced or transmitted in any form by any means, electronic or mechanical, including photocopying, recording, or by any information storage and retrieval system, without permission in writing from the Publisher.

MACMILLAN is a registered trademark of Macmillan, Inc.

Food Styling by Elizabeth Duffy
Prop Styling by Randi Barritt

Photography Credits

BELLE MEAD HOT GLASS STUDIO & GALLERY
(Cake stands, cake plates)
884 Route 206
Belle Mead, NJ 08502
(908) 281-0802
Contact: Bob Kuster

CHARMING HOME
(Antique dishes and cake servers)
358 Springfield Avenue
Summit, NJ 07901
(908) 598-1022
Contact: Nikki Mazer Garden

Library of Congress Cataloging-in-Publication Data available on request.

ISBN: 0-02-861234-5

Manufactured in the United States of America

10 9 8 7 6 5 4 3 2

Interior design by Nick Anderson

ACKNOWLEDGMENTS

The cover of this book says that it was written by Dede Wilson, but it certainly was more of a collaborative effort than that. These pages are dedicated to all of those behind this project.

Thanks to Maureen and Eric Lasher, my literary agents. Not only did Maureen pluck me out of relative oblivion, but she planted the seeds for the wedding cake idea and found me a caring publisher. More than that, she guided the creation of my proposal without which this book would not exist. I cannot thank her enough.

My sincere gratitude to Justin Schwartz, my editor at Macmillan, who changed my life forever. I have always wanted to write a cookbook and knew that I could; Justin gave me that chance. I hope he is as happy with this book as I am. It has been a joy working with him. He is attentive and professional, genuine and congenial. All authors should be so lucky; I have an editor who is also a friend.

Liz Duffy is a food stylist extraordinaire. This book is visually as much hers as mine. Her patience, ideas, and hard work were phenomenal. Liz, thank you from the bottom of my heart.

Dennis Gottlieb is a photographer with a vision. His boundless enthusiasm was sustaining and his artist's eye brought my cakes to life. Thom Lang, Dennis' assistant, provided an amazingly calming, steady presence. Thanks to Joyce Sangirardi, whose surprise visits and hours of help at the photo shoot made our lives a little bit easier and to Randi Barritt, who chose such lovely props. I thoroughly enjoyed our visits to the flower market.

Lisa Ekus, who started out as a client, has become a friend, mentor, advisor, and occasional employer. My career has been molded and formed by her vast knowledge and the connections I have made through her. Thank you Lisa, for all that you have shared.

Thanks to Michael Beacom, Amy Gordon, and Jennifer Griffin in the editorial department, Alexandria Greeley, copy editor, Nick Anderson, designer, Iris Jeromnimon, jacket designer, and Tracey Moore, production editor, for taking such care with my baby. I truly felt as though they cared as much about the book as I did.

My heartfelt thanks to Adrienne Welch who came aboard during the final months and gave her editorial expertise and support. Thanks also to Kathleen Hackett for personal and professional advice.

To my dad, Moses Acosta, and my deceased mom, Barbara, for always supporting me in whatever endeavor I chose. They gave me a wonderful culinary foundation without which I would not be where I am today.

Mary McNamara is my culinary doppelganger and one of my best friends. Her palate and cooking skills are formidable and I gain so much from our brainstorming sessions and frequent baking frenzies. I owe her thanks, too, for her recipe testing. Her comments helped clarify these recipes.

Robin Jaffin, who has been with me for virtually my entire culinary career, has supported me emotionally and spiritually throughout. There is no other person I would have gone into business with and our departed bakery is still close to my heart.

Thanks to Liz Cantor, my first baking assistant, and to Sunny Caldwell and Derek Alwes for testing recipes and giving their frank, instructive comments, which helped strengthen the book.

Thanks also to Emily Lea, who believed in me when others didn't and helped bring my bakery to fruition; I will always be grateful. If it were not for

my bakery, this next step of book writing might not have happened.

I am grateful to Nick Seamon, who, in my early career years, gave me a job with freedom to experiment to my heart's desire. A large part of my baking foundation comes from my years with The Black Sheep Deli and Bakery in Amherst, Massachusetts, and I will never forget that.

My culinary zeal and knowledge is constantly being fed by those preceding me and around me. Whether they know it or not, these bakers and cooks have all greatly influenced my work: Maida Heatter, whose illustrative writing style always inspired me and gave me something to strive for. She is my muse. Alice Medrich, with her clean, elegant, European style, is present in much of my work. Rose Levy Beranbaum has lent motivation through her books and personally. Thanks to Susan Purdy; if it were not for her article on wedding cakes, I might never have been able to do this book. Thanks to Flo Braker, for telling me about the Schlesinger library and always being available on the other end of the phone. Carole Walter, whom I only briefly met, took the time to write me a note with her encouragement. Carole Bloom, a newfound peer, whose reference book is a godsend, has always been willing to chat. Thanks to Nick Malgieri, always ready to answer questions with insightful answers. Marcel Desaulniers' books have provided stimulus. Betty Rosbottom, new neighbor and friend, has influenced me with her prolific ideas and warm teaching style. Also thanks to all the friends I have met through the International Association of Cooking Professionals (IACP). This organization has provided me with numerous contacts and myriad opportunities.

I am thrilled to have found Laura Baddish, *publicist par excellence*. Her enthusiasm, energy, and forward thinking are marvels to behold. A nod to Nach Waxman of Kitchen Arts and Letters, who told me to think about how I use cookbooks and then to write from that perspective.

Harry, my husband, lent invaluable computer expertise and has been there to calm me down when nothing else would (and even make me laugh) . . . even though he kept wishing I were testing steaks and pork chops instead of sweet things. He also diligently supported our entire family financially while I was getting myself up on my feet. Thank you, schmoopie.

Ravenna, my daughter, is a budding chef who currently works as my *sous chef* quite happily. Thank you for brewing me endless pots of tea during the writing of this book.

To Freeman, one of my cherished twins, who lustily eats anything I make him. That willingness to experiment is a quality that I truly admire.

And to Forrester, his dimpled brother, who loves helping in the kitchen and is a chocoholic supreme (those genes come from me). No one looks better draped in ganache.

CONTENTS

Introduction xi

1. Getting Started 1

2. How to Create a Wedding Cake 9

3. The Cakes 17

4. Cake Accompaniments 125

5. The Basics 129

6. Finishing Touches 151

7. Equipment 177

Resources 185

Bibliography 191

Index 193

INTRODUCTION

As long as there are weddings, there will be a need for wedding cakes. The wedding cake is a symbolic centerpiece at most weddings and its importance does not seem to diminish with time. Some bridal couples may choose to throw the bouquet while others may refrain; some will perform the first dance; others will eschew music and dancing altogether. But virtually all of them will want a cake to commemorate their marriage, joy, and love. Whether it is a young couple in their twenties, a same-sex couple establishing their union, or two eighty-year-old grandparents who are finding love for the second time, they all want to celebrate their joining with an important moment, which often culminates with the cutting of the wedding cake and a frosting-rich kiss.

I am a firm believer that wedding cakes need not always be a white cake with a vanilla buttercream frosting. Quite the contrary, cakes should reflect the tastes, beliefs, and desires of the bridal couple. Back when I started baking, I didn't have such formed ideas about wedding cakes and what they should be. But obviously, the seeds were planted because the first wedding cake I ever made was just such a reflection of the couple. It was June 15, 1985, and I was involved in the organization of a wedding for a local veterinarian and his assistant, the bride-to-be. Both of these people obviously loved animals, and it was mentioned to me that they had a particular fondness for chocolate and for sheep. The result was a four-tier basket-weave cake with a chocolate-almond interior. On the top of the uppermost tier, I laid an expanse of green marzipan to represent a pasture, and on top of the "grass" were bride-and-groom marzipan sheep. The groom came complete with a black marzipan top hat and bow tie, and the bride was resplendent with a pink marzipan bow in her tail and a wisp of veil upon her head. The cake was such a personal, intimate statement that it really made an impact on the guests and the bridal couple alike. I believe the cake can be as personalized as a bride's dress or a groom's choice of best man.

I also strongly believe that a cake is a cake first and foremost, and it is meant to be eaten. It is initially taken in with the eyes and should therefore be aesthetically pleasing to the viewer, but it is ultimately meant to be savored. Hence, you will not find cakes in this book that only concentrate on the outer decoration, leaving behind the very important interior and how it will taste. I do consider my cakes works of art, but they are edible, transitory art, meant to be eaten and enjoyed, to provide second helpings when requested and to fulfill the visual, tactile, and gustatory desires of the wedding party.

With these thoughts in mind, neither do I want the reader of this book to be afraid or confused about how to create these cakes. This book is meant to be used as a springboard to your own style. Of course, making one of the recipes verbatim is fine if at first you do not feel comfortable using your own imagination. But the recipes are presented in such a fashion to get you thinking on your own, creating that perfect cake for your own personal needs and occasions. If you can bake a single-layer cake and frost it, then with some time and practice, you can create the cakes in this book.

HOW TO USE THIS BOOK

If you are a seasoned pro, then by all means turn right to the recipes and start baking. However, I suggest everyone read the Getting Started chapter at least once because it tells you what to do. I review certain techniques and professional tips that will ensure the best results. The chapter entitled How to Create a Wedding Cake details the process I follow from brainstorming a concept to delivering and serving a cake. This chapter tells you how to implement your knowledge.

The Cakes chapter is the first one to present actual recipes with the individual cakes designed for this book. Each cake is labeled "Easier," "Moderate," or "Complex," denoting the level of expertise needed. Feel free to make them as is, or alter them to suit your taste. If you decide to follow the recipe word for word, be sure to read it in its entirety before starting to bake. The various components within each recipe are listed in the order of use.

Then comes Cake Accompaniments, which includes recipes for sauces, fillings, and whipped cream additions; the little extras that make the cakes a total culinary experience.

The Basics chapter that follows contains "building blocks" used throughout the book. These are the recipes you will need when creating your own cakes.

Finishing Touches tells you how to sculpt chocolate flowers and marzipan fruit, how to make gilded decorations, and how to apply buttercream. This chapter gives directions for cake assembly and, finally, instructions on how to cut the cake to serve your guests.

The Equipment chapter lists basics as well as unusual items. Here you will find important information on mixers, icing spatulas, cardboard rounds, and much more.

The Resources section lists businesses and a brief inventory of what each carries. One of my pet peeves is referring to resource lists in cookbooks and having to make many expensive long distance calls to find out which of the companies carries the item I am looking for. I have tried to take the guessing out of this game.

·I·

GETTING STARTED

Components

Although each complete cake in this book is presented as a total package, with cake, filling, exterior buttercream, and general design orchestrated to work together, by all means, pick and choose! If you see a cake you like, feel free to combine it with the filling of another. Use your judgment about whether the new combination is appealing to the palate and to the eye.

To help you develop your own combinations, I will share some tips about how I create wedding cakes for my clients. First, I usually choose a basic cake, based on the flavor the customer likes, such as chocolate, vanilla, or lemon. Then, I play around with different filling ideas and exterior buttercream flavors. When I have chosen all of the flavors and textures, these usually suggest an appropriate decoration. For instance, a chocolate cake might be decorated with chocolate curls or chocolate cake crumbs; an almond génoise might be decorated with toasted, caramelized almonds. Occasionally, I start with a decorative idea first and work backwards. Since flavor is the most important aspect of the cake, I approach my cakes from a pastry chef's, not a cake decorator's, point of view.

Many of the components can be made ahead and frozen, which is important to note. For cake assembly, I remind you to have all components ready, including thawing and readying any frozen components. Buttercream, for instance, should be defrosted, warmed, and whipped to proper consistency before you start assembling the cake.

Cake Layers and Cake Tiers

To clarify the directions in the recipes themselves, you must understand the difference between what makes up a cake tier and a cake layer; they are not the same. Most of the cakes use two thinner two-inch cake pans, which yield two cake layers (sandwiched with filling) to make up one, thick cake tier. Some of the cakes, most notably the truffle cakes, the cheesecakes, and the coffee cake, are baked as one thick tier in a deep three-inch pan and are not split or filled before decorating. Therefore, my definition of a cake layer is a layer of cake, which with other cake layers and filling, makes up a whole tier of cake. A tier is the completed unit of cake, sometimes filled, sometimes not, ready for decoration.

Serving Sizes: Scaling Up and Scaling Down

Most of the recipes in this book are meant to serve 65 to 100 guests. Others are scaled to serve more or fewer people. If you are absolutely enamored with the White Chocolate Satin Apricot Cake with White Chocolate Flowers and Grapes (page 121), but are serving a different number of people, then follow a few simple steps to adapt that particular recipe to your specifications.

If you need more cake, just make an extra-large tier (for the largest size given in the recipe) and have the caterer or banquet manager cut it up behind the scenes. This way it doesn't have to upset the balance of the tiers. If you need less cake, eliminate one of the tiers, if the remaining sizes create a shape that pleases you. However, if you need to totally refigure a cake, you will need to understand pan volumes and how many servings each pan yields. With all of this information, you can determine approximately how many times a recipe for a 10×2-inch pan needs to be multiplied to fill a 12×2-inch one and it will tell you how many the new expanded or concentrated version will serve. Please refer to the charts below.

Sometimes the amounts needed will not mesh exactly with the increase or decrease of the recipe yields. Always select the larger amount. If there is batter leftover, pour into muffin tins or other baking pans. Most of the cakes can be frozen, but most likely, you'll just want to eat the extras as snacks. Serving sizes are approximate. If you are also having a dessert buffet, you may not need as much cake. If the cake is the only dessert, you may want a slightly larger cake.

Serving Size Chart

Traditionally, wedding cake serving sizes are small, because the cake is the showpiece and is no longer considered dessert. But I do consider my cakes as dessert; they are good enough to eat. That is the point of this book. Therefore, I figure on larger pieces per person, which means each tier serves fewer than a catering book or other baking book might tell you. I also assume that you will be eating the top layer. The tradition of saving this layer and freezing it for the first anniversary is quaint, but hardly delicious. If a couple likes the idea, I suggest making them a small cake for their anniversary identical to the one they are ordering. Fresh cake is always better.

If you are planning to use the cake as the primary dessert, possibly with fresh fruit as an accompaniment, then use this chart literally. If the cake is part of a dessert buffet, or follows an extravagant feast, then each tier can be cut into more and smaller pieces. These serving sizes are based on tiers that measure between three and four inches high. This chart is for round tiers only, which are the predominant shapes used in the book. See the cake cutting diagrams on page 176.

SERVING SIZE CHART

Round Tier	Number of Servings
4"	Serves 4
5"	Serves 6
6"	Serves 8–10
7"	Serves 10–12
8"	Serves 12–16
9"	Serves 16–22
10"	Serves 23–34
12"	Serves 36–48
14"	Serves 47–66

Popular Tier Combinations

6", 9", 12"	Serves 60–80
6", 10", 14"	Serves 78–110
8", 12"	Serves 48–64
6", 8", 12", 14"	Serves 103–140
6", 10", 12", 14"	Serves 114–158

CAKE PAN VOLUME CHART

Pan Size	Volume
Round	
5" × 2"	2⅔ cups
5" × 3"	3½ cups
6" × 2"	3¾ cups
6" × 3"	5 cups
7" × 2"	5¼ cups
7" × 3"	8 cups
8" × 2"	7 cups
8" × 3"	9 cups
9" × 2"	8⅔ cups
9" × 3"	14 cups
10" × 2"	10⅔ cups
10" × 3"	14 cups
12" ×2"	15½ cups
12" × 3"	22 cups
14" × 2"	21 cups
14" × 3"	28 cups
Rectangular	
10½" × 15½" × 1"	10 cups
12½" × 17½" × 1"	12 cups
11" × 7" × 2"	8 cups
13" × 9" × 2"	15 cups
Square	
8" × 8" × 2"	8 cups
9" × 9" × 2"	10 cups
10" × 10" × 2"	12 cups
12" × 12" × 2"	16 cups
14" × 14" × 2"	24 cups

Measuring Ingredients

Baking and producing a beautiful finished cake is really what this book is about. Baking the cake components well means your buttercreams will go on more smoothly and the final texture, taste, and overall experience will be as optimal as it can be. To accomplish this, your ingredients must be precisely measured and the cakes baked following particular procedures.

Dry ingredients should be measured with the properly calibrated cups. Metal or plastic cups that you fill to the rim are exact. I store my dry ingredients, such as flour and sugar, in airtight containers. I stir flours before using to aerate them, especially the cake flour, which tends to clump. Then I use the "dip and sweep" method, which is just what it sounds like. I dip the correctly sized measuring cup into the container and then, using the blunt edge of a knife or an icing spatula, I sweep the excess off the top, back into the container. If you shake or tap the measuring cup, the dry ingredient will settle, becoming denser and heavier, and therefore skew your results. I also dip my measuring spoons into containers of baking powder and baking soda and "dip and sweep." Because baking soda often clumps, sift your soda occasionally to prevent this; measuring out little hard balls of leavener is not accurate. I reserve one bowl on my work space for my sifted ingredients. My sifter lives in this bowl and when I need sifted ingredients, I sift them into the bowl. This keeps my surface clean. A good alternative is to sift your dry ingredients onto a large piece of parchment paper. Then you can just pick up the parchment and use it to help funnel the ingredients into your mixer.

Liquids such as honey, oil, liqueurs, water, or lemon juice should be measured in liquid measuring cups. The commonplace Pyrex cups with volume amounts marked on the side and with spouts for pouring are meant for this purpose. Place your measuring cup on a level surface and pour your ingredient up to the mark indicating the amount you need. When measuring sticky ingredients, like honey or corn syrup, lightly spray the interior of your measuring cup with cooking spray; this lets the full amount of honey slide out without leaving a residue sticking to the bottom of the measuring cup.

Ingredients such as butter and chocolate are easier to weigh than measure by volume so I have given weights for these as well as certain other ingredients. Therefore, you will need a scale to make these recipes. I have a small one that weighs in ounces up to one pound and I have another that weighs up to 25 pounds. Most professional pastry chefs weigh everything—dry goods, liquids, dried fruit, fats, and so on. However, I am addressing the needs of all bakers, so I have adopted this blend of approaches. When practical, I have included a volume measurement with the weight. (See page 181 for more information.)

Pan Preparation

Pan preparation is important. A cake that releases easily from its pan will have beautiful sides with all of its crust's integrity intact. I use a vegetable oil–based cooking spray, such as PAM™, most often. I lightly spray the sides and bottom of the pan (it must be free of dents), cut out a parchment piece to fit the bottom of the pan, insert it, and lightly spray the top of the parchment. This does the trick for most cakes. Where I mention "prepare pans with cooking spray and parchment paper," I am referring to this procedure. Check individual recipes for any special pan treatments—for instance, sponge cake pans are ungreased.

Clarified Unsalted Butter

For some recipes, there is no substitute for clarified butter, which you can make yourself. Start with more of solid butter—25 percent is a good average—than the amount of clarified butter you need, because the butter volume reduces during the process. Melt the butter slowly in a saucepan without stirring. A scum may appear on the surface as it melts; simply remove the scum by skimming it off with a spoon. Be careful not to stir the mixture.

When the butter appears clear, look carefully; the milk solids, which are white, will be clumped on the bottom of the pan. Remove from the heat and gently pour off the clarified butter, leaving the milk solid residue in the bottom of the pan. You may find it easier to skim the clarified butter off the top using a ladle. Discard the solids. Store the clarified butter in a covered container in the refrigerator, where it will keep for months. Heat gently to restore fluidity.

Baking Techniques, Times, and Oven Temperature

After you have measured and weighed your ingredients carefully, and prepped your pans, it is time to pop your cakes in your preheated oven. Ovens have different capacities. If you have a larger oven, you may be able to place two racks in the oven at once, creating a top and bottom level. These recipes were tested on the middle rack of an oven. If you choose to bake on two levels at once to save time, know that the heat will not be the same on both racks. You may have to shift the lower cake to the upper rack and *vice versa* half way through the baking time.

I do not suggest this, for several reasons. First of all, some cakes are very sensitive and will deflate when jostled. Also the more often and longer you leave the oven door open, the more heat you will lose; this will affect the way the oven performs. Some cakes, such as the cheesecakes, bake in a water bath. Moving large pans of hot water around is difficult and can too easily result in burns. I prefer to bake on one middle rack, shifting the cakes gently front to back once during baking to encourage even baking. Sliding them along the same rack to the other side is not as drastic a movement as taking them out and moving them vertically. With careful attention you can usually accomplish this same-rack shifting without affecting the batter. If you must use multiple racks at once, be aware that the cakes may bake at different times than stated. For almost all of the cakes in this book, I used Magi-Cake Strips, a wonderful invention that helps your cakes bake evenly and stay level. See the Equipment chapter for a detailed description.

Baking times are approximate. Invest in a high-quality oven thermometer and test your oven temperature. The recipe may call for a 350°F oven, but when you set your oven to 350°, it may be as much as 50° off. A 25° variance is quite common in home ovens. Simply adjust your dial up or down to compensate and use the thermometer to check your adjustments frequently. I leave mine in my oven at all times.

Assuming your oven is set correctly, the times I have given you will be very nearly, if not exactly, correct. But remember, time is only one way of assessing doneness. In all cases, I have given you visual clues as well. Most of the cakes will be done when they "test clean." To do this, stick a toothpick into the center of the cake, all the way to the bottom of the pan, and remove. Look closely at the toothpick. No wet batter or overly moist crumbs should cling to it. I do not like to use the metal picks sold as cake testers because I find that they come out clean even when the cake is still underdone. For another clue, look at the cake's edges. They will usually be slightly more golden than the center of the cake and the sides will just be starting to pull away from the sides of the pan. Another technique that combines visual and tactile assessment is to press the center of the cake very lightly. Your finger will make a slight depression that should spring back up when you remove your finger. If you use all the available clues, you should have no problem being able to tell when a cake is done.

There are exceptions. The truffle cakes are unique and cheesecakes demand their own treatment. Tips for these cakes will be given in the individual recipes.

Cooling, Wrapping, and Storing Components

It may seem obvious that you need to cool a cake after it is baked, but how you cool it will affect the final result, especially its texture. When you take a cake out of the oven, the cake pan still contains plenty of heat. By placing the pan on a rack, the heat can disperse quickly and evenly from both the pan and the cake.

After the cake has cooled in the pan on a rack for about 10 minutes, turn the cake out onto the rack to continue the cooling process. Some cakes, like the cheesecakes and truffle cakes, need different handling. Check individual recipes for specific information. Generally, to remove the cakes from the pans, run an icing spatula around the perimeter of the cake, always pressing out toward the pan, not in toward the cake. You do not want to shave off any of the cake's beautifully straight sides. Then turn the pan over, holding it over the rack; the cake should come right out. If the parchment has stuck to the cake, peel it off to let all steam escape from the cake.

When the cake has completely cooled, it may be filled and frosted, or it should be wrapped thoroughly. First, take a cardboard round that is the same size as the cake and place it underneath the cake. Wrap the cake with plastic wrap, making sure to cover all surfaces. This will probably take two layers unless you have extra-wide commercial wrap. Then, wrap the cake in foil, covering and sealing all sections. You want to create as airtight a package as possible.

Most of the cake components in this book can be made one month ahead and frozen, but do not freeze for more than one month. Even if you are making the cakes one week ahead, store in the freezer, not the refrigerator. The freezer will actually keep the cakes moister. The only times I refrigerate cakes are when they are a refrigerator type cake, like a cheesecake, or after the cake has been assembled, when it will be chilled overnight. The buttercream or glaze traps in the moisture so the cakes will not dry out. If you are going to freeze your layers, give the smaller tiers an extra protective layer by slipping them into a resealable plastic bag with the air squeezed out. For the largest tiers, which won't fit in bags, simply double wrap in plastic and then double wrap in foil. Some of the cakes freeze better than others and that information is given with the individual recipes. If the cakes will be sitting only overnight before filling and decorating, they may remain at room temperature.

Italian Meringue Buttercream can be frozen. I place it in airtight plastic containers with little airspace and freeze up to four months, but I usually use them within a month. They will store in the refrigerator for a week. They can pick up off flavors from the refrigerator so make sure to seal the tops well.

Look in the headnotes of individual recipes for storage information on other specific components.

Melting Chocolate

Much of the chocolate in these recipes is melted, which you can do in several ways. First, always start with finely chopped chocolate. The classic way to melt chocolate is to place the chopped chocolate in the top of a double boiler (*bain-marie*), or in a heat-proof bowl that fits over a pot. Add water to the bottom of the double boiler but don't let the water touch the bottom of the chocolate bowl. Bring the water to a simmer and stir the chocolate occasionally until it is almost completely melted. Turn the heat off and continue to stir. The residual heat will melt the remaining chocolate.

Another way to melt chocolate, and the one I employ most often for dark chocolates, is with the microwave. To do this successfully, you must be familiar with your particular microwave oven. They come in various wattages, which affects how quickly they work; the higher the wattage, the higher the heat, so to speak. I do not like to melt milk or white chocolates in the microwave because you do not have the same degree of control over the heat source as you do on top of the stove. You also loose the ability to keep a constant eye on the melting procedure, which I find crucial with these more persnickety chocolates.

For dark chocolate, chop it finely, place it in a Pyrex bowl, and set the microwave oven at about one-third power (30 percent). For one pound of chocolate, heat the chocolate, uncovered, for 3 to 5 minutes, checking and stirring at each interval until the bulk of the chocolate is melted. Then remove from the microwave and continue to stir, using the residual heat to complete the melting process.

Make sure you stop and check your chocolate frequently with a rubber spatula. The chocolate may look like it is still in solid pieces, but the center melts first and you need to gently stir the chocolate to encourage even melting.

Whichever method you use for melting chocolate, note that bittersweet and semisweet chocolates should not be heated above 120°F; milk and white chocolates, not above 110° to 115°F.

Using a Pastry Bag

You will need to use a pastry bag for every cake in this book and I assume that you are familiar with its use. I use the polyester Featherweight Decorating Bags by Wilton, most often in the 14-inch and 16-inch sizes. When a bag is new, its opening is small. Cut it to allow the insertion of a coupler.

Never overfill a bag during use. Your hands will warm the contents, so limit the time you work with buttercream. Fill the bag about ⅓ full with the desired filling, twist the top closed, and proceed as directed in individual recipes.

A good way to familiarize yourself with various tips is to make a batch of buttercream, set out a piece of parchment paper, and practice making patterns on the paper. You will find that by holding many tips in one direction, then another, you will be able to make various shapes. Often just a quarter turn of the tip angle will produce a totally new look. You can refer to a cake decorating book for specific information, but do not be afraid to just jump in and experiment. Discard the practice parchment paper when you are through.

Learn from my experience. For years, I kept my bags in a drawer that also contained loose tips and other potentially sharp objects. When I used my bags, I often had little holes in them that allowed buttercream to seep out the sides, making a mess. I realized that the bags became pierced during storage. Store yours safely away from anything that could puncture the surface.

Making a Parchment Cone

Parchment cones are easy to make and come in handy when you do not want to wash out a pastry

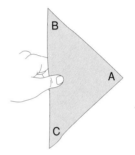

Step 1

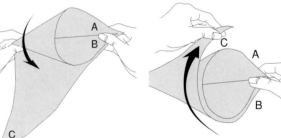

Step 2   *Step 3*

Shell

Reverse Shell

Bead

Rope

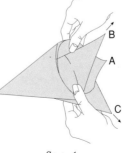

Step 4

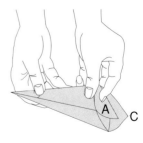

Step 5

bag or don't have one handy. I always use a parchment cone, for example, when decorating with melted chocolate.

Start with a triangle cut from parchment paper. You should have two equal shorter sides and one longer side (see diagrams). The center of the long edge will form the point of the cone. Holding the triangle in front of you, with the long side facing left, place your left thumb and index finger on the center point of the long side. Take the top corner and fold it down curling it under itself, pulling it towards the right, until the tip meets up with the point opposite the long side. Take the last extended corner from the bottom and wrap it around the entire outside of the cone so that it meets up with the first two tips. Jiggle back and forth so that the fit is perfect and the point is tight. Fold the section with the three corners in towards the center of the cone. The cone is ready to fill.

Never overfill the cone. Fill it up about halfway, then fold the open edge over itself several times to make a seal. Snip off the point with sharp scissors. For most chocolate work you need only a tiny opening; make a larger opening prior to filling to use with tips. Discard the cone when you are finished.

Buttercream, Syrup, and Filling Amounts

I hope you will be using this book to come up with your own combinations of cakes, fillings, and buttercreams. This chart is designed to aid the design process by listing fairly accurate amounts of filling, syrup, and buttercream components. I say "fairly accurate" because these amounts will work, but you may perhaps like a thicker layer of filling, which means you would need more of it, or less syrup, which means you would need a smaller amount. If you want the filling, buttercream, and decorative buttercream to be the same component, just add those figures together for the total amount of buttercream you will need.

FOR A CAKE CONSISTING OF:

8-inch and 12-inch tiers
3 to 5 cups syrup
2 to 4 cups filling
10 to 12 cups buttercream for crumb coat and final coat
4 to 6 cups buttercream for decoration

6-, 9-, and 12-inch tiers
4 to 6 cups syrup
3 to 5 cups filling
12 to 14 cups buttercream for crumb coat and final coat
5 to 7 cups buttercream for decoration

6-, 10-, and 14-inch tiers
6 to 8 cups syrup
4 to 6 cups filling
13 to 15 cups buttercream for crumb coat and final coat
6 to 8 cups buttercream for decoration

6-, 8-, 12-, and 14-inch tiers
7 to 9 cups syrup
5 to 7 cups filling
14 to 16 cups buttercream for crumb coat and final coat
7 to 9 cups buttercream for decoration

· 2 ·

HOW TO CREATE
A WEDDING CAKE

THE SIX PLANNING STAGES

I divide the creation and implementation of making a wedding cake into six basic categories:

Stage One is the Initial Planning Stage. You determine the date, budget, number of guests, level of formality for the reception, flavor preferences, existence of any food allergies, and any important associated information. Of course, all of this information applies to cakes intended for birthdays, anniversaries, or showers as well.

Stage Two is the Creative Process. Admittedly one of the most fun parts, this is when you take the basic information from the first stage and start applying it to the development of an actual cake. At this point, if you are unfamiliar with any of the recipes or procedures, I suggest that you make one small tier, using all of the components you have decided on. You can do this as far ahead as possible to help you understand what is demanded of you for the larger, final cake. If you do this close to someone's birthday, you can use the cake for that celebration.

Stage Three involves preparing the Time Schedule and Ingredient and Equipment List. Your ingredient and equipment list will be made from your final decisions involving Stages One and Two. The time schedule will detail which components can be made ahead, which must be done at the last minute, and in what order you should accomplish each task.

Stage Four is the actual Baking and Decorating. This stage is the heart of the entire preparation process and the one where your individual skills and creative eye will come into play.

Stage Five is Storage and Transportation. In all likelihood the cake will need 24 hour's storage, and you must make arrangements for this. Transportation is no small matter either, because you will need proper containers to safely transport the cake from one location to another.

Stage Six is Serving the wedding cake.

Stage One

THE INITIAL PLANNING STAGE

The Initial Planning Stage is necessary for obtaining important information from the bridal couple.

Consider the following questions, even if you are designing the cake for yourself:

WHAT DATE IS THE EVENT? From this information, you will know the season as well as the day of the week, and the latter is very important for logistical planning. For instance, if you are delivering a cake late on a Sunday, make sure that you have prepared for any last-minute needs, since stores may be closed early in the day. Or, if the wedding is on Sunday morning, you have to take into consideration that there might be church traffic near your delivery site.

HOW MANY GUESTS? During the planning stage, only an approximate number is needed—for instance, 100 to 125 guests. Be sure to include musicians, photographers, and clergy, as they will want cake as well. The final count should be provided two weeks prior to the event to give you needed time to order special ingredients. Ask the couple if they plan to save the top tier. Although I discourage this, since eating one-year-old cake is no way to celebrate an anniversary, many couples want to, for tradition's sake. If they do, you will need to discount the top tier from your size calculations and have a larger cake. (See Size Chart in the Getting Started chapter, page 3.)

WHAT IS THE TIME OF THE RECEPTION? The time is important to know for delivery purposes and will lead to other questions. For instance, if the party runs from 2:00 P.M. to 5:00 P.M., does that mean a late lunch? Perhaps not. It may be a champagne-and-dessert reception, in which case you'll need more cake. Is the reception from 5:00 P.M. to 10:00 P.M.? This may mean a very long hors d'oeuvres reception, followed by a formal dinner, including a dessert buffet. All of these things affect your cake design.

HOW FORMAL WILL THE RECEPTION BE? If the party is a relaxed, outdoor country wedding, taking place midday, then the cake might reflect the overall relaxed mood. If it is a formal evening affair, something altogether different will be in order.

WHAT IS THE BUDGET? Knowing how formal the reception will be might give you some insight. Generally, a formal affair is usually more expensive and the cake budget will be correspondingly larger. Some couples may have not thought about this because the caterer's budget included a cake. But if the couple has decided to get something custom-made, they may not have discussed cake costs. Likewise, if you are making the cake for yourself or a friend, then it is important for you to determine how much money you can and want to spend. Remember, your food costs will be much lower than if you had purchased a cake, so maybe you will be able to afford a cake covered in roses. This would have been prohibitively expensive otherwise.

WHICH FLAVORS DO THE COUPLE PREFER AND DO THEY HAVE ANY FOOD ALLERGIES? Some couples will come to you with fairly well-formed ideas about what they want. For example, they may have always dreamed about having a chocolate cake, or they may think that Mother's spiced pound cake is the only

option. More likely, they will ask for suggestions. Ask them about what other food is being served; this may help you guide them. For example, if the food has a completely Mexican theme, then a cake made with Mexican chocolate would be appropriate. Or if the food is very rich, a lighter cake with an airy filling might be in order. Alcohol is a separate and sensitive issue. I often add liqueurs to my cakes, but this will not be appropriate for couples who do not drink. Be sensitive about this topic, and comply with any requests.

You may not have thought about food allergies, but they do exist, and obviously if the groom is allergic to chocolate and you are informed of this early on, you can save time and skip over those chocolate suggestions entirely. When asking about allergies—for example, to chocolate, nuts, or citrus—remember that the average wedding reception has 120 guests and you cannot possibly satisfy everyone's taste preferences or needs. But I do think it is important for the bride and groom to feel as though they have what they want personally. It is their day.

Some couples will not be able to decide and may ask for several flavors within one cake. This can work if you combine them judiciously. For instance, a layer of chocolate cake alternated with a layer of orange pound cake flow nicely when tied together with a vanilla, or even a mocha, frosting. This combination works because each of the three flavors works together in any combination. But three different cake flavors are too many. It is difficult to find so many flavors that will work harmoniously, especially when adding a possible fourth flavor in the buttercream. Also guests will see the different flavors and will want to try a bit of each, and figuring out your size calculations in this situation is a nightmare. Even with two flavors, you will probably need more cake because of such a problem. You should always avoid certain combinations, such as a layer of a delicate vanilla génoise with a filling of orange curd and a layer of chocolate mint. The mint would overpower the vanilla and orange, and you will not have created a balance. Let your palate and knowledge of flavors be your guide.

Stage Two

THE CREATIVE PROCESS

Many people ask me how I come up with ideas about how a cake will look. Believe it or not, I do most of the creative process in bed, right before I go to sleep. I like to close my eyes, and in a relaxed state, I daydream about what the cake might look like. In this way, I take the basics determined during the Initial Planning Stage—such as cake and buttercream flavors and the level of formality—and then I let my imagination soar. I envision dark red roses on the cake with a small ring of caramelized almonds around the base; then I imagine removing the roses and substituting another flower, mentally playing with the colors and patterns. But inspiration can come from anywhere, and you should be receptive to things around you. Maybe the bride has a favorite piece of jewelry that might inspire a design, or you may wish to copy the pattern of the lace curtains in your dining room. Think about how you respond to beautiful objects in your environment, and don't be afraid to gather ideas from anywhere. The colors in a sweater or the shades of a sunset can all provide fodder for the wedding cake designer.

This is also the stage during which you should consider the season, location, and time of the reception. Most weddings take place during the warm summer months, but other seasons can provide a starting point for the design. For instance, a decadent Chocolate Raspberry Truffle Cake would be great for a New Year's Eve wedding. A White Chocolate Satin Apricot Cake with White Chocolate Flowers and Grapes will echo springtime if served then. Or Poppyseed Cake with Orange Marmalade Filling and Grand Marnier Buttercream is perfect for supporting a bounty of summer fruits, and a Pumpkin Cake with Crystallized Ginger, Walnuts, and Dried Cranberries is ideal to help celebrate a fall wedding. The autumnal colors of burnt orange and deep red with the brown tones of the nuts inside the cake invoke the flavors and hues of this colorful season. Take the design one step further; use caramelized walnuts on the exterior, too. Or create leaves out of marzipan or chocolate and scatter them over the cake.

Play around with ideas. It may help you to sketch as you go along. The couple may have requested pillars, or a stacked cake, but perhaps they have left this up to you or are looking for your suggestions. Several sketches, each showing a different configuration, will help them.

Once you know which components your cake requires, bake a small 6-inch tier, using all of the necessary ingredients and procedures. Do this weeks or, preferably, months ahead, so that you can fine-tune any aspects of the design. If one or two of the steps are difficult for you, this preplanning allows you to practice. You will also get to actually taste the cake this way and determine if it is what you had in mind for the occasion.

Stage Three

TIME SCHEDULE AND INGREDIENT AND EQUIPMENT LIST

A Time Schedule is very important because it lets you see, at a glance, which steps need to be done when and in which order. You will have already decided which recipes, which pans, and which special equipment you need, and all of this belongs on your list. Below is a sample of the Time Schedule and Ingredient and Equipment List. Your knowledge of cake size and type will help you determine the amount of food. You must determine your time schedule from working backwards from the desired serving time and this affects all your decisions. For instance, if the couple plans to serve the cake at 3:30 P.M., then you must get the cake to the premises by 2:30 P.M. at the latest to allow time for set-up. This means that you must leave your storage site by 2:00 P.M., and that is how you must work backwards.

CAKE: *Three-tier chocolate almond cake, mocha filling, chocolate ganache, caramelized almonds outside, crystallized lavender roses and lemon balm leaves with gold pillars*

TWO WEEKS BEFORE: Order or buy chocolate, almonds, flour, and whatever nonperishable ingredients you do not have. Buy plastic separator plates, pillars, and spray-paint gold. Research where to purchase unsprayed lavender roses and order them.

ONE WEEK BEFORE: Spray-paint plates and pillars. Toast and caramelize almonds; store in an airtight container.

FOUR DAYS BEFORE: Make buttercream and ganache. Grind almonds for cake. Measure out dry ingredients for cake.

TWO DAYS BEFORE: Bake cake layers.

ONE DAY BEFORE: Decorate cake. Crystallize roses.

DAY OF EVENT: Transport cake. Assemble on site.

Stage Four
BAKING AND DECORATING

By this time, you should be so organized that the actual baking should proceed without glitches. If you have never made the recipe before, make one small tier first, several weeks in advance, so that you will be familiar with all the procedures outlined. Allow yourself time to do the job well. Lay out your ingredients and check them off as you proceed. I have baked cakes forgetting the sugar, and believe me, there is nothing quite as frustrating as having to go back to the beginning. Concentrate on the task at hand and all will go well.

As scientific and accurate as baking a cake is, the decoration process involves creativity. You should adhere to certain tried-and-true methods to make your job easier, but this is also where your individual style comes through. Refer to the chapter on Finishing Touches for ideas. As far as creativity is concerned, I believe that each cake has its own personality and it begins to come through during the decorating process. For example, you may see a picture of a cake with a beautiful matte white buttercream and with perfect full-blown red roses cascading down the side, and want to re-create it. When you start decorating, you notice that the buttercream is not matte, but has a satin sheen, and that the roses that were available to you were mostly tight buds and a different shade of red than those in the photograph. Your first inclination might be to panic, but don't. Look at the creative possibilities that are presented. The cake can become your own. You may find that the sheen of the cake contrasts even more beautifully with the velvet quality of the roses, and that the textures and shapes of the closed and half-closed roses are more interesting. The key is to work with what you have and to not be afraid of experimenting. Maybe you thought that three roses would look good on top, but when it actually comes time to arrange them on the cake, four roses seem more aesthetically appropriate. The personality of the cake will start to come through, and by working with it, as opposed to only wanting to adhere to a preconceived notion, the results will be better.

Stage Five
STORAGE AND TRANSPORTATION

Most of the cakes in this book will be made over the course of three or four days. During that time, you will need various types of storage. After the cakes have been baked, filled, and have received a crumb coating of buttercream, you will need many refrigerated surfaces. For a completed stacked cake, you will need one large and tall space, usually refrigerated. If the cake design has pillars, it will be transported in an unassembled state. This means that your home storage must be flexible as the tiers will all be separate and take up a lot of surface space.

The best place to start is with the bottom tier. If it is 14 inches wide, then it will probably be sitting on a 18-inch Masonite or wooden round (or some other rigid platter). Therefore, you need an area approximately 20 inches around in the refrigerator, or wherever, to allow for the base and any decorations. You do not want it to touch anything. You also do not want to store your exquisite creation with any strong-tasting or pungent foods or substances. Briny olives, odorous cheeses, and garlic-laden dressings are delicious, but should not be near a cake.

You also need to be aware of the storage facilities at the reception site. If you are going to deliver the cake very early and it will need refrigeration, call ahead and tell the banquet room organizer or caterer about your needs. Hotels or other large facilities probably have several walk-in refrigerators. Select one free of odors and one that is not used frequently. Chefs and assistants will run in and out of heavily used ones and they are no place for a delicate wedding cake.

Outdoor weddings present their own set of problems. More than half of the cakes that I have made and delivered had an outdoor tent as their destination. Refrigeration will sometimes be available but more often, it is not. If the wedding is in a private yard, speak with the owners of the house about an extra refrigerator. Make sure the caterer has not already planned to store anything in it, and measure its interior dimensions yourself beforehand so there is no confusion as to its capacity. Very occasionally, the caterer will have a large enough operation to have a refrigerated truck or other such portable unit. Negotiate with them for a space. If no refrigeration is available, the next best option is an air-conditioned room, or at least a very cool one, like a clean basement or garage.

There is a possibility that no refrigeration or cool spot will be available. In this case, you must work very closely with the caterer on the timing of dessert. Ask them beforehand when they plan to serve dessert. If you are not attending the wedding, ask if you can call during the festivities at some point to see how things are progressing, obviously leaving yourself enough time to travel to the reception site. Arrive as close to serving time as possible, allowing a certain period of time for guests to view the cake. The amount of time that you can afford to let the cake sit out will depend on the type of cake and the weather. Worst-case scenario: If the cake has meringue or egg yolk buttercream, and the temperature is in the 90s, then allow no longer than half an hour for the cake to be unrefrigerated. In a case like this, I'll put the cake in my freezer for an hour before delivering it so that the buttercream is as cold as possible without being actually frozen. Of course, this is because I have an upright freezer that can accommodate a wedding cake.

Transportation is as important as the taste of the cake or the color of the flowers. You need a vehicle and some sort of storage container(s) to hold the cake in the vehicle. I finally bought myself an expensive, restaurant-grade storage unit in which to transport my cakes, but for 10 years, I did without one. If you are going to assemble a cake on pillars at the reception site, then you are dealing with separate layers and they can be put into several different containers—coolers and insulated boxes are perfect. The cakes should go straight from the refrigerator into the boxes with a freezer pack. Knowing the dimensions of your refrigerator is important, but so is knowing the sizes of your tiers and the size of the finished cake, so carefully measure everything first, including the car.

Even if you have figured out your storage-box situation, you still need to fit these containers, or one large container, into your car. A flat surface is a must. Some hatchbacks will suffice; usually you need a station wagon, if not a van. Plan ahead. Also, obviously the best-case scenario is to hitch a ride on a refrigerator truck belonging to the caterer, but this is rarely feasible. Whichever vehicle you use must have air conditioning if the delivery is being made in warmer months. Even though the cake is in an insulated box, you want conditions working for you, not against you.

Of course, some cakes do not have to be coddled as much as others in warm weather, and with such cakes, the logistics will be easier. However, you still want a strong, protective container in which to transport the cakes.

Do not underestimate these considerations. You have spent many hours creating your cake, and you should take care that it is around long enough to be eaten and enjoyed.

One caveat: Right before I load a cake into my van, I place a sign in the rear window that says "Caution: Wedding Cake on Board." Then I drive as slowly as I need to, with my flashers on. I have delivered cakes this way, and without a sign, and drivers are much more courteous if they understand why you are holding up traffic and displaying your flashers.

Also remember that accidents can occur. Minor touch-ups may be needed at the reception site as the cake may have been nicked during transportation. Always have extra buttercream with you with the appropriate tips, icing spatulas, pastry bags, and anything else you may need. If your cake has chocolate filigree work, marzipan flowers, chocolate leaves, or the like, always pack extras of these, too. Anticipate the worst-case scenario, plan well, drive slowly, and all should be fine.

Stage Six

SERVING

It is not unusual for me to become friends with the clients I work with and I often am invited to the reception or to help serve my artwork. When this happens, it is easy to control the situation. I know how many servings each tier is supposed to yield, I know what each layer contains, and I can answer questions about the cake. Usually, you will be leaving the cake in the hands of the caterer or the restaurant staff. They need to know what they are serving, its temperature requirements, the yield of every layer, the flavors and ingredients, and whether or not the couple wants to save the top tier. All of these things are important for different reasons. For instance, caterers follow certain guidelines for serving cake. Their charts will have a different number of servings per tier than yours do. If

the cake is a cheesecake, they should be ready to cut the cake with a hot knife or a piece of string or unflavored dental floss, to get the cleanest-looking pieces. Also, a guest may have a food allergy and ask about the ingredients in the cake. The servers need to be informed in order to answer such questions intelligently. The best way to relate this information to the servers is to write it down in a concise and informative way.

Remember, you want your cake to be appreciated and enjoyed to its fullest, and if it is carelessly slopped onto a plate, or if it is not served at the proper temperature, your efforts will not be fully appreciated. And don't forget to bring your camera. You should have a few photos of all the cakes you make for future reference.

·3·
THE CAKES

HONEY MAPLE CARROT CAKE WITH PECANS AND RAISINS

COMPONENTS

Honey Maple Carrot Cake
Two 6 × 2-inch layers
Two 10 × 2-inch layers
Two 14 × 2-inch layers

....

28 cups Honey or Maple Syrup
Buttercream (page 143 in
Basics chapter)

....

10 cups chopped toasted
pecans for exterior (page 147 in
Basics chapter)

....

Greenery and Flowers
Miniature sunflowers
Ambiance roses
Protea
Lisianthus
Dendrobium orchids
Lilies

....

MAKES 100 SERVINGS

E A S I E R

❖

This moist, spicy carrot cake is sweetened with a blend of honey and maple syrup. Some folks eschew refined sugar so these liquid sweeteners are a great alternative. I use a mix of the two so that neither one is really dominant. The cake, based on oil, not butter, is a great keeper and can be made several days ahead. Plump raisins are delicious; little hard dried fruit nuggets are not. If yours are not fresh and moist, plump them in hot water for 30 minutes before using. You also have a choice when it comes to the flour. You may use all whole wheat pastry flour, all regular white cake flour, or a 50/50 blend of the two.

This is the one cake in the book that is mixed by hand. It may seem difficult, but it is not. The oil and sweeteners combine easily and stirring in the dry ingredients takes no time at all. The batter is also quite forgiving. Don't like raisins? Leave them out. Love nuts? Double the quantity of nuts, using two different varieties, if you like—walnuts and pecans are great together.

Staying with the no-white-sugar-theme, the buttercream is also made from a blend of the two sweeteners. The sides of the cake are covered with chopped toasted pecans.

HONEY MAPLE CARROT CAKE

This oil-based batter is easy to whip up. You may freeze the cakes for up to a month, or keep well wrapped at room temperature for up to four days.

FOR TWO 6 × 2-INCH CAKE LAYERS
1½ cups unsifted whole wheat pastry flour
1½ teaspoons baking powder
1½ teaspoons baking soda
¾ teaspoon salt
1½ teaspoons ground cinnamon
¾ teaspoon ground nutmeg
¾ pound whole carrots
½ cup canola oil
⅓ cup honey
⅓ cup maple syrup
3 large eggs
⅓ cup dark raisins
1⅓ ounces pecans (about ½ cup), toasted and chopped

Preheat the oven to 350°F. Prepare two 6 × 2-inch pans with cooking spray and parchment paper.

Sift the flour, leaveners, salt, and spices together; set aside. Wash and peel the carrots. Trim both ends and grate, using the medium grating attachment of your food processor or the large holes on a hand grater. Set aside.

In a large bowl, combine the oil, honey, and syrup, whisking together well. Add the eggs, one at a time, whisking well after each addition. Add the dry ingredients, stirring just until the mixture is well blended. Stir in the carrots, raisins, and nuts.

Pour the batter into the pans and bake about 35 to 45 minutes or until a toothpick tests clean. Cool, place on cardboards, and wrap with plastic wrap and foil.

FOR TWO 10 × 2-INCH CAKE LAYERS

3¾ cups unsifted whole wheat pastry flour

1 tablespoon plus 2 teaspoons baking powder

1 tablespoon plus 2 teaspoons baking soda

1¾ teaspoons salt

1 tablespoon plus 2 teaspoons ground cinnamon

2 teaspoons ground nutmeg

2 pounds whole carrots

1¼ cups canola oil

¾ cup plus 2 tablespoons honey

¾ cup plus 2 tablespoons maple syrup

8 large eggs

¾ cup plus 2 tablespoons dark raisins

3½ ounces pecans (about 1⅛ cups), toasted and chopped

Prepare two 10 × 2-inch pans with cooking spray and parchment paper. Proceed as above for the 6-inch cakes. Bake about 45 to 55 minutes. Cool, place on cardboards, and wrap with plastic wrap and foil.

FOR TWO 14 × 2-INCH CAKE LAYERS

7½ cups unsifted whole wheat pastry flour

3 tablespoons plus 1 teaspoon baking powder

3 tablespoons plus 1 teaspoon baking soda

1 tablespoon salt

3 tablespoons plus 1 teaspoon ground cinnamon

1 tablespoon plus 1 teaspoon ground nutmeg

4 pounds whole carrots

2½ cups canola oil

1¾ cups honey

1¾ cups maple syrup

16 large eggs

1¾ cups dark raisins

7 ounces pecans (about 2⅓ cups), toasted and chopped

Prepare two 14 × 2-inch pans with cooking spray and parchment paper. Proceed as above. Bake about 55 to 65 minutes. Cool, place on cardboards, and wrap with plastic wrap and foil.

GREENERY AND FLOWERS

I used approximately 2 miniature sunflowers, 6 roses, 3 sprays of protea, 2 lisianthus stalks, and 2 lily stalks. A small bunch of assorted flowers was placed on the cake top. Then, single flowers were placed here and there on the lower tiers. Rose petals were literally tossed upon the cake to fall as they chose. Refer to photo for placement ideas.

ASSEMBLY

Have all components ready. Cover an 18-inch-round Masonite board with decorative foil. Fill and crumb coat all layers. Chill well, then apply final coat of buttercream. While the frosting is still soft, scoop up the nuts and press them around the cake's sides. Chill all tiers.

Center and stack tiers on Masonite board, using dowels for internal support. On upper, and lower edges if desired, make a simple shell border using star tips #16, #17, and #18 for the top, middle, and bottom tiers respectively. Refrigerate overnight.

Place the flowers on the cake shortly before serving. Scatter rose petals on and around the cake along with the flowers. Serve the cake at room temperature.

CHOCOLATE ALMOND TORTE WITH SUGARED NUTS

COMPONENTS

Chocolate Almond Torte
Two 6 × 2-inch layers
Two 10 × 2-inch layers
Two 14 × 2-inch layers

....

18 cups Bittersweet Chocolate
Ganache, 4 cups for filling and
14 cups for glazing (page 145
in Basics chapter, also see
this recipe)

....

10 cups Sliced Sugared
Almonds, use sliced nuts,
natural or blanched (page 149
in Basics chapter)

....

Equipment
4 spiked pillars
7-inch separator plate
(all painted gold)

....

Greenery and Flowers
Red roses
Lemon leaves

....

MAKES 100 SERVINGS

E A S I E R

❖

This is a wonderful chocolate cake, not too sweet and very moist. Most of the flour in the cake has been replaced with toasted, ground almonds providing an interesting, nubby texture. The small amount of flour is correct.

The cake is filled and covered with chocolate ganache and the bottom edges are decorated with sugared, sliced almonds. I chose to separate the top tier with gold pillars, which play up the golden color of the almonds. The cake is dark, suave, and sophisticated. The dark red roses only add to the drama. You may crystallize the roses, or leave them fresh for their deep, blood-red color as we did in the photo. The velvety quality of the fresh blooms looks wonderful against the ganache.

CHOCOLATE ALMOND TORTE

This component may be made one month ahead and frozen.

....

FOR TWO 6 × 2-INCH CAKE LAYERS

5$^{1}/_{2}$ ounces semisweet chocolate, finely chopped

5$^{1}/_{2}$ ounces blanched almonds (about 1$^{2}/_{3}$ cups), lightly toasted

3$^{3}/_{4}$ tablespoons unsifted all-purpose flour

5$^{2}/_{3}$ ounces unsalted butter, at room temperature

$^{3}/_{4}$ cup sugar, divided into $^{1}/_{2}$ cup and $^{1}/_{4}$ cup

6 large eggs, separated

$^{1}/_{4}$ teaspoon salt

Preheat the oven to 350°F. Prepare two 6 × 2-inch pans with cooking spray and parchment paper.

Melt the chocolate in a double boiler (*bain-marie*) or in the microwave. Set aside and cool until room temperature.

Meanwhile, place the almonds and flour in the container of a food processor fitted with the metal blade. Pulse on and off repeatedly until the almonds are ground to a fine meal. The flour should prevent the natural oils in the nuts from turning the mixture into almond butter. Check the bowl every 15 seconds. Process until fine, but do not let the nuts become soft and gummy.

In your mixing bowl, use a flat paddle to cream the butter. Add $^{1}/_{2}$ cup of the sugar gradually and continue to beat until light and fluffy on medium-high speed. Add the yolks one at a time, beating well after each addition. Scrape down once or twice. Beat in the melted chocolate until it is thoroughly incorporated. Add the almond-flour mixture on low speed and mix until batter is well blended. Set aside.

In a clean, grease-free bowl, with a clean balloon whip, beat the whites on low speed until frothy. Add the salt. Continue to beat until soft peaks form. Add the remaining $^{1}/_{4}$ cup sugar gradually and whip until stiff, but not dry, peaks form. Fold $^{1}/_{4}$ of the meringue into the chocolate batter to lighten it. Fold in the remaining whites thoroughly, taking care not to deflate them. No white streaks should remain.

Divide the batter between the two pans and spread tops smooth with a small offset spatula. Bake about 30 to 40 minutes or until a toothpick comes out with some moist crumbs. Do not overbake. Cool, place on cardboards, and wrap with plastic wrap and foil.

FOR TWO 10 × 2-INCH CAKE LAYERS

13¾ ounces semisweet chocolate, finely chopped

13¾ ounces blanched almonds (about 4⅛ cups), lightly toasted

⅔ cup unsifted all-purpose flour

14½ ounces unsalted butter, at room temperature

1¾ cups plus 1 tablespoon sugar, divided into 1¼ cups and ½ cup plus 1 tablespoon

15 large eggs, separated

½ teaspoon salt

Prepare two 10 × 2-inch cake pans with cooking spray and parchment paper. Proceed as above for the 6-inch tier. Bake about 40 to 50 minutes. Remember, a toothpick inserted in the cake should come out with some moist crumbs sticking to it. Cool, place on cardboards, and wrap with plastic wrap and foil.

FOR TWO 14 × 2-INCH CAKE LAYERS

Prepare two 14 × 2-inch cake pans with cooking spray and parchment paper. Make the 10-inch cake recipe twice, once for each pan; do not double the recipe. Bake about 65 to 70 minutes. Do not overbake. Cool, place on cardboards, and wrap with plastic wrap and foil.

BITTERSWEET CHOCOLATE GANACHE

The 4 cups of ganache for the filling should be of a soft spreading consistency. The 14 cups of ganache for the exterior of the cake should be pourable. The same ganache formulation can be used; it is just a matter of manipulating the temperature. Ganache can be made one month ahead and frozen.

GREENERY AND FLOWERS

The red roses add drama to this cake, not to mention expense. Make sure to account for them in your budget. I used about 18 roses; order some "seconds" from your florist—they're cheaper—to pull apart and scatter on the table near the cake. Buy them one to two days before use and store them in the refrigerator. You can manipulate how they look—for tight buds, keep the roses chilled; for open buds, place the roses in warm water to encourage the petals to open.

The lemon leaves are dark green and glossy. Buy a bunch from your florist, requesting smaller ones, if possible.

ASSEMBLY

All components should be ready. Cover an 18-inch-round Masonite board with decorative foil. Have one 7-inch separator plate and 4 spiked pillars painted gold.

Fill the tiers with the spreadable ganache. Pour the ganache over all the individual tiers set over a wire rack. Precise directions are given in the Finishing Touches chapter under Glazing with Ganache, page 156.

Before refrigerating the cakes, and while the ganache is still tacky, scoop up the nuts and press them onto the sides of the cakes. The Finishing Touches chapter gives detailed instructions on page 156. In the photo, you will note that the nuts come ¼ of the way up the sides of the cake. If your ganache is applied unevenly, and there are many unsightly drips, feel free to completely cover the sides with the sugared nuts. Chill well.

Place the bottom tier in the center of the covered Masonite board. Center the middle tier on top, using dowels for internal support. Place the top tier on its separator plate. Refrigerate the cake overnight. Assemble the cake at the event site. Place the red roses and greens on the cake right before displaying it. Serve the cake at room temperature.

PUMPKIN CAKE WITH CRYSTALLIZED GINGER, WALNUTS, AND DRIED CRANBERRIES

COMPONENTS

Pumpkin Cake
Two 6 × 2-inch layers
Two 9 × 2-inch layers
Two 12 × 2-inch layers
Two 14 × 2-inch layers

7 cups Cranberry Buttercream

12 cups toasted and chopped
walnuts, about 2½ pounds
(page 147 in Basics chapter)

25 cups White Chocolate
Cream Cheese Frosting (page
144 in Basics chapter)

Equipment
12 spiked pillars
7-inch separator plate
10-inch separator plate
13-inch separator plat
(all painted gold)

Greenery and Flowers
Crocosnia
Hypericum berries

MAKES 125 SERVINGS

E A S I E R

❖

This cake is a symphony of colors: russet-orange cake speckled with nuggets of toasted brown nuts and ruby red cranberries; a creamy pink-red Cranberry Buttercream filling; and an ivory White Chocolate Cream Cheese Frosting. It has the understated simplicity of pumpkin quick breads, but the crystallized ginger and cranberries raise it to new heights. I thank one of my best friends, Mary McNamara, for the filling. I was testing the cake component—at the time without the cranberries—and asked Mary what she thought would go well with it. Without missing a beat, she said, "cranberry butter-cream." As soon as she said that, I immediately thought of the dried cranberries for the cake as well. Voila! This is how recipes are born. I envision this cake at a fall New England country wedding, but use it as you see fit.

In keeping with the rustic theme, these cake tiers could be simply stacked. I have chosen to tier them with lots of greens. I think it makes an interesting example of a homey cake that can be given a special treatment.

One note on ingredients: Dried cranberries are now sold nationwide by Ocean Spray as Craisins. And, for the pumpkin, many supermarkets only carry solid-pack pumpkin in the fall. You should check for ingredients before embarking on this project.

CRANBERRY BUTTERCREAM

6 cups prepared Italian Meringue Buttercream (page 139 in Basics chapter)
1½ cups prepared Cranberry Purée (recipe follows), at room temperature

Let the buttercream reach room temperature. Place it in a mixing bowl. With the balloon whip, beat the buttercream until light and fluffy. Add the purée, a few spoonfuls at a time, on low speed, allowing the buttercream to absorb the purée after each addition. When all the purée is added, beat the buttercream mixture well on high speed until combined. Store it in an airtight container in the refrigerator. Reconstitute the mixture like regular Italian Meringue Buttercream, as described in the Basics chapter, page 139.

CRANBERRY PURÉE

MAKES 1½ CUPS

2⅔ cups raw cranberries, fresh or frozen (the equivalent of ¾ of a 12-ounce package)
¾ cup sugar
¾ cup water

Place all ingredients in a medium, nonreactive saucepan. Stir the mixture to combine. Bring it to a simmer and cook for about 15 minutes, or until most of the berries have popped open.

Pour the berries into a food processor and purée the mixture until it is smooth and well blended. This will begin to break down the somewhat tough skins of the cranberries. For the silkiest purée, press the mixture through a strainer or a food mill.

Cool to room temperature and store in an airtight container in the refrigerator. Make sure the purée is cool before adding it to buttercream.

PUMPKIN CAKE

You may make this one month ahead and freeze it, but I prefer to make it two days ahead and store it tightly wrapped at room temperature.

FOR TWO 6 × 2-INCH CAKE LAYERS	FOR TWO 9 × 2-INCH CAKE LAYERS
1¹/₂ cups unsifted cake flour	3 cups unsifted cake flour
1 teaspoon baking soda	2 teaspoons baking soda
1 teaspoon baking powder	2 teaspoons baking powder
1 teaspoon ground cinnamon	2 teaspoons ground cinnamon
pinch ground nutmeg	¹/₄ teaspoon ground nutmeg
pinch ground cloves	¹/₄ teaspoon ground cloves
¹/₂ teaspoon salt	1 teaspoon salt
1 tablespoon plus 1 teaspoon chopped crystallized ginger	2 tablespoons plus 2 teaspoons chopped crystallized ginger
1¹/₄ ounces walnuts (about ¹/₂ cup), chopped	2¹/₂ ounces walnuts (about ³/₄ cup), chopped
¹/₃ cup dried cranberries	²/₃ cup dried cranberries
1 cup solid-pack pumpkin	2 cups solid-pack pumpkin
¹/₂ cup sugar	1 cup sugar
¹/₂ cup light brown sugar	1 cup light brown sugar
¹/₂ cup canola oil	1 cup canola oil
2 large eggs	4 large eggs

Preheat the oven to 350°F. Prepare two 6 × 2-inch cake pans with cooking spray and parchment paper.

Sift together the flour, baking soda, baking powder, cinnamon, nutmeg, cloves, and salt. Toss the ginger, walnuts, and dried cranberries with the dry ingredients. This will prevent them from sinking to the bottom of the pan.

Place the pumpkin, sugars, and oil in the bowl of your mixer. With the flat paddle, combine them on medium speed and add the eggs, one at a time, beating after each addition. The mixture should be smooth and homogenous.

Add the dry mixture in 4 batches, scraping the batter down after each addition. Beat just enough to combine the wet and dry ingredients; do not overmix.

Divide the batter evenly between the pans. Bake about 35 to 45 minutes, or until a toothpick tests clean. The cake will turn golden and have a fragrant aroma. Cool, place on cardboards, and wrap with plastic wrap and foil.

Prepare two 9 × 2-inch cake pans with cooking spray and parchment paper. Proceed as above for the 6-inch cake. Bake about 40 to 50 minutes. Cool, place on cardboards, and wrap with plastic wrap and foil.

FOR TWO 12 × 2-INCH CAKE LAYERS

Prepare two 12 × 2-inch cake pans with cooking spray and parchment paper. Double the recipe for the 9-inch cake. Instead of using your mixer, whisk all of the wet ingredients together in a large stainless steel mixing bowl. Proceed with the recipe, making the entire batter at once in the same bowl. Despite the large quantity, the batter is actually very easy to make by hand. Alternatively, if you prefer, make the recipe for the 9-inch cake twice using your mixer. Bake for approximately 45 to 55 minutes. Cool, place on cardboards, and wrap with plastic wrap and foil.

FOR TWO 14 × 2-INCH CAKE LAYERS

7$\frac{1}{2}$ cups unsifted cake flour

1 tablespoon plus 2 teaspoons baking soda

1 tablespoon plus 2 teaspoons baking powder

1 tablespoon plus 2 teaspoons ground cinnamon

$\frac{2}{3}$ teaspoon ground nutmeg

$\frac{2}{3}$ teaspoon ground cloves

2$\frac{1}{2}$ teaspoons salt

$\frac{1}{3}$ cup chopped crystallized ginger

6 ounces walnuts (about 2 cups), chopped

1$\frac{2}{3}$ cups dried cranberries

5 cups solid-pack pumpkin

2$\frac{1}{2}$ cups sugar

2$\frac{1}{2}$ cups light brown sugar

2$\frac{1}{2}$ cups canola oil

10 large eggs

Prepare two 14 × 2-inch cake pans with cooking spray and parchment paper. Proceed as above for the 12-inch cakes, mixing the batter by hand in a mixing bowl. Bake about 50 to 60 minutes. Cool, place on cardboards, and wrap with plastic wrap and foil.

GREENERY AND FLOWERS

To accentuate the casual nature of this cake, I have tucked a plethora of greenery and some flowers between the tiers, filling up the gaps completely. In the photograph, we used approximately 18 stalks each of the crocosnia and hypericum berries. The photo will give you an idea of quantity.

ASSEMBLY

Have all components ready. Cover an 18-inch-round Masonite board with decorative foil. Have 7-, 10, and 13-inch separator plates and 12 matching spiked pillars painted antique gold. Fill the tiers with the Cranberry Buttercream. Crumb coat with White Chocolate Cream Cheese Frosting. Chill all tiers well.

Apply a final coat of frosting and press the nuts around the sides in a triangular pattern while the frosting is still soft (see photo). Alternately, cover sides completely with nuts. Place the bottom tier on the Masonite board. Place top tiers on their respective separator plates. Apply a simple shell border on the bottom edges of each tier. I used a #16 star tip for the top tier, #17 star tip for the next tier, and a #18 star tip for the bottom two tiers. Refrigerate overnight.

Assemble the cake at the event site. Place plenty of greenery in between the spaces, completely filling them up. Tuck the flowers in between the greens. Serve the cake at room temperature.

CHOCOLATE RASPBERRY CAKE

COMPONENTS

Sour Cream Chocolate Cake
Two 6 × 2-inch layers
Two 10 × 2-inch layers
Two 14 × 2-inch layers
(page 134 in Basics chapter)

6 cups Italian Meringue
Buttercream, raspberry variation
(page 141 in Basics chapter)

23 cups Italian Meringue
Buttercream, chocolate
variation (page 141 in
Basics chapter)

10 cups Chocolate Curls
(page 167 in Finishing
Touches chapter)

Equipment
8 spiked pillars
7-inch separator plate
11-inch separator plate
(all painted gold)

Greenery and Flowers
Birds of Paradise
Lisianthus
Lilies
Ivy

MAKES 100 SERVINGS

E A S I E R

❖

I remember when I was about 10 years old my mom was having a dinner party and for dessert she planned to serve chocolate ice cream and raspberry sherbet—in the same dish! I remember vociferously protesting and screwing my face up in disgust. Either flavor was fine with me, but separately.

I have grown up, and thankfully, my palate has matured as well. Now I love chocolate and raspberries in many guises. This cake is comprised of Sour Cream Chocolate Cake layers with a Raspberry Buttercream filling that is made with fresh or individually quick frozen (IQF) fruit. The exterior is all chocolate buttercream and curls.

CHOCOLATE CURLS

For this cake, you want the more informal type of curls. Simply follow the directions for Chocolate Curls in the Finishing Touches chapter, page 167. Make the type that you simply shave off a block of chocolate.

GREENERY AND FLOWERS

The purple and orange color scheme provided by the flowers is dramatic and unusual. I used 1 bird of paradise, 6 lisianthus stalks, and 8 lily blossoms. One bunch of ivy was used to decorate the columns.

ASSEMBLY

Have all components ready. Cover an 18-inch-round Masonite board with decorative foil. Have 7-inch and 11-inch separator plates and 8 spiked pillars painted gold.

Fill tiers with a layer of Raspberry Buttercream and crumb coat with a thin layer of chocolate buttercream. Chill all layers. Apply a final coat of chocolate buttercream and apply the chocolate curls to the sides of the tiers while the buttercream is still soft. Chill again.

Affix the tiers to their separator plates and the bottom tier to the Masonite board. Apply a simple leaf border along the upper edges, using #66, #67 and #68 tips respectively for the smallest, middle, and bottom tier. Chill overnight.

Assemble the cake on site and arrange flowers before setting the cake out for viewing. Serve the cake at room temperature.

SAVORY SMOKED SALMON CHEESECAKE WEDDING CAKE

COMPONENTS

Smoked Salmon Cheesecake
One 6 × 3-inch cake tier
One 9 × 3-inch cake tier

3/4 cup chopped chives

1 ounce smoked salmon

Extra springs of Italian parsley

Strips of lemon zest

2 regular or 1 long hothouse
cucumber

70 Dill Toasts

Lemon leaves (optional)

MAKES 35 SERVINGS

E A S I E R

❖

Of all the cakes in this book, this may be the most unusual. A nondessert cake at a wedding, you ask? Why not, I say. This is perfect for a second wedding reception. Perhaps you are getting married at city hall, or just inviting close family members to be present for your exchange of vows. The small reception might be at your apartment or home, not at a banquet hall. You must feed the guests, and that's where this cake comes in.

It is a cheesecake flavored with salmon, lemon, cream cheese, and fresh dill. It is essentially the same hors d'oeuvre presented in my friend Betty Rosbottom's First Impressions *book, but she never envisioned it stacked as a wedding cake! It is served with thin toast triangles and sliced cucumbers and makes a welcome treat at such a reception party. Serve with plenty of chilled champagne, a selection of other finger foods, and perhaps an array of small fruit tarts or other sweet treats.*

SMOKED SALMON CHEESECAKE

FOR 6 × 3-INCH TIER

1/4 cup dried unflavored bread crumbs

2/3 cup grated Parmesan cheese, divided into 1/2 cup and 2 tablespoons plus 2 teaspoons

2 tablespoons unsalted butter, at room temperature

1 pound cream cheese, at room temperature

2 large eggs

2 tablespoons chopped chives

2 tablespoons chopped fresh Italian parsley

1 teaspoon lemon zest

1/4 teaspoon salt

Freshly ground black pepper, to taste

1/2 cup sour cream

6 ounces smoked salmon, finely chopped

Preheat the oven to 350°F. Prepare a 6 × 3-inch solid cake pan with cooking spray and parchment paper.

Blend together the bread crumbs, 2 tablespoons plus 2 teaspoons Parmesan cheese, and butter in a small bowl. Press the mixture into the bottom of the cake pan, making an even layer. Set aside.

Place the cream cheese in the bowl of your mixer. With the flat paddle, beat the cream cheese on medium speed until light and fluffy. Beat in the remaining Parmesan cheese. Add the eggs, one at a time, beating well after each addition. Scrape down the mixture once or twice. Beat in the chives and parsley, lemon zest, and salt and pepper. Mix well. Stir in the sour cream by hand and fold in the chopped salmon.

THE WEDDING CAKE BOOK

Pour the batter into the pan and smooth the top with a small offset spatula. Place the cake pan in a larger pan filled with 1 inch hot water. Bake about 30 to 40 minutes. The cake should be set around the edges, but still creamy and soft in the middle. Turn the oven off and let the cake cool in the oven. Remove the cake from the oven, cool completely on a rack, then refrigerate it overnight or longer. This may be prepared 2 days ahead. Wrap it tightly with plastic wrap and store in the refrigerator, still in its pan.

FOR 9 × 3-INCH TIER

½ cup dried unflavored bread crumbs
1⅓ cups Parmesan cheese, divided into 1 cup and ⅓ cup

2 ounces (½ stick) unsalted butter, at room temperature
2 pounds cream cheese, softened to room temperature
4 large eggs
¼ cup chopped Italian parsley
¼ cup chopped chives
2 teaspoons lemon zest
½ teaspoon salt
Freshly ground black pepper, to taste
1 cup sour cream
12 ounces smoked salmon, finely chopped

Proceed as above, using one 9 × 3-inch-deep pan. Bake about 40 to 50 minutes. Cool, wrap with plastic wrap, and store in refrigerator, still in its pan.

DILL TOASTS

These are simply dill-seasoned toasts cut into triangles. These are best made early in the day of the event.
Serve the sliced cucumbers with the toasts as an alternative.

35 thin slices white bread
2 ounces (½ stick) unsalted butter
⅓ cup olive oil
2 tablespoons dried dill

Preheat the oven to 350°F. Line a baking sheet with parchment paper.

Remove crusts from the bread and then cut each one in half on the diagonal. Do several at a time by stacking the slices on top of one another and cutting through all of them at once with a sharp, heavy knife.

Melt butter in a small saucepan and stir in the olive oil and dill. Brush both sides of the triangles with the mixture to saturate evenly. Place on baking sheet and bake about 10 minutes, or until golden but not brown. Store at room temperature until needed. Take care not to break them.

ASSEMBLY

Ready a platter large enough to hold the bottom 9-inch tier. Have all components ready, except the toasts, which you make closer to serving time. Unmold both tiers, following the instructions given for Sour Cream Apple Cheesecake on page 115. Place each layer on a cardboard round with the crust layer on the bottom. These "cakes" receive very little embellishment. If the sides need sprucing up, dip an icing spatula in warm water, dry it, and smooth them.

Place the large tier on the serving tray. Center the small tier on top, using dowels for internal support.

Sprinkle the tops of the tiers with chives or other garnish. To make a rose out of the salmon, take a strip of it and roll it in a spiral. Loosen some of the outer coils of the spiral, for a simplified rose. Place it on top with some parsley sprigs and lemon peel. The cake may be refrigerated overnight at this point, if desired, or served immediately.

When ready to serve, place the toasts in a pretty basket and ring the bottom of the cake with the cucumbers and lemon leaves, if desired. Guests can spread the salmon on either toast triangles or rounds of cucumber.

CARAMEL RUM CAKE WITH CARAMELIZED WALNUTS

COMPONENTS

Génoise
Two 8 × 2-inch layers
Two 12 × 2-inch layers
(page 131 in Basics chapter)

6 cups Sugar Syrup, liqueur
variation using dark rum (page
147 in Basics chapter)

21 cups Caramel Buttercream

4 cups toasted, chopped
walnuts for cake sides, about
12 ounces (page 147 in
Basics chapter)

65 Caramelized Walnuts for
border on top inside edge
of tiers (page 150 in
Basics chapter)

Two 3-inch-long Golden Sugar
Molded Cherubs (page 173 in
Finishing Touches chapter,
see also this recipe)

MAKES 45 SERVINGS

E A S I E R

❖

This cake was very popular at an Italian restaurant where I worked. I made it in a long, rectangular shape, but the round shape presented here looks great.

The cake is a basic yellow, buttery Génoise. The layers are soaked with Dark Rum Syrup and it is filled and covered with Caramel Buttercream. The top is decorated with whole, Caramelized Walnuts; the sides, with chopped, toasted walnuts. The combination of tastes and textures with the punch of the rum is truly delicious. This cake should be made for lovers of rum; a nonalcoholic version is not the same.

I have done this cake in a smaller size, perfect for a small wedding or bridal shower. The cake is capped off by two golden cherubs molded out of sugar. If you would prefer to purchase them (ungilded) they can be ordered from Sweet Celebrations (see Resources section, page 189).

GOLDEN SUGAR-MOLDED CHERUBS

Refer to the Finishing Touches chapter, page 173, for Sugar Molding. Make two cherubs that will face each other from molds from Sweet Celebrations. Let them dry and paint with gold powder dissolved with some vodka. Make two to three of each in case of breakage.

If you want to really go for broke, cover them with real gold leaf following the directions in the Finishing Touches chapter. Either variation will last indefinitely if stored in an airtight container.

CARAMEL BUTTERCREAM

MAKES 8 CUPS

4 cups heavy cream

4 cups sugar

2 cups water

1 pound unsalted butter (4 sticks), at room temperature

Pour the cream in a large saucepan and scald. Set aside, keeping warm.

Combine the sugar and water in a large, heavy-bottomed saucepan and stir to combine. Place the pan over medium heat and bring to a boil; wash the sugar crystals down from the sides with a damp pastry brush, if necessary. You may also cover the pan briefly. Steam will develop and wash down the sides of the pan automatically. Do not stir. Swirl the pan occasionally to mix the contents.

The mixture will begin to darken to amber, but do not let it turn darker. At the proper color, remove the pan from the heat. Immediately, but slowly and steadily, pour in the warm cream. If the mixture boils up, use a whisk to stir it

down. If the mixture seizes up, the caramel will harden. To melt it, place the pan on low-medium heat and stir the mixture until smooth.

Remove from the heat and cool in the pan for 10 minutes. Pour into your mixer's bowl and set aside overnight at a cool room temperature or refrigerate until firm; do not let it chill till ice cold.

With a balloon whip, begin to beat the mixture on low-medium speed. If it is too cold the mixture will be too thick to whip. If it is still too warm, it will be soupy. Chill or warm as needed, using some of the tips suggested in the Italian Meringue Buttercream recipe in the Basics chapter (page 139). It should be pale, light in texture, and very smooth.

Add the soft butter two tablespoonful at a time while continuing to whip on high.

The mixture should become soft, creamy, and smooth. Continue beating until the mixture is thick enough to pipe or spread with an icing spatula. Sometimes this buttercream takes a lot of whipping to smooth it out. Be persistent. Use immediately or store in an airtight container in the refrigerator, until needed. Reconstitute like Italian Meringue Buttercream (see Basics chapter, page 139).

ASSEMBLY

Have all components ready. Cover a 14-inch-round Masonite board with decorative foil. Sprinkle all layers with syrup. Fill and crumb coat with Caramel Buttercream. Chill tiers, then apply final coat. While the buttercream is still soft, press chopped walnuts into the sides of the cake. Chill tiers well. Center bottom tier on Masonite board. Center 8-inch tier on top, using dowels for internal support.

Fit a pastry bag with a coupler and a #19 tip and apply a shell border on the upper and lower edge of the 8-inch tier. Change to a #21 tip and do the same for the 12-inch tier. Make one large rosette on the center top of the cake with the #21 tip; this will hold the cherubs. Refrigerate overnight.

Shortly before serving, place Caramelized Walnuts, end to end, along the inside of each top border (see photo). Place the two cherubs in the rosette on the top tier. Serve cake at room temperature.

White Cake with Lemon Curd, Blackberry Curd, and Pressed Flowers

COMPONENTS

White Cake
Two 6 × 2-inch layers
Two 10 × 2-inch layers
Two 14 × 2-inch layers
(page 136 in Basics chapter)

6 cups of Lemon Curd for
the filling (page 142 in
Basics chapter)

6 cups Blackberry Curd
(page 142 in Basics chapter)

29 cups Lemon Curd
Buttercream, a combination of
4⅛ cups Lemon Curd and
25 cups Italian Meringue
Buttercream. Do not use any
lemon zest, which would
interfere with piping.
(page 141 in Basics chapter)

24 Pressed Flowers, plus extra
in case of breakage (page 164
in Finishing Touches chapter)

Strips of lemon zest (optional)

MAKES 100 SERVINGS

MODERATE

❖ ❖

I developed this cake for my Great Aunt Bert's 95th birthday. I didn't know what she liked, but I didn't want to ask her either. It was a surprise and she's the type of person who would say that I shouldn't bother making a cake anyhow. As far as I'm concerned, anyone who reaches that age deserves a party!

I thought that something light and fruity would be best, but I wanted a twist. The color scheme is what came to me first, actually. I thought of a nice light white cake with a lemon filling and something purple. Blackberry curd was the way to go. The pressed flowers were another inspiration. I love working with fresh flowers, and wanted to develop a new way of using them. I had used them fresh and crystallized . . . so what else was there? I thought of dried flowers, but the crumbly texture dissuaded me. This technique, which I think is the most original idea in this book, is very easy to reproduce. Look up the complete directions in the Finishing Touches chapter. For this cake we used pansies and Johnny-jump-ups.

To pick up the colors in the flowers, I chose to add a bit of violet paste color to the borders. Although I usually steer clear of artificial colorings, this is a perfect example of a way I think the added color in the borders enhances in an elegant way, rather than in a distracting one.

Assembly

Torte the cake layers by cutting each layer in half horizontally for four layers per tier—refer to the Finishing Touches chapter, page 153, for instructions. When stacked, every tier will be made up as follows, from the bottom up: cardboard, layer of cake, layer of lemon curd, layer of cake, layer of lemon curd buttercream, layer of cake, layer of blackberry curd, layer of cake, and lemon curd buttercream over all.

Have all components ready. Cover an 18-inch-round Masonite board with decorative foil. Beginning with the largest size, layer the tiers in the order described above. Create a border of buttercream around each curd layer to prevent the curd from seeping out, if necessary (see Finishing Touches chapter, page 154). After you place the top cake layer on each tier, press down gently. Crumb coat with the Lemon Curd Buttercream. Repeat with other tiers. Chill well.

Apply a final, smooth coat of buttercream over each tier and chill again. Place the bottom tier on the covered Masonite board and center and stack the remaining tiers, using dowels for internal support. Tint the remaining buttercream with violet paste color and apply a simple, slightly elongated shell border on the top and bottom edges using a #16 tip for the smallest tier, #17 tip for the middle tier, and #18 tip for the largest bottom tier. Refrigerate overnight.

Just before serving, press the flowers against the sides of the tiers in a decorative way, using the picture as a guide. Prop a flower on top, using lemon zest for support and garnish, if desired. Serve cake at room temperature.

FLAMING BAKED ALASKA WEDDING CAKE

COMPONENTS

One 10 × 2-inch cake layer (you can choose any cake in the book; I like the Sour Cream Chocolate Cake, page 134 in Basics chapter)

2 cups Sugar Syrup, liqueur variation using straight Alizé syrup for a strong passion fruit flavor or, for a nonalcoholic variation, substitute a fruit syrup such as the passion fruit flavor made by Da Vinci (call 1-800-640-6779 for availability) or use Monin brand (see Resources, page 185).

Sorbets
2 pints raspberry sorbet, softened slightly
2 pints mango sorbet, softened slightly
1 pint passion fruit sorbet, softened slightly

7 to 8 cups Italian Meringue Buttercream, without the butter (page 139 in Basics chapter, see also this recipe)

2 tablespoons high-proof alcohol, such as brandy

3 cups Bittersweet Chocolate Sauce, 2 tablespoons per serving (page 127 in Cake Accompaniments chapter)

24 Chocolate-Dipped Spoons

MAKES 24 SERVINGS

MODERATE

❖ ❖

I love this cake. It combines so many things that I look for in a dessert: interesting combinations of flavors, contrasting textures, colors, and temperatures. In my version it blends chocolate cake; raspberry, mango, and passion fruit sorbets; sweet, toasted meringue; chocolate sauce; and a surprising eating utensil: Chocolate Dipped Spoons. These are simple, but really exquisite, elegant, and tasty! I have seen them recently, made with plastic spoons, offered in mail-order catalogs for use with coffee.

I used a specially made ice cream bombe mold to make the dessert pictured. What makes it distinct is its beautifully proportioned shape—it measures 7 inches in diameter on the bottom and is 5 inches deep; its small air-escape hole in the top of the dome; and its base, so that the filled bombe can be frozen easily without the contents spilling out. You may use any round-bottom bowl of similar size. Just make sure that its diameter fits nicely on the cake base. Make sure also that the oven is tall enough to accommodate the cake with the bombe perched on top, and with extra room for the meringue and head space.

Baked Alaska desserts are ephemeral and this recipe is geared towards the smaller, intimate wedding. It will serve a maximum of two dozen guests. The dessert is best served at an indoor evening reception where you will get maximum effect from the dramatic, fiery presentation. This flaming is produced by warming brandy, pouring it into an embedded eggshell, and setting it alight—all last-minute touches, of course.

SORBET

I use Sharon's Sorbet or Häagen-Daz sorbet and find both of them to be excellent. Of course, you may make your own sorbet, if you are so inclined. One word of warning: If you are using purchased sorbets, make sure that the product is frozen solid with no icy covering on the outside of the container. This may indicate poor freezer conditions, involving fluctuating temperatures. This results in a grainy, icy, poorly textured product.

ITALIAN MERINGUE

Make one batch, and stop when the syrup has been added and the meringue whipped and cooled. This is your stable meringue to be used for the Baked Alaska. Do not add any butter.

This should be made immediately before you are ready to coat and bake the dessert—essentially, right before serving. Make sure to save half of one eggshell.

CHOCOLATE-DIPPED SPOONS

Since you are making this for a small number of people, consider using metal spoons—sterling silver, if you can. You can rent them very reasonably. If you prefer, you may use a good quality plastic. These are available in gold or silver colors. You may make these one month ahead and store in an airtight container in the refrigerator or freezer.

1 pound bittersweet chocolate

24 spoons

Melt the chocolate, according to suggested methods. Line a tray with parchment paper for the dipped spoons.

Dip the bowl of each spoon into the chocolate, letting the excess drip back into the bowl of melted chocolate. Coat the entire spoon, or half the spoon bowl (as we did in the photo). Place the spoons down on the parchment paper in the normal way, with the bowl's convex side facing down. Do not let the spoons touch each other. Place the tray in the refrigerator to chill the chocolate. When the chocolate is firm, place the spoons in a single layer in a large, flat plastic container with an airtight lid. If you need to make other layers, separate them with parchment paper or waxed paper.

ASSEMBLY

This entire recipe is all about assembly. It contains several components, but most are made way in advance. Of all the recipes in the book, this one requires good last-minute timing and nerves that go along with pulling off a last-minute production.

For the sorbet, up to one week in advance, line an ice cream bombe mold with a large sheet of plastic wrap. You may need two overlapping pieces. It will help you to unmold the bombe. Smooth out the plastic as well as you can so that it adheres to the inside of the bombe with as few wrinkles as possible. Let the ends hang over the outside.

Using a large, strong spoon, smooth the raspberry sorbet around the sides and bottom of the mold for a layer about 1 inch thick; spread evenly. Line this with another 1-inch-thick layer of mango sorbet. Do not let the two intermingle. If the raspberry sorbet is too soft, freeze it before adding the mango. Fill the center completely with passion fruit sorbet. Place a piece of plastic wrap over top and freeze solid, at least overnight.

This can be done one week ahead. Make sure to wrap it airtight so that no flavors get picked up from the freezer.

Have a heat-proof serving tray ready that is large enough to accommodate the cake.

Preheat the oven to 450°F.

Fan the Chocolate Dipped Spoons on a tray in the refrigerator.

Warm the Bittersweet Chocolate Sauce and pour it in a sauce boat.

Have all components ready and ask the caterer to give you a 15-minute warning before the cake is to be presented.

Place the defrosted cake layer on the tray and sprinkle it with liqueur or syrup. To unmold the bombe, peel away the plastic from the open end of the mold, grab the overhanging plastic ends, and pull up. The bombe should pop out. If it does not, place a warm washcloth around the outside of the bombe mold for one minute and try again.

Place the flat end of the bombe on the center of the cake. Gently, but quickly, peel the plastic wrap off the dome.

Use a large spoon to spread the meringue all over the surface of the bombe and cake. Make sure the meringue goes all the way down to touch the surface of the serving tray or the sorbet will not be insulated. Use the outside of the spoon bowl to make random peaks of meringue all over the dessert; work quickly.

Place half an eggshell on top of the bombe with the open half facing up. The meringue will hold it in place.

Bake until lightly browned, about 5 minutes. Meanwhile, warm the brandy in a small saucepan and set out the warmed sauce and the spoons. Remove the cake from the oven. Pour the brandy into the shell and ignite it.

Dim the lights and present the cake. The alcohol will burn out in a few minutes.

This cake needs to be served immediately in assembly line fashion. Ask a helper to spoon several tablespoonfuls of chocolate sauce on each plate and hand it to you. Place some cake and sorbet on the plate and serve it with a chocolate spoon. This is not the prettiest cake to slice and serve, but I have never heard any complaints and have always garnered much astonished praise from those lucky enough to have this magical dessert.

Also, if you would like to make the completed bombe ahead, you may. The entire dessert, covered with meringue, can be frozen overnight. The one drawback, in this instance, is that the cake will be a bit firm. The bombe can go directly from the freezer into the oven. Make sure the platter can go from freezer to oven as well.

VARIATIONS

This dessert can be varied endlessly and easily. Here are some suggestions:

Use sorbets, ice milks, or ice creams.

White Cake sprinkled with Rum with Coconut, Pineapple and Banana Sorbets. Serve with Bittersweet Chocolate Sauce.

Yellow Génoise sprinkled with Kahlúa with Vanilla, Chocolate and Coffee Ice Creams. Serve with Crème Anglaise.

Chocolate Almond Torte with Vanilla and Chocolate Ice Milks. Serve with Crème Anglaise and Crushed Nougatine.

White Chocolate Cake with Strawberry Sorbet and Vanilla Ice Cream. Serve with Bittersweet Chocolate Sauce and Chantilly Cream or with Raspberry Coulis.

ESPRESSO GÉNOISE

Make the Génoise three or four days before the event. Wrap in plastic wrap or foil and store at room temperature.

FOR TWO 6 × 2-INCH CAKE LAYERS

¾ cup unsifted cake flour

¼ cup unsifted cornstarch

1 tablespoon plus 2 teaspoons finely ground espresso

1 teaspoon vanilla extract

1 teaspoon instant espresso powder (see Note)

5 large eggs

¾ cup sugar

1½ ounces (3 tablespoons) clarified butter (page 4 in Getting Started chapter), warm

Preheat the oven to 350°F. Prepare two 6 × 2-inch cake pans with cooking spray and parchment paper.

Sift together the flour, cornstarch, and ground espresso and set aside. If the espresso cannot sift, stir it in. Dissolve the instant espresso powder in the vanilla and set aside.

Place the eggs, shells intact, in a bowl filled with hot water. Warm them for 10 minutes. Break the eggs into the bowl of your mixer, and add the sugar to the eggs. With the balloon whip, beat on high speed until tripled in volume, light, fluffy, and pale yellow. Quickly, but gently, fold in the dissolved instant coffee.

Sprinkle ⅓ of the dry mixture over the eggs. Using a whisk, fold the dry ingredients into the eggs very gently. Proceed with the remaining dry mixture. Cut down into the eggs with the whisk and fold over gently; this will prevent the egg mixture from deflating.

Slowly and precisely dribble the butter, one tablespoon at a time, over the batter and whisk it in gently, but completely, turning over the batter in broad strokes. Do not speed this step or some butter make sink to the bottom of the cake and create a rubbery layer.

Scrape into the pans and bake about 25 to 35 minutes, or until a toothpick tests clean and the edges just begin to pull away from the sides of the pan. Cool, place on cardboards, and wrap with plastic wrap and foil.

Note: Instant espresso powder can usually be found in specialty food stores and even some supermarkets. Medaglia D'Oro brand is good and is sold nationwide.

FOR TWO 8 × 2-INCH CAKE LAYERS

1 cup plus 2 tablespoons unsifted cake flour

⅓ cup unsifted cornstarch

2 tablespoons plus 1½ teaspoons finely ground espresso

1½ teaspoons vanilla extract

1½ teaspoons instant espresso powder

8 large eggs

1 cup plus 2 tablespoons sugar

2½ ounces (¼ cup plus 1 tablespoon) clarified butter (page 4 in Getting Started chapter), warm

Prepare two 8 × 2-inch cake pans with cooking spray and parchment paper. Proceed as above. Bake about 30 to 40 minutes. Cool, place on cardboards, and wrap with plastic wrap and foil.

FOR TWO 10 × 2-INCH CAKE LAYERS

1¾ cups plus 2 tablespoons unsifted cake flour

⅔ cup plus unsifted cornstarch

¼ cup finely ground espresso

2½ teaspoons vanilla extract

2½ teaspoons instant espresso powder

13 large eggs

1¾ cups plus 2 tablespoons sugar

Scant 4 ounces (scant ½ cup) clarified butter (page 4 in Getting Started chapter), warm

Prepare two 10 × 2-inch cake pans with cooking spray and parchment paper. Proceed as above. This is a large amount, but it will fit into the mixer's bowl. Bake about 30 to 40 minutes. Cool, place on cardboards, and wrap with plastic wrap and foil.

FOR TWO 14 × 2-INCH CAKE LAYERS

Prepare two 14 × 2-inch cake pans with cooking spray and parchment paper. Make the 10-inch recipe twice, once for each 14-inch pan. Bake about 35 to 45 minutes. Cool, place on cardboards, and wrap with plastic wrap and foil.

GREENERY AND FLOWERS

Vanda orchids come in many colors. I used burgundy and maroon to accent the coffee-colored buttercream. These, and the lilies, will probably have to be special-ordered. I used 6 sprays of orchids and 6 lilies for the cake in the photo.

ASSEMBLY

Have all the components ready. Cover an 18-inch Masonite board with bronze-colored decorative foil. Have on hand a 9-inch separator plate and four spiked pillars, all painted a dark brown color.

Sprinkle all the layers with the Espresso Soaking Syrup; fill with the Kahlúa-flavored Egg Yolk Buttercream, reserving the remainder for the decoration. Crumb coat all tiers; chill. Spread a final coat of Espresso Buttercream on all tiers. Chill again.

Center the 14-inch tier on the covered board. Insert dowels for internal support and center the 10-inch tier on top. Place the 8-inch tier on the painted 9-inch separator plate. Center the 6-inch tier on top of the 8-inch tier, using dowels for internal support.

Fit a pastry bag with a coupler and a #16 tip. Fill the bag with Kahlúa Egg Yolk Buttercream and make an elongated scroll on the top and bottom edges of the top two tiers. Repeat this for the bottom two tiers with a #17 tip. Tuck the chocolate-covered espresso beans randomly among the scrolls. Refrigerate overnight.

Transport unassembled and assemble on site by placing the four spiked pillars into the 10-inch tier and stacking the smaller two tiers on top. Decorate with flowers. Serve the cake at room temperature.

GINGER PEACH PECAN COFFEE CAKE

FOR 6 × 3-INCH TIER

STREUSEL

2 tablespoons light brown sugar, packed

1/2 teaspoon ground cinnamon

1 ounce pecans (about 1/3 cup), chopped

1 tablespoon unsalted butter, chilled

1 tablespoon unsifted all-purpose flour

CAKE

1 cup unsifted all-purpose flour

1/2 teaspoon baking soda

1/2 teaspoon baking powder

pinch salt

1/2 teaspoon ground ginger

4 ounces (1 stick) unsalted butter, at room temperature

1/2 cup light brown sugar, packed

1/2 teaspoon vanilla extract

1 large egg

1/2 cup sour cream

1 medium peach

Preheat the oven to 350°F. Prepare one 6 × 3-inch cake pan with cooking spray and parchment paper.

To make the streusel, combine the brown sugar, cinnamon, pecans, butter, and flour in a small bowl. Mix with fingers until crumbly and set aside. You may not use it all for this tier. Reserve excess for larger tiers.

To make the cake, sift together the flour, baking soda, baking powder, salt, and ginger and set aside. Place the butter in the bowl of your mixer and with the flat paddle, beat until creamy on medium-high speed. Add the sugar gradually and beat until light and fluffy. Beat in the vanilla. Add egg, beating well and scraping down the bowl once or twice.

Add the dry ingredients, alternating with the sour cream, in 2 batches, scraping down the batter between additions. Beat just until blended. The mixture will be quite thick.

To peel the peach, drop it in boiling water for 1 minute. Run under cold water and slip off the skin.

Cut it into 1/8-inch-thick slices. Spread half of the batter into the pan and sprinkle with half of the streusel. Place half the peach on top, covering the surface. Repeat with the remaining batter and streusel. With the last half of the peach, make a pretty pinwheel pattern on the surface with the peach slices.

Wrap the pans with the Magi-Cake Strips and bake about 60 to 70 minutes, or until a toothpick tests clean. If the cake begins to brown too much, tent it with foil during the final 10 minutes.

Cool on a wire rack. To remove the cake from the pan, carefully loosen the cake edges from the pan and invert onto the rack, then turn it upright on the rack and cool completely. Place on cardboard, and wrap with plastic wrap and foil, and store at room temperature.

FOR 9 × 3-INCH TIER

STREUSEL

1/4 cup light brown sugar, packed

1 teaspoon ground cinnamon

2 ounces pecans (about 2/3 cup), chopped

2 tablespoons unsalted butter

2 tablespoons unsifted all-purpose flour

CAKE

2 cups unsifted all-purpose flour

1 teaspoon baking soda

1 teaspoon baking powder

1/4 teaspoon salt

1 teaspoon ground ginger

8 ounces (2 sticks) unsalted butter, at room temperature

1 cup light brown sugar, packed

1 teaspoon vanilla extract

2 large eggs

1 cup sour cream

2 medium peaches

Prepare one 9 × 3-inch cake pan with cooking spray and parchment paper. Proceed as above with the following changes: Fill pan with batter, layers of streusel and fruit, reserving some batter and streusel. Place baking core in center and fill with remaining batter, and sprinkle with streusel. Bake about 45 to 55 minutes. If the cake begins to brown too much, tent it with foil during the final 10 minutes.

While cooling, remove the core and cool on the side. This allows the cake to cool more quickly. Remove the cake from pan and the cake plug from core when cool. Insert the cake plug in the hole in the cake, trimming its narrow end, if necessary, so that the plug fits flush with surface. Cool, place on cardboard, and wrap with plastic wrap and foil.

FOR 12 × 3-INCH TIER

STREUSEL

$1/3$ cup light brown sugar, packed

$1^1/3$ teaspoons ground cinnamon

$2^2/3$ ounces pecans (about $3/4$ cup), chopped

4 ounces ($1/2$ stick) unsalted butter, chilled

$1/4$ cup unsifted all-purpose flour

CAKE

4 cups unsifted all-purpose flour

2 teaspoons baking soda

2 teaspoons baking powder

$1/2$ teaspoon salt

2 teaspoons ground ginger

1 pound (4 sticks) unsalted butter, at room temperature

2 cups light brown sugar, packed

2 teaspoons vanilla extract

4 large eggs

2 cups sour cream

2 medium peaches

Prepare a 12 × 3-inch cake pan with cooking spray and parchment paper. Proceed as above, using the baking core, and bake for about 55 to 65 minutes. If the cake begins to brown too much, tent it with foil during the final 10 minutes. Cool, place on cardboard, and wrap with plastic wrap and foil.

VANILLA ICING GLAZE

This is a thick, sweet, drippy icing that you pipe over the top of the tiers, which must be completely cool or the icing will melt. This recipe makes a sufficient amount.

12 ounces (approx. $2^3/4$ cups) confectioners' sugar, sifted

$1/2$ cup heavy cream

1 teaspoon vanilla extract

Place the confectioners' sugar in a large bowl. Add $1/4$ cup of the cream. Begin to whisk and gradually add additional cream to make a smooth, drippy, but pipeable mixture. Whisk slowly to prevent air bubbles. Stir in the vanilla. Use a parchment paper cone to pipe out the icing.

GREENERY AND FLOWERS

Because this cake has no buttercream border along the bottom edge of each tier, you may be able to see the unsightly cardboard rounds. Use your flowers and greenery to mask the seams where the cakes meet the cardboard. I used approximately 12 scabiosa, 8 zinnias, and 2 sprays of bells of Ireland.

ASSEMBLY

Cover a 16-inch-round Masonite board with decorative foil. The cakes and icing should be ready.

Place the bottom tier on the covered board, and center and stack the remaining tiers, using dowels for internal support. Make a parchment cone, fill with icing, snip off a small opening and pipe crisscross designs on top of each of the cake tiers (see photo).

Assemble the cake and pipe icing the day it is served. Leave out unwrapped no longer than three hours and arrange flowers right before setting out for display. Serve cake at room temperature with strong black coffee.

Earl Grey Chocolate Mousse Cake

COMPONENTS

Earl Grey Cake
Two 6 × 2-inch layers
Two 10 × 2-inch layers
Two 14 × 2-inch layers

6 cups Earl Grey Syrup

10 cups Earl Grey
Chocolate Mousse

23 cups Italian Meringue
Buttercream, chocolate variation, adding 1½ teaspoons
bergamot oil (page 141 in
Basics chapter)

2 cups Cocoa Piping Gel

MAKES 100 SERVINGS

M O D E R A T E
❖ ❖

This cake should be called "FDA Approved Cake." I had tasted a chocolate confection flavored with Earl Grey tea and it inspired me to create a cake recipe with the same taste combination. If you have ever tasted Earl Grey tea, then you are familiar with bergamot, which is the citrus family plant that gives the tea its wonderful scent and flavor. I began developing a chocolate cake recipe using strongly steeped tea as the flavoring adjunct, but the flavor did not really come through.

I knew that bergamot was available as an essential oil, which is a very concentrated form of the plant. A few drops added to the cake would certainly punch up the taste. But was it edible and safe?

According to the Federal Drug Administration, Title 21 of Federal Regulation Section 182.20 states that bergamot essential oil is "generally recognized as safe for consumption." Of course, if you were to drink a cup of it, you might not feel too well, but the amounts here are small. Make sure that you buy the essential oil made from an organic source; you can find it at herb stores and health food stores. This is important, because not only do the plant's essences become concentrated during the distillation process, but any pesticides or herbicides will become concentrated as well.

This cake is chocolate through and through, and I gave it some exterior detail by adding free-form squiggles and dots for a contemporary look. I was once asked by an artisan to make him a cake that looked like it had been decorated by the painter Jackson Pollock. This design was the result.

EARL GREY SYRUP

Make this soaking syrup up to one week ahead. Store refrigerated in an airtight container. The superfine sugar dissolves more easily, but you may use granulated sugar instead if you stir it until it is dissolved.

6 cups boiling water
6 tablespoons loose Earl Grey tea leaves
3 cups superfine sugar
³/₄ teaspoon bergamot oil

Pour the boiling water on the tea leaves in a heat-proof, nonmetallic bowl. Stir and steep for 4 minutes. Strain out the tea and discard the leaves. Add the sugar to the tea and stir until dissolved. Cool and then stir in the oil. Store in an airtight container.

EARL GREY CAKE

This is a very straightforward chocolate cake recipe that replaces water with Earl Grey tea. Note that the boiling water called for is slightly more than the amount of tea needed; tea leaves swell and absorb some of the water. Just add the amount of tea called for in the instructions. Make the cake layers two or three days before the event.

FOR TWO 6 × 2-INCH CAKE LAYERS

²/₃ cup boiling water

2 teaspoons loose Earl Grey tea leaves

¹/₂ cup unsifted Dutch-processed cocoa

2 ¹/₄ cups unsifted cake flour

2 teaspoons baking powder

¹/₂ teaspoon salt

6 ounces (1¹/₂ sticks) unsalted butter, at room temperature

1¹/₃ cups sugar

2 teaspoons vanilla extract

¹/₈ teaspoon bergamot oil

2 large eggs

Preheat the oven to 350°F. Prepare two 6 × 2-inch cake pans with cooking spray and parchment paper.

To make the tea, pour the boiling water over the tea leaves in a small heat-proof, nonmetallic bowl. Let steep for 5 minutes. Strain the tea and measure out ¹/₂ cup tea; place in a small bowl. Discard any remaining tea and tea leaves. Whisk the cocoa into the reserved warm tea until smooth and it becomes a thick paste. Set aside.

While the tea is steeping, sift together the flour, baking powder and salt and set aside.

In your mixer's bowl, beat the butter with the flat paddle attachment until creamy on medium-high speed. Add the sugar gradually and beat until light and fluffy. Beat in the vanilla and bergamot oil. Add the eggs one at a time, beating well after each addition; scrape down the bowl once or twice.

Add the tea-cocoa mixture and the dry ingredients alternately in three batches, scraping down after each addition. Blend until well combined.

Scrape the batter into the pans. Bake about 35 to 45 minutes or until a toothpick tests clean. Cool, place on cardboards, and wrap with plastic wrap and foil.

FOR TWO 10 × 2-INCH CAKE LAYERS

1¹/₂ cups boiling water

1 tablespoon plus 2 teaspoons loose Earl Grey tea leaves

1¹/₄ cups unsifted Dutch-processed cocoa

5²/₃ cups unsifted cake flour

1 tablespoon plus 2 teaspoons baking powder

1 teaspoon salt

15 ounces unsalted butter (4 sticks less 1 tablespoon), at room temperature

3¹/₃ cups sugar

1 tablespoon plus 2 teaspoons vanilla extract

¹/₄ teaspoon bergamot oil

5 large eggs

Prepare two 10 × 2-inch cake pans with cooking spray and parchment paper. Proceed as above, measuring out 1¹/₄ cups of tea. Pour the batter into two 10-inch pans and bake about 40 to 50 minutes. Cool, place on cardboards, and wrap with plastic wrap and foil.

FOR TWO 14 × 2-INCH CAKE LAYERS

Prepare two 14 × 2-inch cake pans with cooking spray and parchment paper. Make the 10-inch recipe twice, once for each 14-inch pan. Bake about 50 minutes to 1 hour. Cool, place on cardboards, and wrap with plastic wrap and foil.

EARL GREY CHOCOLATE MOUSSE

Make the mousse one day before you need to fill the layers. It should set at least four hours before spreading, but chilling overnight is fine and allows for more flexibility. The basic recipe (without the bergamot) is similar to one developed by Alice Medrich and is featured in her book Cocolat, *one of my favorites.*

MAKES 10 CUPS

1 cup boiling water

1 tablespoon loose Earl Grey tea leaves

1²/₃ pounds (26 ounces) semisweet chocolate, finely chopped

4 large egg yolks

¼ teaspoon bergamot oil

8 large egg whites

¼ teaspoon cream of tartar

2 tablespoons sugar

1¹/₃ cups heavy cream

Pour the boiling water over the tea leaves in a heat-proof, nonmetallic bowl. Steep for 5 minutes. Strain the tea and measure out ¾ of a cup. Discard any remaining tea or tea leaves. Pour warm tea over the chopped chocolate and melt in a double boiler (*bain-marie*) over hot water or in the microwave. When almost completely melted, remove from the heat and stir with a whisk until all the chocolate is melted and the mixture is smooth.

Whisk in the yolks, one at a time, combining well. Whisk in the bergamot oil.

With a clean balloon whip, beat the whites, on low speed, in a clean, grease-free bowl until frothy. Add the cream of tartar, increase speed and whip until soft peaks form. Add the sugar, 1 tablespoon at a time with the machine still running. Continue to whip until stiff, but not dry, peaks form.

In a separate bowl, with a clean balloon whip, beat the cream on medium-high speed until soft peaks form. Do not overwhip or the texture of the final mousse will be grainy. Start the beating with the machine, if you wish, and finish by hand with a whisk to ensure a soft, smooth whipped cream.

Fold ⅓ of the meringue mixture into the chocolate mixture. Add the remaining meringue and fold until completely blended. Fold in the whipped cream until no white streaks remain. Scrape the mousse into an airtight container and chill until firm, at least 4 hours or overnight.

COCOA PIPING GEL

Clear piping gel pipes very smoothly, stays soft, and can be colored in a variety of ways. Here, it is flavored and colored with cocoa, a recipe I first read about in Rose Levy Beranbaum's The Cake Bible. *You can buy the gel at cake decorating stores or through mail-order. Wilton is one of the easiest brands to find. Make this two hours before needed to allow for cooling. This can be stored in an airtight container at room temperature until needed. You will be using a decorating tip with a small opening so it is imperative that the gel be smooth for piping. If necessary, press it through a strainer while still warm. If the color is too dark for your liking, mix the final product with a bit of the buttercream as we did for the photograph.*

MAKES 2 CUPS

1 cup plus 3 tablespoons piping gel

6 tablespoons hot water

1 cup plus 3 tablespoons Dutch-processed cocoa, sifted

2¹/₄ cups confectioners' sugar, sifted

Whisk all ingredients together in a saucepan. Do not whip too vigorously or air bubbles may form, which will make smooth piping more difficult. Heat over low heat, stirring constantly, until just smooth. Cool completely at room temperature. Place in the pastry bag and pipe.

ASSEMBLY

Have all components ready. Cover an 18-inch Masonite board with decorative foil. Sprinkle cake layers with the Earl Grey Syrup. Fill cakes with a thick layer (approximately ¾ inch) of the mousse. It will be plenty thick enough to spread and stay put. Crumb coat tiers with a layer of the buttercream. Chill all layers, then apply a final coat with the same buttercream.

Place the bottom tier on the covered board. Insert dowels for internal support and center and stack remaining tiers. Fit a pastry bag with a coupler and a #6 round tip. Make a bead border around the base of each tier using the buttercream. Make the decorations with the Cocoa Piping Gel using a pastry bag and a #2 tip. Follow the patterns as shown in the picture, or apply designs of your own devising. Refrigerate overnight. Serve cake at room temperature.

BELLINI CAKE WITH CHAMPAGNE FLUTES

COMPONENTS

White Cake
Two 6 × 2-inch layers
Two 10 × 2-inch layers
Two 14 × 2-inch layers
(page 136 in Basics chapter)

6 cups Sugar Syrup, liqueur variation using peach schnapps (3 cups syrup combined with 3 cups peach schnapps)
(page 147 in Basics chapter)

6 cups Champagne
Peach Filling

23 cups Italian Meringue Buttercream, liqueur variation using peach schnapps (page 140 in Basics chapter)

Equipment
3 champagne flutes
2 seven-inch acrylic disks,
¼-inch thick
7 yards, 3-inch wide
peach-colored ribbon

Greenery and Flowers
Sari roses

MAKES 100 SERVINGS

M O D E R A T E

❖ ❖

*S*ome cakes start with a flavor combination: I was reading a book that referred to "peaches and champagne," which immediately brought to mind the classic Italian cocktail called a Bellini. Invented at Harry's Bar in Venice, the drink consists of sweetened peach purée and champagne. I decided that a summer wedding cake featuring these flavors would be quite appealing. This cake starts with White Cake layers that are sprinkled with peach eau-de-vie or peach schnapps liqueur and filled with a textured champagne-flavored peach purée. The buttercream is also flavored with peach liqueur to accentuate the fruitiness. I use Dekuyper brand schnapps, which is clear and will not color the buttercream; peach brandy is too dark. The top tier is set apart from the rest of the cake by champagne flutes, which further hint at the flavors inside. The ribbons on the champagne glasses and covering the board actually echo an ancient tradition. In the seventeenth century, ribbons—then called love knots—were used to decorate the bridal bed with certain colors denoting particular wishes such as happiness, fertility, or a long marriage.

The success of this recipe depends on the peach taste. The peach liqueur will always be fragrant and fruity, but to have a good flavor in the purée, use ripe or fresh-frozen peaches. Individually quick frozen (IQF) peaches, such as the Red Valley brand, have no additives though they are peeled. Canned peaches will not do. The peach jam used in the filling must also be of a good quality with a high fruit content. Less expensive brands are mostly sugar. Look at the label—peaches should be listed before any sugars.

CHAMPAGNE PEACH FILLING

This filling depends on the quality of the peaches and jam, as mentioned above. The champagne does not have to be expensive, but I do recommend a brut, or the overall result will be too sweet. I tested the recipe with Freixenet, which can be bought by the split (small bottle). This can be made up to 4 days ahead.

MAKES 6 CUPS

3 cups peach jam (36 ounces)
3 cups diced peaches (either freshly peeled or IQF, defrosted and drained)
1 tablespoon unsifted cornstarch
2 tablespoons cold water
⅓ cup champagne

Combine the jam and the diced fruit in a heavy-bottomed, nonreactive saucepan. Cook over a low heat, stirring, until it simmers and continue cooking for 10 minutes. The mixture will reduce and thicken.

Meanwhile, dissolve the cornstarch in the water. Stir this mixture into the hot fruit. Raise the heat and boil for one minute. Remove from the heat. Stir in the champagne. Cool completely and store in an airtight container in the refrigerator. When chilled the filling firms, and it spreads easily over the cake layers.

Vanilla Sponge Cake with Raspberry Mousse Filling, Italian Meringue, and Crystallized Flowers

COMPONENTS

Vanilla Sponge Cake
Two 6 × 2-inch layers
Two 10 × 2-inch layers
Two 14 × 2-inch layers

....

8 cups Sugar Syrup, liqueur variation using peach schnapps (4 cups syrup plus 4 cups peach schnapps) (page 147 in Basics chapter)

....

10 cups Light Raspberry Mousse

....

23 cups Italian Meringue Buttercream, without the butter (page 139 in Basics chapter, see also this recipe)

....

14 cups Raspberry Coulis, 2 tablespoons per serving, to be spooned onto the plates (page 127 in Cake Accompaniments chapter)

....

2 dozen Crystallized Flowers and Mint Leaves (page 163 in Finishing Touches chapter)

....

MAKES 100 SERVINGS

MODERATE
❖ ❖

This is what I call an "enlightened cake." It is lighter in calories than the average wedding cake, due to the elimination of added fat to the cake, filling, or frosting. I also call it enlightened because instead of trying to create a light wedding cake with ersatz ingredients, I used a classic sponge cake with whole eggs, but no added fat from butter or oil. The cake is a bit drier than a classic American butter cake, but I like its texture as a change of pace. The yogurt-raspberry mousse filling adds flavor, color, and moisture. It is made from a mixture of puréed raspberries, some gelatin dissolved in cranberry juice, and low-fat vanilla yogurt. Susan Purdy has a similar mousse in her low-fat dessert cookbook, Have Your Cake and Eat It Too, *and I have based this on her recipe. You can add even more moisture to the cake with the optional Peach Schnapps Syrup sprinkled on the layers. The frosting is simply an Italian Meringue Buttercream without the butter added. It is a shiny, snowy-white, billowy creation, a bit sweeter than the traditional buttercream version. It is easy to make and to work with, as far as decoration is concerned, but it must be used immediately after it is made. Its texture also firms on the cake differently than the traditional buttercream rendition. While the traditional version is buttery, this one is marshmallowy. If the bride is on a low-fat diet, and does not want to compromise, even on her wedding day, then this is the cake to serve.*

Note that the tiers are offset, not centered. The additional Raspberry Coulis, served on the side, adds flavor, color, and moisture.

LIGHT RASPBERRY MOUSSE

Make and refrigerate the mousse at least one day, even up to three days, ahead. This gives it time to firm. You can also make this to serve as a low-fat dessert on its own, maybe with fresh raspberries sprinkled on top. Defrost the raspberries in the refrigerator overnight, in the bags in a bowl of warm water, or on low in the microwave.

MAKES ABOUT 10 CUPS

Three 12-ounce packages individually quick frozen, unsweetened raspberries
3 tablespoons unflavored gelatin (one packet is just short of 1 tablespoon)
1 cup cold water
1 cup cranberry-raspberry juice
3/4 cup superfine sugar
3 cups low-fat vanilla yogurt

Defrost the raspberries. Place the berries and any juice in the container of the food processor fitted with the metal blade and purée for about 15 seconds. Strain out the seeds, if desired.

Meanwhile, sprinkle the gelatin over the cold water in a small pan and stir to combine. Let sit 5 minutes until the gelatin has softened. Add the cranberry-raspberry juice and heat on very low heat. Stir until the gelatin dissolves. Do not boil. Add the sugar and continue to heat, without boiling, until the sugar dissolves. Stir it a few times to facilitate the process.

Remove from the heat and pour into a bowl that is set in a larger bowl filled with ice and ice water. Add the purée and whisk into the gelatin mixture. Cool the mixture, stirring over the ice until it is as thick and viscous as an egg white, for about 30 minutes.

When the mixture is thick, pour off any liquid whey from the yogurt and stir the yogurt into the gelatin mixture gently, but thoroughly, with a whisk. Cover the bowl and chill overnight or store in an airtight container in the refrigerator.

Vanilla Sponge Cake

Make this cake the day before you are going to assemble it. Its lack of fat allows it to dry out more quickly than a butter cake. However, my recipe tester Mary McNamara swears that the cake was still good three days after baking.

FOR TWO 6 × 2-INCH CAKE LAYERS

5 large eggs, separated

3/4 cup plus 1 tablespoon sugar, divided in half
(6 1/2 tablespoons and 6 1/2 tablespoons)

3/4 teaspoon vanilla extract

3/4 cup plus 1 tablespoon cake flour, sifted

1/4 teaspoon cream of tartar

Preheat the oven to 350°F. Prepare two 6 × 2-inch cake pans with parchment paper; do not coat with cooking spray.

In the bowl of your mixer, with a balloon whip, beat the yolks and 6 1/2 tablespoons sugar on high speed until pale yellow and thick. A broad ribbon should form when the balloon whip is lifted. Beat in the vanilla. Stir in the flour by hand until the mixture is evenly combined.

In a clean, grease-free bowl, with a clean balloon whip, beat the whites on low speed until frothy. Add the cream of tartar and beat on medium-high speed until soft peaks form. Add the remaining 6 1/2 tablespoons sugar gradually. Continue to beat, increasing the speed, until stiff, but not dry, peaks form. Do not overbeat.

Fold about 1/4 of the meringue mixture into the rest of the batter to lighten it up. Then, fold in the remaining meringue.

Spread the batter in the pans, smoothing tops with a small offset spatula. Bake about 30 to 40 minutes, or until a toothpick tests clean. Do not overbake this cake as it contains little fat to keep it moist.

Cool on a rack for 10 minutes. To release from the pans, loosen sides with a small spatula, pressing away from the cake. Invert onto rack and set aside at room temperature to cool completely. Place on cardboards and wrap with plastic wrap and foil. Let sit at room temperature overnight.

FOR TWO 10 × 2-INCH CAKE LAYERS

12 large eggs, separated

2 cups sugar, divided in half

2 teaspoons vanilla extract

2 cups cake flour, sifted

1/2 teaspoon cream of tartar

Prepare two 10 × 2-inch cake pans as described above. Proceed as for 6-inch cake recipe. Add the flour in batches and stir in thoroughly. Bake about 35 to 45 minutes. Cool, place on cardboards, and wrap with plastic wrap and foil.

FOR TWO 14 × 2-INCH LAYERS

Make the 10-inch recipe twice; once for each 14 × 2-inch pan. Bake about 40 to 50 minutes. Cool, place on cardboards, and wrap with plastic wrap and foil.

Italian Meringue Frosting

Follow the recipe for Italian Meringue Buttercream on page 139 in the Basics chapter, but eliminate all of the butter. You will whip the whites, pour over the sugar syrup, and then whip the frosting until cool. You will need 23 cups total. Make about 18 cups initially for the crumb coat and the final coat. While the layers chill, make another batch for the decoration. Use immediately after making.

Greenery and Flowers

The crystallized flowers and mint leaves were placed in a cascade on the cake pictured. I added a small silver vase to the top of the cake to hold a few more flowers. Use the photo for placement ideas.

Assembly

Have all components ready. Cover an 18-inch-round Masonite board with decorative foil.

Sprinkle the layers with the Peach Schnapps Syrup and fill tiers with ½ inch of raspberry mousse, smoothing with an offset spatula. Spread almost to the edges, leaving about ¼ inch free of mousse.

Crumb coat with a layer of the Italian Meringue. Immediately apply a thick final layer of the frosting over all. Smooth out the sides with a spatula warmed in hot water and dried. Chill all the tiers.

Have your small batch of decoration frosting ready. Spread some on the Masonite board and center the 14-inch tier on top of it. Stack the top two tiers in an offset configuration (see photo), using dowels for internal support.

Fit a pastry bag with a coupler and a #16 star tip. Fill the bag with frosting and make a reverse shell border around the top and bottom edges of the top tier. Use a #17 tip for the middle tier and an #18 tip for the bottom tier. Refrigerate cake overnight.

This cake may be decorated before or after transporting to the event site. About two hours before serving, remove the cake from the refrigerator, and adorn it with flowers. The cake should be served at room temperature. Spoon Raspberry Coulis on plates and place the slices on the coulis.

Meanwhile, sift together the cake flour, baking powder, and salt and set aside.

In the bowl of your mixer, cream the butter with the flat paddle attachment until creamy and smooth. Add ¾ cup sugar gradually and continue to beat on medium-high speed. Scrape down the bowl once or twice and cream until very light and fluffy. Add the vanilla, beating to combine. Add the yolks, one at a time, beating well after each addition and scraping down the contents once or twice. Set aside.

In a clean, grease-free bowl, with a clean balloon whip, beat the egg whites on low speed until frothy. Add the cream of tartar, increase speed to medium-high, and continue to whip until soft peaks form. Add ¼ cup sugar gradually and whip until stiff, but not dry, peaks form. Do not overbeat.

In a large bowl, combine the butter-egg yolk mixture with the sifted dry ingredients alternately with the poppyseed mixture. Do this by hand, gently folding in the dry and wet until all ingredients are thoroughly combined. Fold in the whipped whites carefully, retaining the volume provided by the meringue.

Scrape into the pans, smoothing the tops with an offset spatula. Bake about 40 to 50 minutes, or until a toothpick comes out clean. Cool, place on cardboards, and wrap with plastic wrap and foil.

FOR TWO 9 × 2-INCH CAKE LAYERS

⅔ cup poppyseeds

1½ cups whole milk

3 cups unsifted cake flour

1 tablespoon baking powder

⅔ teaspoon salt

6 ounces (1½ sticks) unsalted butter, at room temperature

2 cups sugar, divided into 1½ cups and ½ cup

1½ teaspoons vanilla extract

6 large eggs, separated

½ teaspoon cream of tartar

Prepare two 9 × 2-inch cake pans with cooking spray and parchment paper. Proceed as above for 6-inch layers. Bake about 50 to 60 minutes. Cool, place on cardboards, and wrap with plastic wrap and foil.

FOR TWO 12 × 2-INCH CAKE LAYERS

Prepare two 12 × 2-inch cake pans with cooking spray and parchment paper. Make the 9-inch recipe twice, once for each 12-inch pan. Bake about 55 to 65 minutes. Cool, place on cardboards, and wrap with plastic wrap and foil.

GREENERY AND FLOWERS

I used approximately 1 pint strawberries, 3 half-pints raspberries, 1 pint blueberries, 1 pint blackberries, 5 bunches of champagne grapes, 18 cherries, and 1 bunch of mint leaves for the cake in the photo. If you can find fruit with stems and leaves intact, the effect will be spectacular. Make sure all fruit is at the peak of freshness.

ASSEMBLY

Have all components ready. Cover an 18-inch-round Masonite board with decorative foil. Fill the tiers with the Marmalade Buttercream and crumb coat with the Grand Marnier Buttercream; chill all tiers. To make the pattern you will need a #48 basket-weave tip, which will make all the broad, flat, horizontal lines, and a plain round #6 tip, which will provide the vertical lines. The #48 tip has one smooth side and one ridged side; I use the ridged side.

Fit the tips on individual pastry bags so you can use both tips simultaneously. To start, pipe a vertical line with the #6 tip, going from the bottom of the tier to the top. With the #48, pipe horizontal lines, each about one inch long, crossing the vertical line. Make the first one parallel to the top edge of the cake, the next one the width of a basket weave below it, and repeat with remaining lines. The last one should not be at the bottom edge; leave room for another strip between it and the bottom, which you will make next. (Refer to the illustration for guidance). Pipe another vertical line to the right of the horizontal lines, slightly overlapping the edges of the horizontal ones. Then pipe more horizontal lines across this filling in the spaces formed by the previous horizontal lines. This set of horizontal lines will be started just to the left of the second vertical line and go for an inch toward the right. Repeat this pattern, working all around the cake. As you approach the end, space it so that the last set of horizontal lines complements the first set. The piping may take a while; it is

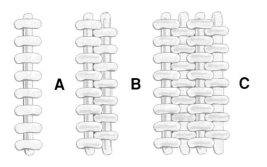

Making a basket weave.

best to only put a little bit of buttercream in each bag at a time because the extended time that your hands spend wrapped around the bags will overheat the buttercream. For the tips to pipe clean shapes, keep the buttercream cool. You can stop at any time to chill the tier and the buttercream and resume later. When you are finished, chill the tier and repeat the procedure with the other tiers. Chill all tiers well.

Center the bottom tier on the Masonite board. Center the tiers on top of one another, using dowels for internal support. Pipe a rope border with the #6 tip along the top edges. Chill overnight.

Arrange the fruit and mint immediately before setting the cake out for display. Serve the cake at room temperature.

GREENERY AND FLOWERS

These exotic flowers work perfectly with the tropical flavors of the cake. I used approximately 2 sprays of oncidium orchids, 4 sprays of dendrobium orchids, and 2 sprays of cattleya orchids. Place a bunch of flowers on the top, and nestle the rest around the pillars and the base of the cake.

ASSEMBLY

Have all components ready. Cover an 18-inch-round Masonite board with decorative foil. Have 7-inch and 11-inch clear acrylic separator plates and 8 matching spiked pillars. These acrylic ones are particularly nice and can be purchased from Parrish's (see Resources section, page 188).

Sprinkle the layers with the passion fruit syrup. Fill the tiers with a layer of Coconut Buttercream, sprinkling some chopped macadamias on top of the filling before setting the top layer in place. Crumb coat with more coconut buttercream and chill. Apply a thick final coat of buttercream on all tiers. Don't worry about making it very smooth because it will be covered with coconut. You need enough for the coconut to stick to.

Holding each tier, supported by cardboard, in your left hand, scoop up the coconut with your right hand and gently press it into place covering the surface of each tier. Reverse the procedure if you are left-handed. Repeat with all tiers. See specific instructions in the Finishing Touches chapter, page 159. Place the bottom tier on the Masonite board. Place top two tiers on their respective separator plates. Refrigerate overnight.

Assemble the tiers on site shortly before serving. Nestle the caramelized nuts randomly amongst the coconut, as shown in the photo, and arrange flowers, as desired. Serve the cake at room temperature.

TAHITIAN VANILLA BEAN POUND CAKE WITH ORCHIDS AND FRUIT

COMPONENTS

Pound Cake
Two 6 × 2-inch layers
Two 10 × 2-inch layers
Two 14 × 2-inch layers
(page 130 in Basics chapter,
see also this recipe)

6 cups Vanilla Pastry Cream
(page 146 in Basics chapter)

Fresh fruit layer

23 cups Italian Meringue
Buttercream, vanilla variation
(page 140 in Basics chapter)

24 gold dragées

Greenery and Flowers
Dendrobium orchids in magenta,
white, magenta and white, and
gold with fuschia speckles
Boxwood greens

MAKES 100 SERVINGS

M O D E R A T E
❖ ❖

In my opinion, a rose is not just a rose, and vanilla beans are not just vanilla beans. Bourbon beans are harvested for most of the vanilla extract that you find on supermarket shelves. When it comes to beans, however, you have a choice. Both bourbon beans (including those from Madagascar, and the islands of Comoro or Reunion) as well as Tahitian beans are available for the home cook. I love the extremely fragrant, floral Tahitian beans and this recipe showcases them nicely. Each type of vanilla is derived from different species of the orchid plant (Vanilla planifolia *and* Vanilla tahitensis) *and that is why I chose to decorate this cake with this most beautiful of flowers. Many orchid flowers are considered edible such as the vanda and dendrobium. Another plus is that these flowers hold up quite well out of water, allowing for an extended display time for the cake. Note that dendrobium orchids were used on the previous cake as well, to a much different effect.*

This cake is made for the vanilla lover. With the vanilla beans scattered throughout the cake and pastry cream filling, the vanilla essence truly shines forth. The fresh fruit filling adds color and texture to the cake without in any way distracting from the vanilla. You may eliminate the pastry cream filling and use buttercream instead if you want to remove the extra component. Increase amounts of buttercream accordingly.

TAHITIAN VANILLA BEAN POUND CAKE

You may make the cake one month ahead, wrap it well, and freeze it. I make mine three days before the event. This allows one full day of rest before decorating. This cake keeps quite well and its flavor improves with a little aging.

Follow directions for Pound Cake, in Basics chapter, page 130, making the following changes:

For the 6-inch layers, use 1 Tahitian vanilla bean. Split the bean open and scrape out the seeds into a small bowl, using a blunt knife or spoon tip. Add the vanilla extract and stir with a fork to break up the sticky seed clumps. Add this to the butter-sugar mixture and beat thoroughly to disperse the vanilla seeds. Proceed as directed with the rest of the recipe.

For the 10-inch layers, add 1½ Tahitian vanilla beans. For the 14-inch layers, use 3 beans. Proceed as above.

ALMOND BANANA CAKE WITH AMARETTO BUTTERCREAM AND MARZIPAN LEAVES

COMPONENTS

Almond Banana Cake
Two 6 × 2-inch layers
Two 10 × 2-inch layers
Two 14 × 2-inch layers

32 cups Italian Meringue Buttercream, liqueur variation using Amaretto (page 140 in Basics chapter)

Marzipan Leaves and Acorns, (page 148 in Basics chapter for marzipan recipe and page 169 or 172 in Finishing Touches chapter for shaping leaves, see also this recipe)

Lemon leaves (optional)

MAKES 100 SERVINGS

C O M P L E X
❖ ❖ ❖

*T*his is a moist, fruity cake made with banana purée and almond extract. The almond flavor is further intensified by Amaretto liqueur in the buttercream and decorations of the marzipan leaves falling down the sides of the cake. I made a cake just like this for a couple who contracted with me more than two years prior to their wedding. Believe it or not, the flavor of the cake wasn't decided upon until a mere two weeks before the wedding. Things do happen like this with clients. You have to walk a fine line between allowing the couple to walk all over you, and strong-arming them into a decision. Be gracious, offer guidance, and if it is getting dangerously close to the wedding date, issue an ultimatum in the nicest possible way. The result of those panicked brainstorming sessions at the last minute just may yield a successful and intriguing concept, like the cake presented here.

These cakes layers are only a tad over one inch thick, which will yield tiers that are about 2 1/2 inches high, a bit shorter than most in the book. If you want to make three layers for each tier for an extra-thick cake, go ahead; adjust your buttercream amount accordingly, too, as there will be more cake to fill and cover. With the marzipan decorations, which are quite rich, I prefer a thinner tier. One note on bananas: The average 7-ounce banana yields approximately 1/2 cup of purée. Figure the number of bananas needed accordingly.

ALMOND BANANA CAKE

You may make this cake three or four days ahead.

FOR TWO 6 × 2-INCH CAKE LAYERS

3/4 cup banana purée (2 small bananas)

1/4 cup buttermilk

1 cup plus 2 tablespoons unsifted cake flour

3/4 teaspoon baking powder

1/4 teaspoon baking soda

pinch salt

2 ounces (1/2 stick) unsalted butter, at room temperature

2/3 cup sugar

1/2 teaspoon vanilla extract

1/4 teaspoon almond extract

1 large egg

1 ounce natural almonds (about 1/3 cup), coarsely chopped (optional)

Preheat the oven to 350°F. Prepare two 6 × 2-inch cake pans with cooking spray and parchment paper.

Place the bananas in a food processor fitted with the metal blade and purée. Whisk the banana purée and the buttermilk together in a small bowl. Set aside. Sift together the cake flour, leaveners, and salt. Set aside.

In your mixer's bowl, beat the butter with the flat paddle attachment until creamy. Add the sugar gradually, beating well until light and fluffy on medium-high speed. Beat in the extracts. Add the egg, beating well.

Add the wet and dry ingredients alternately in two batches, beating well after each addition and scraping down the bowl once or twice. Make sure the batter is well blended. By hand, gently fold in the nuts, if using, with a few broad strokes.

Pour the batter into the pans. Bake about 30 to 40 minutes, or until a toothpick tests clean. Cool, place on cardboards, and wrap with plastic wrap and foil.

FOR TWO 10 × 2-INCH CAKE LAYERS

2 cups banana purée (4 medium bananas)

$^2/_3$ cup buttermilk

$2^3/_4$ cups plus 1 tablespoon unsifted cake flour

2 teaspoons baking powder

$^2/_3$ teaspoon baking soda

$^1/_3$ teaspoon salt

5 ounces (1$^1/_4$ sticks) unsalted butter, at room temperature

1$^2/_3$ cups sugar

1$^1/_4$ teaspoons vanilla extract

$^2/_3$ teaspoon almond extract

3 large eggs

2 ounces natural almonds (about $^2/_3$ cup), coarsely chopped (optional)

Prepare two 10 × 2-inch cake pans with cooking spray and parchment paper. Proceed as above for 6-inch cake recipe. Scrape the batter down several times when adding the dry and wet ingredients so that the batter will combine smoothly and thoroughly. Bake about 40 to 50 minutes. Cool, place on cardboards, and wrap with plastic wrap and foil.

FOR TWO 14 × 2-INCH CAKE LAYERS

Make the 10-inch cake recipe twice, once for each 14-inch layer. Bake about 45 to 55 minutes. Cool, place on cardboards, and wrap with plastic wrap and foil.

MARZIPAN LEAVES AND ACORNS

The Marzipan recipe in the Basics chapter may be made a month ahead. Instructions for making leaves are in the Finishing Touches chapter. The leaves should be made a day or two before needed to retain some of their suppleness. I used a variety of sizes.

If you want to tint half of the leaves green, as in the picture, you will also need some green paste color. I prefer to use some of the more subtle green colors such as moss or juniper. The popular leaf green is jarringly bright, at least to my eye. You can also blend colors, if you like.

For the acorns, Elizabeth Duffy, the fabulous food stylist who helped make all of the cakes for the photographs in this book, came up with this idea. Simply roll light green marzipan into an acorn shape. Take some brown-tinted marzipan, roll it into a ball, flatten it out into a disk and use it to make the nut's cap and stem. Use small, sharp scissors to snip the cap to give it texture.

ASSEMBLY

Have all components ready. Cover an 18-inch-round Masonite board with decorative foil. Fill and crumb coat with buttercream; chill. Apply smooth, final coat of buttercream and chill again. Center the largest tier on the board. Center and stack top two tiers, using dowels for internal support.

Fit pastry bag with a coupler and #2 tip. Fill with buttercream and draw leaf shapes randomly on the cake. Chill well.

Arrange the Marzipan Leaves on the cake so they are adjacent to and complement the piped leaves (see photo). Use the photo as a guide for placing the marzipan acorns. The marzipan leaves and acorns may be set on the cake the night before and may be refrigerated with the cake. Lemon leaves may ring the bottom of the cake, if desired. Serve cake at room temperature.

GIANDUJA TRUFFLE CAKE

COMPONENTS

Gianduja Truffle Cake
One 6 × 3-inch tier
One 10 × 3-inch tier
One 14 × 3-inch tier

12 cups Bittersweet Chocolate
Ganache, 10 cups for pouring,
2 for piping (page 145 in Basics
chapter)

Nuts, Greenery, and Fruit
Hazelnuts in the shell
Fresh figs
Lychees
Crab apples
Seckle pears
Cape gooseberries

Gold Powder

16 cups Chantilly Cream,
2 tablespoons per serving,
start with 8 cups heavy cream
(page 126 in Cake
Accompaniments chapter)

MAKES 125 SERVINGS

C O M P L E X

❖ ❖ ❖

Gianduja (jon-doo-ya) is an Italian mixture of milk chocolate and hazelnuts; I use the Callebaut brand (which can be mail-ordered from N.Y. Cake and Baking Distributors, page 187, or found in many specialty food stores). This truffle cake combines gianduja with semisweet chocolate to make a rich and creamy cake. It is topped with bittersweet ganache, gold-dusted hazelnuts in the shell, greenery, and fruit. Although this is a variation of the Chocolate Raspberry Truffle Cake, it tastes so different and has different preparation techniques, I felt it deserved to be a recipe on its own.

This cake is quite rich because of its dense, truffle-like texture and ingredients. It is so moist that you may make it one week ahead and store it in the refrigerator, unglazed but wrapped tightly. Glaze it the day before you plan to serve it. This cake needs an accompaniment of Chantilly Cream to help cut the richness.

GIANDUJA TRUFFLE CAKE

Make this component up to one week ahead.

FOR ONE 6 × 3-INCH TIER
6 large eggs
½ pound bittersweet chocolate
½ pound gianduja
8 ounces (2 sticks) unsalted butter

Preheat the oven to 375°F. Prepare one 6 × 3-inch pan with cooking spray and parchment paper.

Place the whole eggs, shell intact, in a bowl filled with hot water for 10 minutes.

Meanwhile, place the chocolates and butter in the top of a double boiler (*bain-marie*) and melt. Alternatively, melt the chocolate and butter in the microwave at half power for 5 to 8 minutes, checking and whisking together every 2 to 3 minutes. Allow the mixture to cool slightly, stirring occasionally, for 10 minutes. It will remain warm, but the excess heat will have dissipated.

Crack the eggs into the bowl of your mixer, and with a clean balloon whip, beat on high until tripled in volume, or until pale yellow and light and spongy, and it holds a soft peak. This will take about 5 minutes on highest speed.

Add ¼ of the egg mixture to the cooled chocolate, gently combining by hand with a whisk. Egg streaks may remain. Add the remaining eggs and fold them in, first with a whisk and then with a large rubber spatula. The batter will deflate a bit, but try to retain as much volume as possible. The mixture will be smooth, thick, and evenly colored.

Scrape the batter into the prepared pan placed in a larger pan filled with 1 inch of hot water. Bake for about 15 minutes, or until the surface loses its sheen.

FRUITCAKE

May be made one month ahead; make at least one week ahead.

FOR ONE 6 × 3-INCH TIER

1½ pounds mixed fruits: dark and golden raisins, currants, dried dates, figs, cherries, cranberries, apricots, pineapple, and candied lemon and orange peels

3 tablespoons sherry plus extra for saturation

3 tablespoons honey

¾ cup plus 2 tablespoons unsifted cake flour

pinch baking soda

½ teaspoon ground cinnamon

pinch ground cloves

3¾ ounces unsalted butter (almost 1 stick), at room temperature

⅓ cup plus 1 tablespoon light brown sugar

2 large eggs

5 ounces mixed walnuts and pecans (about 1¼ cups), chopped

Preheat the oven to 275°F. Prepare one 6 × 3-inch cake pan with cooking spray and parchment paper.

Leave the raisins, currants, cherries, and cranberries whole. Dice the remaining fruit. Combine all the fruits with the sherry and honey in a nonreactive bowl and toss to mix evenly. Cover with plastic wrap and soak the fruit overnight, or up to two days, at a cool room temperature. Stir a few times during soaking.

Sift dry ingredients and set aside.

Cream the butter in your mixer's bowl using the flat paddle attachment. Add the brown sugar gradually and beat until light and fluffy on medium-high speed. Beat in the eggs.

Add the dry ingredients in three batches, beating well, but briefly, after each addition. Scrape down the batter once or twice to encourage even mixing. Stir in the fruits, all their liquid, and the nuts. Fold in two of the charms, reserving the others for the remaining tiers.

Scrape into the pans, smoothing the top with a small offset spatula. Bake about 2 hours, 5 minutes to 2 hours, 15 minutes or until a toothpick tests almost clean. If the cake begins to brown too much, tent it with foil during baking.

Cool in pans on racks for 10 minutes. Turn out of the pans, cool completely, and place on cardboards.

FOR ONE 9 × 3-INCH TIER

2¾ pounds mixed fruits (see above for suggested mixture)

⅓ cup sherry plus extra for saturation

⅓ cup honey

1¾ cups plus 2 tablespoons unsifted cake flour

⅓ teaspoon baking soda

¾ teaspoon ground cinnamon

⅓ teaspoon ground cloves

7⅓ ounces unsalted butter, at room temperature

¾ cup plus 2 tablespoons light brown sugar

3 large eggs

10 ounces mixed walnuts and pecans (about 2½ cups), chopped

Prepare one 9 × 3-inch cake pan with cooking spray and parchment paper. Proceed as above for the 6-inch tier, adding eggs one at a time and beating well after each addition. Remember to fold in several charms. Bake about 2 hours, 25 minutes to 2 hours, 35 minutes. If the cake begins to brown too much, tent it with foil during baking. Cool as directed above.

FOR ONE 12 × 3-INCH TIER

5⅓ pounds mixed fruits (see above for suggested mixture)

⅔ cup sherry, plus extra for saturation

⅔ cup honey

3¾ cups unsifted cake flour

⅔ teaspoon baking soda

1⅔ teaspoons ground cinnamon

⅔ teaspoon ground cloves

15 ounces (3¾ sticks) unsalted butter, at room temperature

1⅔ cups light brown sugar

6 large eggs

1¼ pounds mixed walnuts and pecans (about 5¼ cups), chopped

Prepare one 12 × 3-inch cake pan with cooking spray and parchment paper. Proceed as above with the following changes: Cream the butter and sugar in the mixing bowl and beat in the eggs one at a time. Add sifted ingredients and combine. Turn batter out into a large bowl and add the fruit and nuts (the entire amount will not fit in a standard mixing bowl). Combine the batter with the fruits and nuts, using a large spatula or your hands. Stir in remaining charms. Bake about 2 hours, 55 minutes to 3 hours, 5 minutes. If the cake begins to brown too much, tent it with foil during baking. Cool as directed above.

PREASSEMBLY—SATURATING

To saturate the cooled cakes with sherry, use a long wooden skewer to make several holes in the cooled cakes. Slowly sprinkle sherry over the layers. You want to evenly saturate the tiers. On average, you will add about 2 tablespoons to the 6-inch tier, ¼ cup to the 9-inch tier, and ½ cup to the 12-inch tier. Wrap the cakes up in cheesecloth moistened with more sherry and place them in plastic bags or wrap well with plastic wrap. Store them at room temperature.

Every day, take the cakes out of the bags and sprinkle them with more sherry, saturating the cheesecloth in the amounts referred to above. On day one, sprinkle the tops; day two, sprinkle the bottoms. Keep alternating every other day. Remember, you want even saturation, not a wet, soggy cake. Replace the cakes in the bags or plastic wrap and set aside until the next day.

Every day, turn the cakes so that the layers are rotated and are stored on their bottoms and tops alternately. This will encourage even absorption. The saturation process takes some baking intuition in assessing how much sherry to use. If you sprinkle lightly and evenly, then the cakes can easily take more sherry every day. If you remove the cakes from their plastic wrap and they seem overly moist, wait until the next day to add more sherry. If you have made the cakes a week ahead, you may very well add a little sherry every day. If you make the cakes one month ahead, adding sherry every two to four days will do the trick initially. For the last week or two, you may only have to add sherry twice a week. It is fairly easy to tell if the cakes are retaining moisture, so trust your intuition.

ROYAL ICING

The Royal Icing should be prepared immediately before it is needed (see Assembly directions).

You will have to make the royal icing twice. First, at least two days before assembly, make a small 2-cup batch; refer to the Basics chapter, page 144, for the recipe for flooding the cake drum. Thin the icing with water so that it flows freely and pour it over the cake drum. It will spread out and cover the top. Pick up the drum and tilt it gently to encourage the icing to flow out to the edges. Do not smooth top with a spatula, but wipe the edges to clean up the sides. Set aside on a flat surface at least 48 hours to dry solid. When dry, affix a ½-inch-wide ribbon around the edges of the drum,

using some royal icing as glue; reserve some from your first batch. Or, if you prefer, cover the drum with dark red, green, or silver decorative foil. It is important to use a ½-inch-thick cake drum because this cake is heavy and needs the support.

Make a second 8-cup batch of royal icing just before beginning final cake assembly. I prefer to use fresh royal icing for this step; you must make sure it is free of lumps or it will not go through the tiny #1 tip.

ASSEMBLY

Have all components ready. Cover each tier with a layer of marzipan; refer to the Finishing Touches chapter, page 157, for complete directions. The fruitcake should be moist enough so that the marzipan adheres readily. You may make a single, large layer of marzipan, or piece it together with a top disk and side strips. The royal icing will help camouflage any seams. However, a

single layer is best and the smallest tier, at least, should be covered in this way.

Center the largest tier on the covered board. Center and stack the remaining tiers, using wooden dowels for internal support. Fit your pastry bag with a coupler and a #1 (or #0 if available) tip. Fill the bag with perfectly smooth royal icing. Using the picture as a guide, make a lacy pattern, covering the tiers completely. This is really just a free-form squiggle; just don't overlap any of your lines. Use a #6, #7, and #8 round tip to make a bead border at the base of each tier, using the smallest tip for the top tier, the #7 for the middle tier, and the #8 for the bottom tier. If you need extra help covering any marzipan seams, make a bead border along the top edges as well.

The cake may sit at room temperature for up to one week at this point because the marzipan will seal in moisture. However, I prefer to assemble this cake the day before serving as the fruitcake has already aged properly. Place the cake in a large box to keep it free of dust. Do not refrigerate.

To make marzipan holly leaves, simply follow directions in the Finishing touches chapter (page 169 or 172), using a holly leaf cutter and tinting the marzipan a rich green. The berries are simple: Tint marzipan with red paste coloring and roll into small balls. Arrange the marzipan holly leaves and berries, before setting it out for display. Serve small pieces, because this cake has a very concentrated flavor and dense texture.

Please note that the charms are not expensive and are sold for about $20. They greatly enhance the uniqueness of the cake. Of course, the cake will be just as tasty and pretty to look at without them.

MARZIPAN CHOCOLATE CAKE WITH APRICOT FILLING AND COGNAC

COMPONENTS

Marzipan Chocolate Cake
Two 6 × 2-inch layers
Two 9 × 2-inch layers
Two 12 × 2-inch layers

4 cups Sugar Syrup, liqueur variation using cognac (page 147 in Basics chapter)

8 cups high-quality apricot preserves for filling, at room temperature for easy spreading

9 pounds Marzipan, for covering tiers (textured rolling pin was used for photo) (page 148 in Basics chapter)

5 cups Bittersweet Chocolate Ganache, for piping (page 145 in Basics chapter)

10 ounces melted semisweet chocolate, for piping to make lattice

Equipment
8 trimmable pillars
7-inch separator plate
10-inch separator plate
(all painted dark brown)

18 Marzipan Roses in various sizes (page 170 in Finishing Touches chapter)

24 Chocolate Leaves, in various sizes (page 172 in Finishing Touches chapter)

MAKES 80 SERVINGS

COMPLEX
❖ ❖ ❖

This cake is a variation of the "Spanish Vanilla" cake that the Culinary Institute of America (CIA) teaches to its pastry students. At first, it may not seem obvious what is Spanish and what is vanilla about this recipe. The prominent flavors come from the almond paste and the chocolate. This so intrigued me that I called upon Marcus Farbinger, the team leader of the pastry program at the CIA. He explained that the cake is basically a pound cake of German origin and that the almond paste was probably originally added to the batter to improve its keeping qualities, as well as to flavor it. Almonds and vanilla, both used in the cake, were brought to that part of the world via the trade routes, which went through Portugal, Spain, and on up to northern Europe long ago. Since the ingredients were often originally from Spain, and its neighbors, the cake's name was given as a tribute to the origins of its ingredients. Nick Malgieri, Director of the baking curriculum at Peter Kump's School of Culinary Arts in Manhattan, added that the cake recipe is probably about 150 years old. Before that time, chocolate was not available in that section of Europe. Also, the method of incorporating shaved chocolate to the batter, according to Malgieri, is very indicative of the area and times. The chocolate at that time was much harder and drier. Since it probably didn't melt very well, the way to incorporate a chocolate flavor into a cake was in this manner.

The cake is an extremely moist pound cake with almond paste and toasted, ground almonds in the batter. Shaved chocolate is folded in, giving the batter a tweed-like appearance. The cake is sprinkled with cognac, filled with apricot preserves, and covered with marzipan. For the photo, we covered the cake with a lattice of chocolate to accentuate the chocolate flavor within. The chocolate ganache border is rich and luscious, like the cake itself. The tiers are supported on short pillars. Serve smaller pieces of this cake.

bowl. Whip the 20 egg whites in two separate batches: Whip 10 whites with ½ cup sugar until they form stiff, but not dry, peaks. Scrape them onto the batter in the bowl. Repeat with the second batch of 10 egg whites and another ½ cup sugar. While this is whipping, fold the first batch into the batter to lighten it; fold in remaining meringue. Proceed as above. Bake about 80 to 90 minutes. Cool, place on cardboards, and wrap with plastic wrap and foil.

ASSEMBLY

Have all components ready. Cover a 16-inch-round Masonite board with chocolate-brown paper. Have ready 7-inch and 10-inch separator plates and 8 short, trimmable pillars, each painted a dark brown color.

Torte each 12-inch layer in half—each complete tier is composed of four cake layers. Place the bottom layer, cut side up, in front of you, sprinkle it with cognac syrup, and spread it with preserves. It is fine if an occasional chunk of apricot remains in the preserves in the interior layers. Place the second cake layer on top of the preserves, sprinkle it with cognac syrup, spread with preserves, and repeat with the third layer. Place the fourth layer on top and sprinkle it with cognac syrup. Brush some preserves on the tops and sides of the entire tier, without any chunks of fruit. This will help the marzipan adhere. Repeat with the remaining tiers and layers.

Following the instructions in Finishing Touches, page 157, roll out a piece of marzipan large enough to cover the 6-inch tier. Cover this small tier with the marzipan, trimming the bottom flush with the bottom of the cardboard; you should not see any cardboard at all. Repeat with the 9-inch and 12-inch tiers. Piece marzipan together, if necessary, for largest tier as described in Finishing Touches chapter, page 157. Place the top two tiers on their respective separator plates. Center the bottom tier on the Masonite board.

Fill a parchment cone with some melted chocolate and snip a tiny opening. Make a lattice design on the top of each tier. Do not let any drip down the sides. If it does, do not try to wipe off; you'll make a chocolate smear on the cake. Simply refrigerate the cake; the chocolate will harden and you can peel it away. You will have to use a few parchment cones to finish all three layers. Chill all the tiers.

Fit a pastry bag with a #8 round tip. Using the ganache at room temperature, pipe a small bead border on the top and bottom edge of each tier. The border around the top edge should completely enclose the chocolate lattice. Chill again, preferably overnight.

Transport the tiers unassembled, stack them with pillars on site, and place flowers and leaves on the tiers, as desired. Serve the cake at room temperature.

Buttermilk Spice Cake with Vanilla Buttercream and Marzipan Sweets

COMPONENTS

Buttermilk Spice Cake
Two 6 × 2-inch layers
Two 9 × 2-inch layers
Two 12 × 2-inch layers

26 cups Italian Meringue
Buttercream, vanilla variation
(page 140 in Basics chapter)

1 miniature pumpkin

4 dozen Marzipan Sweets
(page 148 in Basics chapter)

MAKES 65 SERVINGS

C O M P L E X

❖ ❖ ❖

This is a very old-fashioned cake, firm, velvet-crumbed, and flavored with cinnamon, cloves, nutmeg, ginger, and cardamom. The buttermilk makes it tender. The spices are not overpowering, but you will definitely know you are eating a spice cake. I prefer to fill and cover this cake with Vanilla Buttercream because I think that its somewhat neutral vanilla flavor does not distract from, or compete with, the cake. Spices, with their warm tastes, make me think of warm colors, so the offset cake is decorated with marzipan fruits and vegetables in autumnal colors: apples, pears, pumpkins, carrots, squash, leaves, plums, oranges, nuts, figs, cherries, lemons, apricots, and bananas. These marzipan sweets can be made up to one month ahead if stored properly in an airtight container. My good friend, Suzanne Lo Manto, made these. She is an accomplished artist, but this was her first time ever sculpting with marzipan! Amazing.

BUTTERMILK SPICE CAKE

The buttermilk in this cake makes for an extremely velvety crumb. You may make this cake one month ahead, wrap it well, and store it in the freezer.

FOR TWO 6 × 2-INCH CAKE LAYERS

3 cups unsifted cake flour

1 teaspoon plus one pinch baking soda

1½ teaspoons ground cinnamon

¾ teaspoon ground nutmeg

¼ teaspoon ground cloves

¼ teaspoon ground ginger

¼ teaspoon ground cardamom

¼ teaspoon salt

6 ounces (1½ sticks) unsalted butter, at room temperature

¾ cup sugar

2 large eggs

1 cup plus 2 tablespoons buttermilk

Preheat the oven to 350°F. Prepare two 6 × 2-inch cake pans with cooking spray and parchment paper.

Sift the cake flour, baking soda, spices, and salt and set aside.

Place the butter in the mixing bowl, and with the flat paddle, beat butter until creamy on medium-high speed. Add the sugar gradually and beat until light and fluffy. Add the eggs, one at a time, beating well and scraping down after each addition.

Add the dry mixture and the buttermilk alternately in three batches, scraping down the bowl once or twice. Beat briefly, but thoroughly, so that the batter is well blended.

Apply a thick, smooth, final coat of buttercream. Pattern the sides, using a combing tool (decorator's comb). Apply the extra dacquoise crumbs to the bottom of each tier, coming up about 1 to 1½ inches along the sides. Chill the tiers.

Place the top two tiers on their respective separator plates. The plates are the same size as the tiers, which means the plates are invisible after assembling. Place the bottom tier on the Masonite board.

Transport the cakes in this state and assemble with columns at the site, trimming them so that the tiers appear to float above one another. Decorate with flowers before serving. Serve the cake at room temperature.

CHOCOLATE RASPBERRY TRUFFLE CAKE

COMPONENTS

Chocolate Raspberry Truffle
Cake
One 6 × 3-inch tier
One 8 ×3-inch tier
One 10 × 3-inch tier
One 12 × 3-inch tier
One 14 × 3-inch tier

20 cups Bittersweet Chocolate
Ganache, 15 cups for glazing
and 5 cups for piping
(page 145 in Basics chapter)

6 loose leaves gold leaf
(page 174 in Finishing Touches
chapter, see also this recipe)

Equipment
12 spiked pillars
7-inch separator plate
9-inch separator plate
11-inch separator plate
(all painted gold)

2 pints fresh raspberries
for decoration

21 cups Chantilly Cream,
2 tablespoons per serving, start
with approximately 10½ cups
heavy cream (page 126 in Cake
Accompaniments chapter)

MAKES 175 SERVINGS

COMPLEX
❖ ❖ ❖

If you like chocolate, deep, dark and rich, with very little else to distract you, then look no further. Flourless chocolate cakes are found on many restaurant menus and in bakeries nationwide. I am a big dark-chocolate fan, so when I had my bakery, I searched for a rendition that suited my palate. The version in Rose Levy Beranbaum's The Cake Bible *is scrumptious, and this cake is based upon hers. I like my cake a bit deeper, so I have reformulated the amount of ingredients per pan. Also, I prefer to bake mine in a solid-bottomed pan; I don't like the risk involved in baking cakes in springform pans and water baths. Maybe most importantly, this cake is speckled throughout with pockets of tart, juicy raspberries. The technique used for adding the raspberries to the batter is unusual, but fun. Just follow the instructions and make sure the raspberries are ultra-fresh, plump, and dry, with no hint of mold or excess moisture. Do not substitute frozen raspberries.*

The baking procedure is unusual as well. The heat is high and the baking time short. You have to trust my instructions because the first few times you make this cake, its loose pudding-like texture defies common sense. Basically you are just heating the batter enough to firm up the protein in the eggs. The chocolate and the butter, after all, are solid at room temperature. You'll see that after the cakes are chilled overnight, they are quite firm. If your oven is calibrated correctly, the baking times should be exactly right as written. If you are in doubt about the cake's doneness, use the visual clues as your guide. The cake will have lost its sheen and the sides will pull away from the pan if gently tilted. One great thing about this cake is that you can make the layers up to five days ahead. Do make sure that you have a pan large enough to hold the 12-inch layer in a water bath. I use a 16-inch-round cake pan, but you may have a roasting pan that works quite well.

The cake is one solid layer of truffle cake—no fillings to distract you. The outside is drenched with a bittersweet ganache. The raspberries on the outside mirror the inside and the gold leaf is extravagant and elegant. This would be perfect for a New Year's Eve wedding (assuming you can get fresh raspberries) or for any evening extravaganza. The cake should be served with Chantilly Cream. Believe it or not, the whipped cream cuts the richness of the cake and provides a welcomed contrast in texture. I do not consider the cream optional.

30 large eggs

5 pounds semisweet chocolate

2½ pounds (10 sticks) unsalted butter

2½ cups fresh raspberries

Proceed as above, but prepare one 14 × 3-inch cake pan with cooking spray and parchment paper. If the amounts are too difficult for you to handle, make the 10-inch cake recipe twice. Bake 30 minutes. Cool. Cover with plastic wrap and refrigerate overnight.

RASPBERRIES FOR DECORATION

The most important thing here is that the berries are as fresh as can be. There should be no mold or moisture present, and they should have a nice shape. If they are old, they will be wet and have lost their shape. Since you will be setting them randomly on top of the finished cake, you don't want them to fold over on themselves or ooze.

GOLD LEAF

Refer to the Finishing Touches chapter on Gold and Silver Leaf, page 174. You will be using loose gold leaf for this cake. As you are going for a free-form abstract shape, it is not as nerve-wracking or tedious as some exacting gold leaf applications. Use the photo as a guideline and place bits of gold on top of the cake with tweezers or a dry brush. The moisture of the ganache will help the leaf to adhere quite easily.

ASSEMBLY

Have all components ready, except the Chantilly Cream, which you prepare at the last minute. Cover an 18-inch-round Masonite board with gold foil. Have ready 7-, 9-, and 11-inch separator plates and 12 spiked columns all painted gold.

To unmold the cakes, the technique is similar to the one described for unmolding the cheesecake (page 115). Starting with the 14-inch tier, look at the cake in the pan. Is it nice and flat? Or, as sometimes happens, are the edges slightly raised? Use a sharp, small paring knife to trim off any excess from the top edge. You want the surface to be as level as possible. Run the bottom of the pan under hot water. The cake will not fall out when you invert it. The warmth from the water will loosen up the cake from the sides and bottom of the pan. Warm a spatula under hot water and dry. Run the spatula around the sides of the cake, pressing towards the pan. Take a 14-inch cardboard and place it on top of the cake. Turn the cake over, holding the cardboard in place by looping your fingers down around the bottom (which is the open side). Make a few quick twisting motions and you should feel the cake begin to slip out. If it doesn't, repeat the warm water step. When it starts to slide down and out of the pan, lower the cake to the table and gently lift off the pan completely. Peel off the parchment; the perfectly flat bottom of the cake will now be the top. If the cake is lopsided, flip back over using another cardboard round to facilitate the process and trim some more off that side. Don't try to trim the original bottom as it will be perfectly flat and you don't want to ruin its surface. Once you are finished trimming, flip over again and you'll have the flat bottom facing up; you are ready to glaze. Set aside and repeat with remaining tiers, using appropriately sized cardboard.

Place the cakes on racks and glaze with pourable ganache (see Finishing Touches chapter, page 156, for detailed instructions). Chill well.

Center the bottom 14-inch tier on the Masonite board. Center the 12-inch tier on top using dowels for internal support. Mount top three tiers on their respective separator plates.

Fit a pastry bag with a coupler, fill with chilled, pipeable ganache and pipe a very simple bead border around the top edge of each tier. Use a #8 round tip for the two smaller tiers, #10 tip for the two middle tiers, and #12 tip for the bottom tier. Pipe a bottom border using #12 tip at the base of the 14-inch and 12-inch tiers. Place bits of gold randomly on the surfaces of the cake. Refrigerate overnight.

Assemble the cake on site, putting the pillars and tiers into place. Arrange raspberries, as desired. Keep refrigerated until 1 hour before serving time and serve with Chantilly Cream.

Honey Lavender Cake

COMPONENTS

White Cake
Two 6 × 2-inch layers
Two 10 × 2-inch layers
Two 14 × 2-inch layers
(page 136 in Basics chapter)

7½ cups Lavender Syrup

29 cups Honey Maple Syrup
Buttercream, using honey only,
preferably lavender honey
(page 143 in Basics chapter)

Royal Icing/Silver Leaf
monogram, optional

MAKES 100 SERVINGS

C O M P L E X
❖ ❖ ❖

This cake has a very unusual taste. You will either love it or hate it. Some palates just don't appreciate flowery tastes. Make a small cake and brush it with the Lavender Syrup to determine your preference. It may sound surprising, and it is, but the floral lavender flavor is quite interesting and mysterious. Paired with the Honey Buttercream and the neutral White Cake, it is a sophisticated blend of flavors. Dried lavender flowers can be purchased in herb stores or in many larger health food markets that sell spices and herbs in bulk. The flavors are old-fashioned to me so I chose a white-on-white decor with a Victorian feel. The optional silver (or gold) monogram on the top of the cake is a nice touch.

FOR OPTIONAL MONOGRAM

A monogram made out of royal icing and coated in silver leaf is very beautiful and, like the flavor of this cake, quite unexpected. Look for typefaces (fonts) that you like in books and magazines. Just photocopy the one(s) you want and size up or down, as needed. Use the first letter of the couple's combined last name or an intertwined monogram of their two first initials or two last initials. To intertwine the letters, make photocopies and cut out sample letters, laying them next to each other and/or overlapping slightly and photocopy again to create a new double monogram. You may also sketch them from scratch. The finished monogram may be made a month ahead if kept completely dry. Use a Blue Magic insert (see Equipment chapter, page 178).

MONOGRAM

1 cup Royal Icing (page 144 in Basics chapter)
Loose silver leaf
1 egg white, lightly whisked

Have the Royal Icing ready. Take a piece of parchment paper and lay it over the monogram. Trace the monogram onto the parchment. To insure against breakage; repeat six times. Do not choose a font that is overly frilly because the extra-fine lines are hard to reproduce with icing.

Place the parchment on a cookie sheet. Fit a pastry bag with either a #1 or #2 tip and fill with Royal Icing. The smaller tip is better for very intricate designs. Make a complete outline of the letter(s), working slowly and accurately. Repeat for other samples. By the time you finish the last one, go back and fill in the first. Flood the interior of the outlines with more icing, thinned with a few drops of water, if necessary. Repeat for all samples.

The monograms must dry overnight. Place the cookie sheet with the monograms in the oven with the heat off. Even if you do not have a pilot light, the oven is a dry environment. Twenty-four hours of drying, at least, is best.

Test for dryness by touching with a finger. Monograms should be quite hard and should lift off without breaking.

Leave them in place for gilding. Refer to the Finishing Touches chapter (page 174) for detailed instructions for working with silver leaf. I usually gild three of my most perfect monograms so that I have two backups. If you have an intertwined monogram, make one of the letters silver and leave the other white for contrast.

For a much easier silvered look, dissolve silver powder in vodka and paint on.

Leave on parchment until needed. Use a small offset spatula to help you lift the monogram up and gently place it on top of the cake.

LAVENDER SYRUP

The color is a beautiful pale purple. Make up to one week ahead. This recipe will make the amount you need.

MAKES 7 ½ CUPS

5 cups water

3 cups sugar

¾ cup dried lavender flowers

Combine all ingredients in a medium, nonreactive saucepan and stir. Heat over medium low, bring to a simmer, and cook for 15 minutes. Remove from the heat and strain through a fine cheesecloth. If you use a fine-mesh metal strainer, small bits of the lavender may filter through; cheesecloth is better. Store in an airtight container and refrigerate until needed.

ASSEMBLY

Have all components ready. Cover an 18-inch-round Masonite board with decorative foil. Sprinkle the cake layers with Lavender Syrup and fill with Honey Buttercream. Crumb coat with the same buttercream and chill well. Coat with a final, very smooth coat of Honey Buttercream. Chill again until firm. Center the bottom tier on the covered board. Assemble the remaining tiers, centered one on top of the other, using dowels for internal support.

For the decoration, follow the photo, using a #16 tip to make a double shell border on the top edge and a single shell border on the bottom edge of the 6-inch tier; use #17 tip for the 10-inch tier; and use #18 tip for the 14-inch tier. Use a #16 tip to make small rosettes on the sides of the top and bottom tiers. Refrigerate overnight.

Lay monogram (if using) on top of the top tier when you take the cake out of the refrigerator. Serve the cake at room temperature.

CROQUEMBOUCHE

COMPONENTS

150 puffs Pâte à Choux
(triple recipe this page)

Nougatine
One 10-inch nougatine base
Two 8-inch nougatine disks
8 small nougatine balls

18 cups Pastry Cream, liqueur
variation using Grand Marnier
(page 146 in Basics chapter)

9 cups Caramel

18 to 24 gold Jordan almonds
(purchased from N.Y. Cake and
Baking Distributors,
Resources section, page 187)

Spun Sugar (optional)

7½ cups Bittersweet Chocolate
Sauce, 2 tablespoons per
serving (page 127 in Cake
Accompaniments chapter)

MAKES 50 SERVINGS

COMPLEX

❖ ❖ ❖

This pastry composition, a traditional French wedding cake, is made up of dozens of tiny cream puffs made of pâte à choux. *I have filled them with a pastry cream flavored with Grand Marnier. The addition of the nougatine embellishments is customary; I added the accent of gold Jordan almonds, which can be purchased from cake decorating stores. This pastry is complicated, and it does take some skill, but like any other cake in this book, it can be broken down into components and done in many different stages.*

The baked Pâte à Choux *can be made a month ahead and frozen. The nougatine can be made two weeks ahead if stored in an airtight container. The pastry cream can be made up to four days ahead. But the assembly should be done the morning of the wedding day, or a no more than 6 hours before serving. Otherwise the caramel that binds the puffs together may begin to melt and break down under prolonged refrigeration.*

The clouds of Spun Sugar are optional, but if you can manage it logistically, it makes for an exquisite presentation.

PÂTE À CHOUX

This is the traditional dough used for eclairs, cream puffs, and pastries such as the Saint-Honoré. Do not underbake the puffs or you will be left with soggy, leaden balls. Also, it is worth using bread flour because its higher gluten content will yield better results. You can find it in stores selling bulk flour, or ask a local bakery if you can buy some from them. Many supermarkets carry it as well. If you use all-purpose flour, you will probably need the smaller amount of eggs.

You will have to make this recipe three times. It is scaled to this size for two reasons. First, it is an amount that fits comfortably in the mixer; second, it makes enough puffs to fill up two pans and I assume that you only have one oven with two racks. The range of eggs is important, and they must be beaten in one at a time. Depending on the flour, you may need 7, perhaps 8, eggs, maybe even 9. You want the batter to be smooth, a rich, golden yellow, and firm enough to hold a shape when mounded with a spoon. If in doubt, use 8. These may be made one month ahead and frozen. Store in resealable plastic freezer bags and take care not to place anything on top of them or they will get crushed.

MAKES 50 PUFFS

2 cups water

½ teaspoon salt

6 ounces (1½ sticks) unsalted butter

2 cups unsifted bread flour (also called strong flour or high-gluten flour)

7 to 9 large eggs, at room temperature

Preheat the oven to 400°F. Line 2 baking pans with parchment paper.

Place the water, salt, and butter in the stainless steel mixing bowl. Place the bowl over low heat to melt the butter. Raise the heat to high and bring to a rolling boil; immediately remove from the heat.

Stir in the flour all at once. Keep stirring with a wooden spoon until the batter begins to come together. Place the bowl over low heat and keep stirring, until the batter dries out slightly, about 1 minute. The *pâte à choux* should cleanly come away from the sides of the bowl.

Place the bowl on your mixer and use a flat paddle to beat in the eggs one at a time. Make sure that each egg is incorporated thoroughly before adding the next.

Fit a large pastry bag with a plain round ½-inch tip. Fill it up with the *pâte à choux* and hold the bag straight over the prepared pan, about 1 inch above the surface.

Pipe out small puffs about 2 inches round. Start squeezing, and when the puff is the right size, ease up the pressure on the pastry bag and pull it away from the puff. It will look like a large chocolate kiss. Make some larger and some smaller and space them 2 inches apart on the sheets. Dip your fingers in cold water and pat down the pointed tops.

Bake 25 minutes, or until the puffs are light gold. Reduce the temperature to 350°F and continue to bake for 5 minutes. Take a sharp knife and make a slit in the side of each puff to allow steam to escape and continue cooking for 5 more minutes, or until puffs are high, round, golden brown, and dry.

Cool completely by placing pans on a rack. Place the puffs in large resealable plastic freezer bags and store in freezer until needed. Or, store at room temperature overnight, uncovered, and proceed with assembly.

NOUGATINE

You will need to make this recipe three times. You could, in theory, triple it, but the warm nougatine has to be worked with quickly and it is easier to take it one batch at a time. Make the nougatine base, or présentoir, *for the croquembouche with the first batch, an 8-inch separator disk and 4 nougatine balls with the second, and the last 8-inch separator disk and 4 nougatine balls with the last batch. In each instance, you may have extra nougatine. This can be ground up and added to buttercreams, crushed and used to decorate cakes, or munched on like an upscale peanut brittle. It keeps well in an airtight container with a Blue Magic insert (see Resources section). If kept dry, it lasts for one week, or longer.*

canola oil
12 ounces sliced almonds (natural or blanched, about 4 cups)
3 cups sugar
2 tablespoons plus 2 teaspoons light corn syrup
1 tablespoon fresh lemon juice

Preheat the oven to 200°F.

Prepare a work surface, preferably marble or a large expanse of Formica countertop, by covering with a thin coat of vegetable oil. Oil a large, heavy rolling pin.

Prepare a cake pan, preferably a 10 × 2-inch pan, to use as a mold for the base. Oil the entire outside of the pan and place it bottom up on a work surface. Set aside.

Coarsely chop the sliced almonds and sift out any powdery residue. Place nuts on a sheet pan and place in the oven to warm, but not toast. This will allow the incorporation of the nuts into the caramel without making it seize.

Combine the sugar, corn syrup, and lemon juice in a heavy-bottomed saucepan. Stir to moisten the sugar. Place the pan over low heat and cook, without stirring, until the mixture begins to melt. When it is partially melted, stir it gently to dissolve the sugar. The process is slow—about 20 minutes; use a wooden spoon, which will not burn your hands. Cook until it turns pale amber, but as soon as it begins to color it darkens quickly. It will look slightly cloudy. Stir in the almonds until thoroughly combined.

Immediately pour the nougatine onto the oiled surface and spread it out into an even layer, using the rolling pin. Roll it about ¼ inch thick, without tearing. Let cool enough to handle, maybe as few as 30 seconds, but still warm and pliable.

Pick up the nougatine and drape it over the oiled cake pan. Smooth the sides down along the cake pan and trim the bottom flush with the work surface. Set aside to cool. Reserve excess for another use.

Second and Third Batches

Roll out the nougatine and cut an 8-inch disk out of each batch using the base of an 8-inch cake pan as a guide. With the remaining warm nougatine, roll 8 small uniform balls about the same size as the puffs. These are the little supports that go between the bottom and top segments.

Let all the nougatine cool. The base may be left on the cake pan until needed. Store all pieces in an airtight container with a Blue Magic insert to keep moisture-free.

Caramel

The caramel will hold your creation together: the "sweet cement," as it were. You need a large quantity because it is easier to work with and you want enough to actually dip the puffs in. This should be made immediately before the assembly of the Croquembouche.

MAKES 9 CUPS

7½ cups sugar
1¾ cups water
⅔ cup light corn syrup

Combine all ingredients in a large heavy-bottomed saucepan. Stir to moisten the sugar. Place over medium heat and cook until the sugar melts and the mixture reaches 320°F, about 25 minutes. Wash down the sides of the pot with a damp pastry brush during cooking if crystals are forming. You may also cover the pan briefly at this point. Steam will develop and wash down the sides of the pan automatically. The caramel will turn golden while staying liquid enough for easy dipping.

Immediately remove the pan from the heat and plunge the bottom into a bowl of cold water to stop the cooking. Remove from water and replace on top of the stove over an unlit burner. If the caramel begins to harden, turn the heat on very low to remelt and keep liquid. A flame tamer works well here.

Spun Sugar

I make spun sugar if I know that I have the last-minute time to attend to it. This is a messy procedure. Protect the floor with newspapers before you start. You will need a large cooling rack and an old whisk that you don't mind cutting. To accomplish this, cut the wires about ¼ way down from the rounded end and snip them with wire clippers. This makes a tool to spin the sugar most efficiently.

3¾ cups sugar
1 cup water
⅔ cup light corn syrup

Coat the cooling rack with a light layer of oil and place it over a sheet pan.

Combine all ingredients in a heavy-bottomed saucepan. Place over medium heat and cook until it reaches 310°F (hard crack stage). The mixture will be quite pale in color.

Remove the pan from the heat and plunge the bottom of the pan into a bowl of cold water to stop the cooking. Place the pan on a heat-proof surface next to your cooling rack. Dip your cut-off whisk into the syrup and swiftly wave your arm back and forth across the length of the rack. You may get nice spun threads of sugar, or you may get heavy sugar droplets. If you get droplets, just wait and try again every 10 seconds or so until the temperature is right and you get spun threads. Repeat with all of the mixture. You may need to reheat the sugar as you go along to keep it fluid, but you should be prepared to keep the process moving once the temperature is right.

Coat your hands very lightly with oil, pick up the spun sugar, and arrange it around the base of the Croquembouche. Serve within the hour, or preferably, immediately, and do not try this in a humid environment.

ASSEMBLY

Have all components ready. The *pâte à choux* puffs should be defrosted or already at room temperature and set on a baking tray. If defrosted, dry out in a 350°F oven for 5 to 7 minutes to recrisp. The pastry cream should be chilled and firm and the caramel freshly made. All of the nougatine pieces should be done. You will most likely have to reheat the caramel a few times as you work; keep it fluid, but do not cook or allow to darken further. Reheating in the microwave is a good way to reliquify it without coloring it.

Have a strong tray that is wide enough to hold the nougatine base. Or, cover a 12-inch-round Masonite board with gold foil. Slip the nougatine base off the cake pan and use some caramel to secure the nougatine base to the platter and set aside.

Fit a large pastry bag with a plain round ¼-inch tip and fill the bag with the pastry cream. Insert the tip into each puff and fill with the pastry cream; place filled puffs on baking tray.

Set up your work space as follows: Set the tray of filled puffs to your left, the caramel in the middle, and a sheet pan with a cooling rack on the right. One puff at a time, begin the assembly line: Dip the top of each puff in the caramel, wiping off the excess on the rim of the caramel pan. Place the puffs, caramel side up, on the cooling rack to harden. Repeat with the remaining puffs. The "top" can either be the flat bottom of the puffs, which will give a more uniform end results, or the true top of the puffs for a more rounded, free-form look. For the Croquembouche in the photo, I used the bottoms as the "tops." These become the visible surface.

To assemble the Croquembouche: Place the platter with the nougatine base in front of you. One at a time, dip one side of the puffs in the caramel and place the puff, with the hardened caramel side facing out, on the base. Repeat with more puffs, placing successive puffs right next to the one before, and allowing the fresh caramel to "glue" them together. It is easiest to do this using a pair of tongs. Complete one entire ring along the outer edge of the nougatine base. Fill in the center with a few puffs to make a solid layer, using more caramel. Make sure to use enough caramel so that the puffs really stick together and to the base or previous layer. Use larger puffs for the bottom layers, and progressively smaller ones as you work up.

Make the next ring slightly smaller in diameter than the first, repeating all the steps, including filling in the center of the tower. Keep assembling the tower until the top is about 8 inches in diameter. Try to work it so that you have made at least four layers before you get to this point. The tower will be fairly vertical with only a slight inward angle. Spread some caramel on the top layer of the puffs and place one of the 8-inch nougatine disks on top. Select the nicest, most evenly sized nougatine balls and stick them evenly around the perimeter of the nougatine disk. Use caramel to adhere them together, using 4 to 5, as you prefer. Set the Croquembouche aside and proceed with the top section.

To make the top cone-shaped tower, use the second 8-inch nougatine disk as your base. Proceed as above, continuing to build up the rings of puffs on top of this base and cap the top with one perfect puff saved for the crowning glory. Let the caramel harden.

Spread some caramel on the top of the hard nougatine balls and place the tower segment on top; pick up the 8-inch disk with the cone-shaped tower and place on top of the nougatine balls. Let the caramel harden. You will have one beautiful, towering Croquembouche.

Dip the gold Jordan almonds in the caramel and stick them in randomly. Serve within 4 hours, storing in a cool, dry room. If using spun sugar, place on Croquembouche now and serve immediately.

SERVING

Croquembouche is not easy to serve. The best way is to use two forks to gently pry off two or three puffs at a time. This makes one serving. The puffs are glued together with the caramel and they usually do not pull off in uniform round shapes. They might look a little the worse for wear, but I have never had anyone complain, because they taste absolutely delicious. Although it is not necessary or traditional, I like to serve these with a little Bittersweet Chocolate Sauce.

WHITE CHOCOLATE LEMON BUTTERMILK CAKE WITH SUGAR SEA SHELLS

COMPONENTS

Lemon Buttermilk Cake
Two 6 × 2-inch layers
Two 10 × 2-inch layers
Two 14 × 2-inch layers

6 cups Lemon Curd,
refrigerated overnight to firm
(page 142 in Basics chapter)

23 cups Italian Meringue
Buttercream, chocolate
variation (page 141 in Basics
chapter)

Seaside Decorations

2 dozen Caramelized Sugar
Coral Fans

MAKES 100 SERVINGS

C O M P L E X

❖ ❖ ❖

This combination is for lemon lovers. The cake is a moist, soft buttermilk cake flavored with lemon oil. It has a pronounced lemon aroma and velvety crumb that improves during the second, third, and fourth days, allowing ample preparation time. The filling is a lemon curd, which is similar to the filling you find in lemon meringue pie. White Chocolate Buttercream tops it all off with its pale ivory color and subtle chocolate taste. Two notes on ingredients: The lemon oil is different from lemon extract. It is a specialty product that can be found in gourmet food stores or mail-ordered from Williams-Sonoma. It is actual lemon oil, derived from the flavorful skin of the fruit, with no bitter taste from the pith. It is quite potent and gives a truer lemon taste than extract does. Also, make sure that you use white chocolate made with cocoa butter and not some of the white chocolate "coatings" on the market. These use vegetable oils instead. It is the cocoa butter in a fine white chocolate that gives it that wonderful taste and buttery texture.

As for the decoration, it is perfect for a seaside wedding. The tastes of lemon and white chocolate are summery to me, hence the decor. You could use real shells to decorate the cake—just make sure they are scrupulously clean! I made my own molds using Super Elasticlay (see Note) to make imprints of real starfish and shells. Once these are baked and set, the handmade flexible molds can form sugar and chocolate shells. Cake-decorating supply stores will also have ready-made flexible silicone molds with sea themes (see Resources, N.Y. Cake and Baking Distributors, page 187). Godiva also offer chocolate shells, seahorses, and starfish that you can use. Contact Godiva Chocolatier Consumer Relations, 260 Madison Ave., NY, NY 10016 for information. In the photo, we used some real shells, and some edible ones. Can you tell which are which?

SEASIDE DECORATIONS

If you want to make your own molds, buy the Super Elasticlay and follow the manufacturer's instructions (see Note). Or, purchase sea-theme molds from a cake-decorating supply store. To make molds out of sugar, tempered chocolate, or chocolate plastic, refer to the recipes in the Finishing Touches chapter. Make an assortment of sizes and shapes, and make extra in case of breakage. These can be tinted with food colorings to resemble natural shells, if desired. The golden shells are real shells covered with gold leaf courtesy of my friend Lucy Gerspacher. The coral was made from drizzled caramelized sugar. All of these can be made well ahead of time and stored in airtight containers, except for the coral, which should be made on the serving day.

Note: Super Elasticlay is a soft, nontoxic, off-white clay that can be baked in the home oven. It remains flexible, which makes very easy-to-use molds. You should be able to find it at your local art store. If not, contact Polyform Products Co., 9420 Byron St., Schiller Park, IL 60176, for information. Follow manufacturer's instructions for making molds.

LEMON BUTTERMILK CAKE

You can make this cake one month ahead and freeze it, but it also keeps extremely well at room temperature for days.
Feel free to make this up to four days ahead and store it well wrapped in plastic wrap and foil.
Do not refrigerate it or it will dry out.

FOR TWO 6 × 2-INCH CAKE LAYERS

2¼ cups unsifted cake flour

⅓ teaspoon salt

⅓ teaspoon baking soda

⅓ teaspoon baking powder

6 ounces (1½ sticks) unsalted butter, at room temperature

1½ cups sugar

1½ teaspoons lemon oil

3 large eggs

¾ cup buttermilk

Preheat the oven to 350°F. Prepare two 6 × 2-inch cake pans with cooking spray and parchment paper.

Sift together the cake flour, salt, baking soda, and baking powder and set aside.

Place the butter in your mixer's bowl. With the flat paddle, beat the butter until it is light and creamy on medium-high speed. Add the sugar gradually, beating well between additions. Scrape down the sides of the bowl once or twice. Beat in the lemon oil. Add the eggs, one at a time, beating well after each addition. Beat on high for about 2 minutes, or until the mixture is smooth.

Add the dry ingredients and the buttermilk alternately in three separate batches. Scrape down the bowl between each addition and beat well. This batter has a tendency to clump so at the very end, beat it well for one minute on medium-high for an evenly blended, thick mixture with a satiny sheen.

Pour the batter into the pans, smoothing the tops with a small offset spatula.

Bake about 45 to 55 minutes, until the sides pull away from the pan and look slightly more golden than the center and a toothpick tests clean. Cool, place on cardboards, and wrap with plastic wrap and foil.

FOR TWO 10 × 2-INCH CAKE LAYERS

5⅔ cups unsifted cake flour

¾ teaspoon plus a pinch of salt

¾ teaspoon plus a pinch of baking soda

¾ teaspoon plus a pinch of baking powder

15 ounces (3¾ sticks) unsalted butter, at room temperature

3¾ cups sugar

1 tablespoon plus 2 teaspoons lemon oil

8 large eggs

1¾ cups plus 2 tablespoons buttermilk

Prepare two 10 × 2-inch cake pans with cooking spray and parchment paper. Proceed as above for 6-inch recipe with the following changes: Beat well after the addition of each egg. The mixture will seem soupy, but as the butter-sugar mixture absorbs the eggs, it comes together into a creamy mass. Add the buttermilk and dry ingredients alternately in 5 batches, mixing well after all the ingredients are added. This amount fits easily in the 5-quart mixing bowl.

Bake about 50 to 60 minutes. Cool, place on cardboards, and wrap with plastic wrap and foil.

FOR TWO 14 × 2-INCH CAKE LAYERS

Prepare two 10 × 2-inch cake pans with cooking spray and parchment paper. Make the 10-inch recipe twice, once for each 14-inch pan. Do not double it. Bake about 55 to 65 minutes. Cool, place on cardboards, and wrap with plastic wrap and foil.

CARAMELIZED SUGAR CORAL FANS

This caramelized sugar is drizzled on parchment to resemble real coral. The recipe makes more than you need, but some may break, so use up the total amount. These must be made the day of serving.

MAKES 2 DOZEN FANS

1½ cups sugar

½ cup water

¼ cup light corn syrup

Line a baking pan with parchment paper and set aside. Place all ingredients in a small, heavy-bottomed saucepan and stir to combine. Cook over medium heat, without stirring, until it reaches a golden caramel color.

Wash down the sides of the pot with a damp pastry brush during cooking if crystals are forming. A thermometer will read approximately 315°F when it is done.

Immediately drizzle the caramel on the parchment paper, using a spoon or a fork for different results. This can be done freehand without a pattern. See the photo for ideas of size and shape. Allow the fans to cool. They will peel off the parchment quite easily and can be placed directly on the cake.

ASSEMBLY

Have all components ready. Cover an 18-inch-round Masonite board with dark sea green-blue wrapping paper.

Beginning with the largest size, assemble the tiers as follows. Use the technique of creating a border of buttercream around each curd layer to prevent the curd from seeping out, if necessary. Use 3¾ cups lemon curd for the 14-inch tier, 1½ cups for the 10-inch tier, and ¾ cup for the 6-inch tier. After you place the top cake layer on each stack, press down gently to seal.

Crumb coat the tiers with the White Chocolate Buttercream. Chill well. Apply a thick, final coat of buttercream to all. Use a combing tool (decorator's comb) to make wavy ridges around the tiers. Place the 14-inch tier on the center of the covered board. Center and stack the top two tiers, using dowels for internal support.

Fit a pastry bag with a coupler and a #6 tip, fill it with buttercream, and pipe a bead border at the base and top edges of the top tier. Change to #8 tip for the two bottom tiers. The bead borders should resemble pearls. Refrigerate cake overnight.

Place whichever final decorations you want on and around the cake. Refer to the photo for ideas. Serve the cake at room temperature.

GÂTEAU OPÉRA

If you have ever been to Paris and had the good fortune of eating at any one of the incredible patisseries, you probably encountered the classic Gâteau Opéra. This wonderful cake, melding the flavors of almond, chocolate, and coffee, gave inspiration for the development of this square wedding cake. The cake component is an Almond Génoise sprinkled with Cognac Syrup; the filling is a Cognac Truffle Filling that packs a punch. If you prefer a nonalcoholic filling, use the Whipped Ganache from the Basics chapter, page 145. The exterior is covered with Espresso Buttercream and the cake is decorated with dark Chocolate Filigree decorations. The cake is great without it, but if you like, serve with Crème Anglaise.

COMPONENTS

Nut Génoise,
square almond variation
Two 6 × 2-inch layers
Two 10 × 2-inch layers
Two 14 × 2-inch layers
(page 132 in Basics chapter)

6 to 8 cups Sugar Syrup,
liqueur variation using cognac
(page 147 in Basics chapter)

8 cups Cognac Truffle Filling

28 cups Italian Meringue
Buttercream, espresso
variation (page 141 in Basics
chapter)

6 cups Bittersweet Chocolate
Ganache, at room temperature
for piping (page 145 in Basics
chapter)

Chocolate Filigree Decorations,
(page 169 in Finishing Touches
chapter, see also this page)

3¾ cups Crème Anglaise,
2 tablespoons per serving,
optional (page 126 in Cake
Accompaniments chapter)

MAKES 120 SERVINGS

COMPLEX

❖ ❖ ❖

CHOCOLATE FILIGREE DIAGRAMS

Top tier.   *Middle tier.*   *Bottom tier.*

COGNAC TRUFFLE FILLING

This delicious filling tastes like a decadent, spirited, truffle candy. Combine the ingredients well, and whisk during the cooling period, to evenly blend the ingredients. You may make this one week ahead and store it in an airtight container in the refrigerator. This recipe makes a sufficient amount to fill the tiers.

MAKES 8 CUPS

3 pounds semisweet or bittersweet chocolate, finely chopped

2⅔ cups heavy cream

4 large egg yolks, at room temperature

1 cup cognac

Heat the chocolate and cream in a double boiler (*bain-marie*) over hot water to melt the chocolate, stirring often. Alternatively, melt the chocolate in the microwave, stirring frequently to encourage even melting.

Meanwhile, whisk the yolks and cognac together in a small bowl. When the chocolate mixture is melted and smooth, whisk it for a few minutes to release some heat. Vigorously whisk in the egg yolk mixture thoroughly. Let cool to room temperature, whisking it occasionally to keep the butterfat in the cream properly dispersed.

Scrape into an airtight container and refrigerate. If it is too firm to spread, leave out at room temperature for a few hours or soften slightly in a microwave at very low power. It should be a smooth, spreadable consistency, like peanut butter.

Assembly

Have all components ready. Cover an 18-inch-square Masonite board with decorative foil.

Sprinkle each cake layer with Cognac Syrup and fill each tier with a layer of the Cognac Truffle Filling. Crumb coat the tiers with Espresso Buttercream and chill well.

Apply a final coat of buttercream, making it thick on the sides. Use a decorator's comb to make the designs on the sides of the cake. Place one edge of the comb on the turntable surface and draw horizontally to make level, parallel lines. It can be difficult to make even, square corners. Don't worry, these will be masked with decoration. Chill well.

Center the bottom tier on the covered board. Arrange the top two tiers, angled, as shown in the photo, using dowels for internal support. Apply a shell border with the ganache using a # 16 tip for the top tier, #17 tip for the middle tier, and #18 tip for the bottom tier. Make the borders on top and bottom edges and vertically along the four corners (see photo). Refrigerate the cake overnight.

Transport the cake and assemble on site. Place filigree decorations on cake, using softened ganache to help affix them, if necessary. Use the photo and illustration for guidance or design your own pattern. Serve cake at room temperature with or without Crème Anglaise.

SOUR CREAM APPLE CHEESECAKE

COMPONENTS

Sour Cream Apple Cheesecake
One 6 × 3-inch tier
One 9 × 3-inch tier
One 12 × 3-inch tier

18 cups White Chocolate
Cream Cheese Frosting (page
144 in Basics chapter)

2¹⁄₈ cups Quince Glaze

Assorted tea roses

MAKES 85 SERVINGS

C O M P L E X

❖ ❖ ❖

This is a wonderful cheesecake to make any time. Just try one of the smaller layers. It is a sour-cream enriched cream-cheese cheesecake with a cinnamon-scented graham cracker crust. Between the crust and the cheesecake is a scrumptious layer of caramelized sautéed apples. The entire cake is covered with a White Chocolate Cream Cheese Frosting that masks the cheesecake so that it looks like a regular layer cake. The recipes were tested using Philadelphia brand cream cheese, the regular kind, not the reduced-fat. It is available nationwide and I suggest you use it for best results. Also, make sure that the cream cheese is at room temperature so that you can blend it easily. Creaming the cream cheese is an important step, because after you add the eggs it will be quite difficult to get any lumps out. If the cream cheese is at room temperature when you start, this step should go smoothly.

The first cheesecake wedding cake that I ever saw was made by Rose Levy Beranbaum and highlighted in Martha Stewart's book Weddings. *Her cake, an apricot-flavored one, had a glaze on the top of each tier. I have replicated that idea here in this recipe, using a quince glaze to complement the apple layer. If you cannot find quince jelly, which has a beautiful, pinkish hue, you may substitute apple jelly, which is commonly found in supermarkets. It has a light-golden color.*

Note that I have written this recipe a bit differently than the others in the book. Each size is treated like a cake unto itself, including the crust and the apple layers. I wrote it this way because this is how you will cook it: one tier at a time. You cannot combine the tiers in the oven because of the cooling-off periods. If you prefer, you can sauté the apples and make the graham cracker crusts all at once, but then you have to divide them into unequal parts, which I think is more confusing.

SOUR CREAM APPLE CHEESECAKE

A former assistant of mine, Laura, taught me a great trick to make the graham cracker crumbs for the crust lie perfectly flat in the pan before baking. Take a flat-bottom glass with a small diameter. Use it to press firmly down over the entire surface of the crust. It will compress the crumbs evenly and firmly and give you a professional result. The cheesecakes may be made up to four days ahead.

FOR ONE 6 × 3-INCH TIER

APPLE LAYER

3 apples, peeled, cored, and cut into 1/8-inch-thick slices

3 tablespoons unsalted butter

3 tablespoons packed light brown sugar

1/2 teaspoon ground cinnamon

CRUST

1/2 cup graham cracker crumbs (about 3 1/2 whole 5 x 2 1/2-inch graham crackers), processed in food processor

2 teaspoons sugar

1/4 teaspoon ground cinnamon

2 tablespoons unsalted butter, melted

CHEESECAKE

1 pound cream cheese, at room temperature

2/3 cup sugar

1 teaspoon vanilla extract

2 large eggs

1/4 cup sour cream

Preheat the oven to 350°F. Prepare one 6 × 3-inch pan with cooking spray and parchment paper.

To make the sautéed apples, melt the butter in a medium sauté pan. Add the apple slices and toss to coat. Cook, stirring occasionally, until the apples begin to soften, 1 to 2 minutes. Add the sugar and continue to cook; the sugar will melt and begin to caramelize, with about 5 minutes cooking time. Remove from the heat and stir in the cinnamon; set aside and cool until room temperature. You may do this step one day ahead. Store in an airtight container in the refrigerator. Bring completely to room temperature before using.

To make the crust, place the crumbs in a small bowl. Add the sugar and cinnamon. Blend them briefly with a

fork. Pour the melted butter over the dry ingredients and toss together to blend thoroughly. Pat evenly into the bottom of the pan. Bake the crust for 5 minutes. Remove from the oven and cool pan on a rack. Reduce the heat to 325°F.

Meanwhile, to make the cheesecake, place the cream cheese in your mixing bowl and use a flat paddle to beat the cream cheese until smooth on medium-high speed. Add the sugar gradually and beat until light and fluffy. Scrape the mixture down several times during mixing. This will take about 5 minutes of beating at high speed.

Beat in the vanilla and add the eggs, one at a time, beating well after each addition. Beat until well blended and smooth, scraping down once or twice. Fold the sour cream in by hand with a few broad strokes of a large rubber spatula.

To assemble, scrape the apple mixture onto the crust and spread to cover the entire surface. Pour the cream cheese mixture over the apples so that the fruit remains in an even layer, under the cheesecake batter. Smooth the top of the batter with an offset spatula.

Check that the oven temperature has dropped to 325°F. If it is still high, prop the oven door open for a few minutes. Place the pan in a larger pan filled with 1 inch of hot water. Bake about 1 hour, until the edges are barely tinged with color and the cake center, when shaken very gently, is still soft. Leave the door closed and turn off the oven; the cake cools in the oven and continues to cook slowly. After 1 hour, prop open the oven door to release remaining heat. Let the cake cool inside until the oven is completely cool.

Cover the cake top with plastic wrap and refrigerate overnight, still in the pan. Store in refrigerator until ready to assemble.

FOR ONE 9 × 3-INCH TIER

APPLE LAYER

6 apples, peeled, cored and cut into $\frac{1}{8}$-inch slices

3 ounces ($\frac{3}{4}$ stick) unsalted butter

6 tablespoons packed light brown sugar

1 teaspoon ground cinnamon

CRUST

1 cup graham cracker crumbs (approximately 7 whole 5 × 2$\frac{1}{2}$-inch graham crackers), processed in food processor

1 tablespoon plus 1 teaspoon sugar

$\frac{1}{2}$ teaspoon ground cinnamon

2 ounces ($\frac{1}{4}$ cup) butter, melted

CHEESECAKE

2 pounds cream cheese, at room temperature

1$\frac{1}{3}$ cups sugar

2 teaspoons vanilla extract

4 large eggs

$\frac{1}{2}$ cup sour cream

For the apple layer, follow directions above. You will need a large enough sauté pan to hold the larger amount of apples.

For the crust, proceed as above for 6-inch tier, using a 9 × 3-inch pan. Bake 7 minutes.

For cheesecake, proceed as above. This amount of batter will fit in the bowl of the mixer. Make sure to scrape down frequently during the mixing process to ensure a smooth result.

Bake about 1 hour, 10 minutes, then turn the oven off. Leave the cheesecake in the oven with the door closed for at least another hour or until the oven is cool. Cover the cake top with plastic wrap and refrigerate overnight, still in the pan. Store in refrigerator until ready to assemble.

FOR ONE 12 × 3-INCH TIER

Double the amounts of the 9-inch recipe. Proceed as above for the 9-inch tier. You may sauté the double quantity of apples at once, if you have a large enough pan. The crust is easy enough to make in double size; use a larger bowl to toss the ingredients together and pat the mixture into a 12 × 3-inch pan. To make the cheesecake, prepare the 9-inch recipe twice. Do not try to double it as it will not fit in the mixer's bowl.

Bake about 1 hour, 15 minutes; turn off the oven and cool the cake in the oven, as described above. Cover the cake top with plastic wrap and refrigerate overnight, still in the pan. Store in refrigerator until ready to assemble.

QUINCE GLAZE

The glaze should be prepared immediately before it is needed (refer to assembly directions).

MAKES 2$\frac{1}{8}$ CUPS

2 cups quince jelly or apple jelly

2 tablespoons Calvados (apple brandy)

Place the jelly and alcohol in a small saucepan and melt over low heat, stirring frequently, until gelled lumps melt. Set it over a barely warm burner, so that it remains pourable, but not hot. Prepare the glaze just before it is needed, after the cake has been frosted, assembled, and refrigerated. The cake must be thoroughly chilled before you apply the glaze.

GREENERY AND FLOWERS

The flowers in the photo are field-grown tea roses. I chose a warm, golden pink color to mirror the glaze, but any color could be used. You'll need approximately 18 roses. Use the photo for placement ideas.

ASSEMBLY

Have all components ready. Cover a 16-inch-round Masonite board with colored paper.

To unmold the cheesecakes, have two 14-inch cardboard rounds ready. Run hot water over the bottom of the pan. Warm a spatula under hot water and dry. Run the spatula around the sides of the 14-inch cake, pressing out towards the pan. The warmth from the water will loosen up the cake from the sides and bottom of the pan. Take one cardboard and cover it with plastic wrap and place it on top of the cake. Turn the cake over, holding the cardboard in place by looping your fingers down around the bottom (which is now the open side). Make a few quick twisting motions and you should feel the cake begin to slip out. If it doesn't, repeat the warm water step. When it starts to slide down and out of the pan, lower the cake to the table and gently lift off the pan completely. Peel off the parchment and place the other cardboard round on top. Slip one hand under the bottom cardboard round, with the other hand on the top cardboard. Flip the cake over. Remove the cardboard that is now on the top of the cheesecake. The surface should hardly be marred at all. The plastic should have minimized any damage. If the top is badly marked, smooth it with a spatula warmed in hot water and dried. The cake will be covered with White Chocolate Cream Cheese Frosting, which will cover any imperfections. Place the cheesecake in the refrigerator and continue with the remaining tiers, using appropriately sized cardboard rounds.

Apply a medium-thick coating of White Chocolate Cream Cheese Frosting over each tier. A crumb coat is not necessary. The cheesecake is firm so you may press on it when spreading the frosting. Smooth well and chill thoroughly.

Center the 12-inch tier on the covered board. Center the 9-inch and 6-inch tiers on top, using dowels for internal support.

Fit pastry bag with coupler and #16 tip and fill bag with frosting. Pipe a shell border on the outer edge and inside bottom edge of the 6-inch tier. Use a #17 tip for the middle tier and a #18 tip for the bottom tier. Make sure that the outer edge borders are continuous so that they hold in the glaze. Make the borders small so that you have room left to apply the glaze. Chill until firm.

Have glaze warm, but not hot. Spoon the liquid glaze on the very top of the cake and on the tops of the two bottom tiers (see photo). Refrigerate overnight.

Decorate with roses. Set the cheesecake out for display 30 minutes to one hour before serving.

SACHERTORTE

COMPONENTS

Sachertorte
One 6 × 3-inch tier
Two 10 × 2-inch layers
Two 14 × 2-inch layers

6 cups high-quality apricot preserves for filling, softened
slightly on top of the stove or
for a few seconds in the
microwave; do not melt

6 cups Bittersweet Chocolate
Ganache, soft for spreading
but not runny (page 145
in Basics chapter)

23 cups Italian Meringue
Buttercream, chocolate
variation (page 141 in
Basics chapter)

Equipment
8 spiked pillars
7-inch separator plate
11-inch separator plate
(all painted terra cotta)

4 dozen Chocolate Leaves
(page 168 in Finishing Touches
chapter)

2 dozen apricot roses

12½ cups Chantilly Cream,
2 tablespoons per serving,
begin with 6¼ cups heavy
cream (page 126 in Cake
Accompaniments chapter)

MAKES 100 SERVINGS

C O M P L E X

❖ ❖ ❖

Sachertorte is a classic cake, having originated in Vienna in 1832. It was invented by Franz Sacher, who at the time was the chef for Prince Metternich. All of the traditional Sachertorte recipes that I researched shared certain techniques. They all start with adding egg yolks to the creamed butter-sugar mixture and folding in the whipped egg whites at the end. I proceeded to develop a recipe along these lines and my first attempt worked out quite well. When I increased the recipe to make a larger tier, I realized after placing it in the oven that I had left out the egg yolks! There they were, all 6 of them, sitting in a bowl on the counter. I had creamed the butter and sugar and went directly to folding in the melted chocolate. I decided not to panic, always a good choice. The cake baked exactly as the original had, and looked the same. But when I tasted them side by side, there was a decided difference. The classic formula was a bit drier and spongier. The one without the yolks was moister and the chocolate flavor was more pronounced. The fact that it was moister, but lacked the fat provided by the yolks, intrigued me. I called Nick Malgieri, the best technician I know, and a treasure trove of information. Nick was similarly fascinated by the results, but not as perplexed as I. He explained that an increased chocolate flavor coming through made perfect sense, because the taste of the yolks was not there to compete. As far as the moisture content was concerned, he explained that it really is a fallacy that the moister the batter, the moister the cake. He pointed out to me that indeed some very wet batters result in dry cakes—and it is true, from my experience.

So, I had to decide which recipe to include in the book. The recipe provided is made without the yolks. If you want to create a more traditional Sachertorte, use the same number of yolks as whites, adding them one by one to the creamed butter and sugar mixture, before proceeding with the melted chocolate. Good luck! Experimentation always leads to new knowledge.

Except for the missing yolks, the flavor of this Sachertorte is quite classic. The traditional cake has an apricot glaze or filling covered by a chocolate ganache. This wedding cake has one layer of chocolate ganache on top of a layer of apricot jam. The exterior is covered with a chocolate buttercream. Apricot roses and chocolate leaves echo the interior's flavors. I first saw apricot roses on the December 1985 cover of Bon Appetit *magazine. I still have the issue, now yellowed with age. The irony is that the author of the recipe, Betty Rosbottom, is now, more than a decade later, my neighbor and very good friend. Thanks, Betty! If you prefer, use real roses on the cake. The ones in the photo are called Leonidas. The spiked columns have been painted a dark terra cotta, reminiscent of the apricots. As in Vienna, the cake may be served* mit schlag *(with whipped cream).*

SACHERTORTE

You may make this cake one month ahead and freeze it.

FOR ONE 6 × 3-INCH TIER

4 ounces semisweet chocolate, finely chopped

3/4 cup plus 1 tablespoon unsifted cake flour

4 ounces (1 stick) unsalted butter, at room temperature

2/3 cup sugar, divided into 1/3 cup and 1/3 cup

2/3 teaspoon vanilla extract

4 large egg whites

pinch salt

Preheat the oven to 350°F. Prepare one 6 × 3-inch cake pan with cooking spray and parchment paper.

Melt the chocolate in the top of a double boiler (*bain-marie*). Stir occasionally until smooth. Alternately, melt in microwave. Set aside. Sift the flour and set aside.

In your mixer's bowl, cream butter until fluffy with flat paddle attachment on medium-high speed. Add 1/3 cup sugar gradually and beat until light and fluffy. (Add the yolks at this point, if used). Beat in the vanilla. Add the melted chocolate and beat until blended. Stir in the flour, in three batches, by hand or on very low with the mixer. Scrape down the batter once or twice between mixing.

In a clean, grease-free bowl, with a clean balloon whip, beat the egg whites on low speed until frothy. Add the salt and continue to beat on medium-high speed until soft peaks form. Add the remaining 1/3 cup sugar gradually and continue to whip until stiff, but not dry, peaks form. Fold 1/4 of the meringue mixture into the batter to lighten. Fold in remaining whites. Take care to retain the volume provided by the whites, but fold in thoroughly so that no whites streaks are left.

Pour into pans and smooth tops with a small offset spatula. Bake about 50 to 60 minutes, or until a toothpick tests almost clean, with a few moist crumbs. A thin crackly layer may have formed on top. It can easily be peeled off with your fingers or a sharp knife after cooling, but before wrapping. Cool, place on cardboards, and wrap with plastic wrap and foil.

FOR TWO 10 × 2-INCH CAKE LAYERS

6 ounces semisweet chocolate, finely chopped

1 1/4 cups unsifted cake flour

6 ounces (1 1/2 sticks) unsalted butter, at room temperature

1 cup sugar, divided into 1/2 cup and 1/2 cup

1 teaspoon vanilla extract

6 large egg whites

1/4 teaspoon salt

Prepare two 10 × 2-inch cake pans with cooking spray and parchment paper. Proceed as above for 6-inch layers. Bake about 30 to 40 minutes. Cool, place on cardboards, and wrap with plastic wrap and foil.

FOR TWO 14 × 2-INCH CAKE LAYERS

Make double the 10-inch recipe using two 14 × 2-inch cake pans that you have sprayed with cooking spray and lined with parchment. You may double the recipe and make it all at once. Add flour in several batches, scraping down each time, to facilitate blending. Bake about 35 to 45 minutes. Cool, place on cardboards, and wrap with plastic wrap and foil.

APRICOT ROSES

Buy moist, whole, sulfur-preserved Turkish apricots. Natural ones do not have the nice orange color you want and are not as plump. The roses do take a bit of time to make, but they are not difficult. The roses may be made up to three days ahead and stored in an airtight container in the refrigerator.

MAKES APPROXIMATELY 2 DOZEN ROSES

48 Turkish apricots

Split the apricots in half from edge to edge into two flat disks. Place the halves between parchment paper and roll out flat with a rolling pin. They should be no more than 1/16 inch thick. Roll one of the pieces, sticky side facing in, into a tight roll to form the center of the flower. Wrap another one, again sticky side facing in, around the bud. Continue with 2 to 4 additional apricots, always starting in the center of the last petal so that each overlaps.

Splay out the tops of the outer petals for a more realistic look. Use toothpicks to hold them together at their base, if necessary. Refer to the photo for guidance. For a crystallized effect, sprinkle the roses with sugar.

VARIATION:

You may also make apricot roses by starting with apricot fruit leather. Use a petal-shaped gum paste cutter to cut out the shapes. Follow the directions for Chocolate Plastic Roses in the Finishing Touches chapter, page 170.

ASSEMBLY

Have all components ready, except for the Chantilly Cream. Cover a 16-inch-round Masonite board with decorative foil. Have ready 7-inch and 11-inch separator plates and 8 spiked pillars (all painted terra cotta).

Torte the 6-inch tier in half. Place the cut surfaces facing up on the counter. Spread the one on the left with preserves and the one on the right with ganache. Lift the right one up and turn it over, placing the ganache side on top of the apricot preserves on the other layer. You will have a cake sandwich with a combined layer of preserves and ganache in the center.

Crumb coat the cake with a thin layer of chocolate buttercream. Chill well. Repeat with other cakes. You will have two 10-inch layers and two 14-inch layers. Do not torte them. You treat each layer of the same size as half of the same tier. Place one 10-inch layer on the counter to the left, one to the right and proceed as for 6-inch tier. Repeat with 14-inch layers. Crumb coat with buttercream and chill well.

Apply the final coat of chocolate buttercream. Chill all tiers. Center the 14-inch tier on the Masonite board. Place the top two tiers on their separator plates.

Pipe a simple shell border around the top edge and bottom edge of each tier. Use a #16 for the top tier, #17 for the middle tier, and #18 tip for the bottom tier. Refrigerate the cake overnight.

Transport the cakes unassembled. Make Chantilly Cream as near to serving time as possible. When you are ready to present the cake for viewing, assemble cakes on spiked pillars. Refer to the photograph for ideas, but you may place the decorations on the cake any way you desire. When you serve the bride, the groom and the bridal party, give each of them some of the decorations with their slice. Serve the cake at room temperature with the Chantilly Cream.

WHITE CHOCOLATE SATIN APRICOT CAKE WITH WHITE CHOCOLATE FLOWERS AND GRAPES

COMPONENTS

White Chocolate Cake
Two 6 × 2-inch layers
Two 10 × 2-inch layers
Two 14 × 2-inch layers
(page 137 in Basics chapter)

· ·

6 cups Apricot Lekvar, at
room temperature

· ·

23 cups Italian Meringue
Buttercream, chocolate
variation (page 141 in Basics
chapter)

· ·

18 assorted White Chocolate
Roses in various sizes (page 170
in Finishing Touches chapter)

· ·

18 assorted White Chocolate
Leaves in various sizes (page
168 in Finishing Touches
chapter)

· ·

150 small White Chocolate
Leaves in natural color for bor-
der (page 168 in Finishing
Touches chapter)

· ·

5 bunches White Chocolate
Grapes (page 170 in Finishing
Touches chapter)

· ·

MAKES 100 SERVINGS

COMPLEX
❖ ❖ ❖

This cake (featured on the cover of this book) is comprised of soft, white-chocolate cake layers, a filling of concentrated apricot lekvar (apricot butter), and a covering of satiny, white chocolate buttercream. Although the insides are scrumptious, it is the outside of the cake that will first grab your attention. All of the roses, flowers, grapes, and leaves are made of chocolate plastic. Some are a natural color, while others are brushed with powdered coloring or tinted with paste coloring. These chocolate accents do take time, but you can start them far ahead and store them in an airtight container at room temperature. I have made this cake several times, and it always comes out a little differently—deliberately, of course. Use the photo as a guide, then try your hand at chocolate-flower arranging.

Apricot lekvar is a concentrated spread similar to apple butter, but made of apricots. It can be purchased from a well-stocked supermarket or specialty food store, or you can make your own. If the lekvar flavor is too concentrated for you, simply blend some of it with the buttercream for the filling—you'll need more buttercream in this case.

APRICOT LEKVAR

This concentrated apricot spread may be made up to 2 weeks ahead.
Store in an airtight container in the refrigerator.

MAKES 6 CUPS

12 cups dried California apricots
1½ cups light brown sugar
½ cup lemon juice

Place the apricots in a large saucepan and add enough water to cover. Cook over medium heat for about 20 minutes, or until apricots are very soft. Drain the apricots, reserving liquid. Set the pan aside for later use.

Place the apricots in 2 batches in the bowl of your food processor fitted with the metal blade. Purée by pulsing on and off until the apricots are smooth. Add some of the cooking liquid, if necessary.

Scrape the purée back into the large saucepan and stir in the brown sugar and lemon juice. Cook over low heat, stirring continually, until the sugar is dissolved, about 5 to 10 minutes. Let cool, then store in an airtight container in the refrigerator, until needed.

Assembly

Have all components ready. Cover an 18-inch-round Masonite board with decorative foil.

Fill the tiers with a layer of lekvar and crumb coat with the White Chocolate Buttercream. Chill well and apply a smooth final coat of white chocolate buttercream. Chill well.

Center the bottom tier on the Masonite board. Align and center the top two tiers on the bottom tier, using dowels for internal support. Using a #3 tip, pipe vines randomly all over the tops and sides of the tiers using the buttercream. You may even pipe some vines down onto the cake board. Use the small white-chocolate plastic leaves to make a bottom border on the top two tiers by overlapping them (see photo). Chill well.

Following the photo for inspiration, place flat leaves randomly on the cake, overlapping some. Place the majority of the flowers and grapes on the cake, making a nice cake top with a bunch of them. Reserve some to take with you to the party site for last-minute adjustments. Refrigerate overnight.

Finish any assembly on site before setting the cake out for viewing. Serve the cake at room temperature.

·4·

CAKE ACCOMPANIMENTS

DESSERT SAUCES AND CREAMS

CHANTILLY CREAM

A chantilly cream is simply lightly sweetened whipped cream. For best results, use the richest cream you can find— at least 38 percent unsalted butterfat. If you can find cream with 40 percent butterfat, all the better. Note that whipping cream is not as rich as heavy cream. Heavy cream is specified throughout the book. The other factors that come into play are freshness and whether the cream has been ultra-pasteurized, a process that exposes the cream to high heat to extend its shelf life. But it also alters its fresh dairy flavor and renders it tasting a bit cooked. Avoid this kind of cream, if possible. The label clearly states whether the cream is pasteurized or ultra-pasteurized. Health-food stores often carry pasteurized heavy cream.

To figure how much cream you need, know your serving size. For example, a two-tablespoon dollop of whipped cream will suffice in most instances. Multiply this by the number of cake servings you have and then divide that number in half. This is the amount of heavy cream you need, since the cream doubles in bulk when whipped. The maximum amount that the five-quart KitchenAid mixer can comfortably hold is six cups of liquid cream.

For best results, make sure the cream is well chilled. It also helps to prechill the bowl and balloon whip. Do not overbeat the cream or you will make unsalted butter or grainy overbeaten cream. It is best to stop the mixer shortly before the soft peaks form and finish it off by hand with a large whisk. If you do overbeat, you may be able to save the mixture by adding a little bit of liquid cream and stirring gently. Do not use confectioners' sugar. It has cornstarch added to prevent clumping and will taste starchy in whipped cream.

MAKES 12 CUPS

6 cups heavy cream, well chilled
1/3 to 1/2 cup sugar
1 tablespoon vanilla extract, (optional)

Place the cream, sugar, and vanilla, if using, in the mixing bowl. With a balloon whip, begin to whip on medium-high speed until the cream begins to thicken. Turn the mixer to high speed and beat until soft peaks form. Do not overbeat.

Make this close to serving time. It may be refrigerated for a few hours. Stir gently with a whisk before serving.

CRÈME ANGLAISE

This is a classic vanilla custard sauce, used frequently in fine restaurants as an accompaniment to fancy desserts. Consider using it in place of Chantilly Cream with the truffle cakes. The basic recipe is a vanilla flavor, but there are variations suggested. When making this, remember that custards demand attention. Don't walk away during cooking. This may be made up to 4 days ahead, and refrigerated in an airtight container.

MAKES 5 3/4 CUPS

4 cups whole milk
1/2 vanilla bean, split lengthwise
1 cup sugar
12 large egg yolks
1/4 cup liqueur (optional)

Combine the milk and vanilla bean in a nonreactive saucepan. Bring the mixture to a boil, turn off the heat, and soak the bean for at least 10 minutes. Cover the pan to keep the mixture warm.

Meanwhile, place the sugar and yolks in a mixing bowl and whip with a wire whisk by hand until creamy. Pour about 1 cup of the hot milk over the yolk mixture, whisking constantly; this will temper the eggs. Then add the egg mixture to the pan of milk, whisking all together well.

Cook the mixture over medium-low heat, stirring frequently with a whisk to prevent the mixture from burning on the bottom and boiling over. If tiny bubbles appear around the edges of the sauce, remove from the heat immediately. Use an instant read thermometer and cook the sauce to 175°F. Do not let it boil.

Set a strainer over a bowl and pour the custard through the strainer. Using a rubber spatula, press the sauce through to remove any overcooked solids that may have accumulated.

The bean will be left in the strainer. If you want, scrape its seeds into the sauce, using a blunt knife or the tip of a spoon. Whisk well to disperse sticky clumps of seeds. Stir the sauce over a bowl of ice water until chilled. Refrigerate in an airtight container.

VARIATIONS

ADDING LIQUEUR

To add a liqueur flavor, stir in ¼ cup alcohol—such as Kahlúa, rum, cognac, or Grand Marnier—at the very end of cooking. Experiment with your favorite flavor.

RASPBERRY COULIS

This is a purée of raspberries that complements such cakes as the Vanilla Sponge Cake with Raspberry Mousse Filling and Italian Meringue, page 59. Defrost the berries completely overnight in the refrigerator or for a few hours at room temperature. Do not defrost them in the microwave because the heat will cook the fruit and you will lose some of the fresh color and flavor. Pour off any liquid and reserve it for later use. Store the completed coulis in an airtight container in the freezer up to one month ahead or in the refrigerator up to three days ahead.

MAKES 4 CUPS

Four 12-ounce bags of frozen unsweetened raspberries, thawed

²/₃ cup superfine sugar

Purée the berries in your food processor fitted with the metal blade. Do this in batches, if necessary. Set a strainer over a bowl and pour the purée through the strainer. Discard the seeds. Stir half the sugar into the purée. Taste and adjust sweetness, if desired. If the purée is too thick, add some of the reserved juice, but do not thin too much.

BITTERSWEET CHOCOLATE SAUCE

This is a dark, shiny, silky chocolate sauce perfect for accompanying such cakes as the Flaming Baked Alaska, page 39. The recipe may be scaled up or down directly. It can be made a week ahead and stored in an airtight container in the refrigerator. Before using it, warm briefly in the microwave at medium power or on top of the stove in a double boiler (bain-marie).

MAKES 5 CUPS

12 ounces unsweetened chocolate, finely chopped

3 cups heavy cream

1½ cups sugar

2 ounces (½ stick) unsalted butter

pinch salt

1 teaspoon vanilla extract

Place all ingredients, except the vanilla, in a heavy-bottomed saucepan. Heat over medium heat, stirring frequently and taking care not to scorch the chocolate. Heat until the chocolate is melted and the sugar dissolved. The sauce should be shiny and smooth. Remove from the heat and stir in the vanilla. Cool to room temperature. Refrigerate in an airtight container.

Plating Techniques

Once you have cut your cakes, you may think that your job is over. At country weddings, or any wedding of lesser formality, slicing, plating, and serving the cake may be enough. But for more formal, seated affairs, you should set your presentation apart with a plate decorated with sauces, confectioners' sugar, cocoa, or other final flourishes.

Know that any plating technique takes time and you want to be sure that you have an assembly line set up with one person applying the plate accouterments, another placing the cake on the plates, and a third person handing out the plates at a buffet, or placing them on trays for the wait staff. Of course, some of these steps can be done ahead of time.

Sauces

Place the sauce of your choice, such as berry coulis, chocolate, or crème anglaise, in a squeeze bottle. Apply the sauces on the plates, before the cake, in squiggly free-form designs, dots, or a defined pattern that you have decided upon. One sauce can be used, or more than one for a colorful, and flavorful effect. *Grand Finales*, a book on plating techniques, is a wonderful reference (see Bibliography, page 191).

Dry Ingredients

Confectioners' or powdered sugar, cocoa, and cinnamon can all be dusted onto plates for a pretty look. A fine-meshed strainer can work for this technique, but a dredger is best. Thoroughly dried edible flowers can be pulverized in a coffee grinder or spice mill. They will have subtle colors that look quite unusual on the plate.

Gold and Silver Powder

These powders are made of actual gold and silver (see Gold and Silver Leaf in the Finishing Touches chapter, page 174). They are expensive and extravagant and I use them on a plate only when I am serving a cake that is adorned with gold or silver leaf. I then dust the bride's and groom's plates with some extra powder for a nice touch.

Chocolate Initials

To make these, put melted chocolate in a parchment cone and pipe initials of the bridal couple on the edge of each plate. The first letter of their last name or combined last names is appropriate. Do this ahead of time so you can chill the plates to firm up the initials. To gild the lily, gild the initials, at least on the plates going to the blessed couple.

A Note on Fresh Fruit

Regardless of the type of cake, be it an elegant chocolate extravaganza, or a light white cake with lemon curd filling, I like to serve fresh fruit with my cakes. There are several reasons for this. First of all, I hope that the cake presented is the cake of the bridal couple's dreams, but it may not jibe with the likes of the entire guest list. Some folks may be allergic to chocolate, others may be on a diet, and some may be trying to avoid fat or sugar. Whatever the reason, most guests appreciate the addition of fresh fruit so that they can have some with their cake or in place of it.

I'm not talking anything fancy here. I usually suggest a simple mixed fruit mélange with cut melons, berries, and grapes (and exotic fruit, if desired). Or, if the season allows, go for a big basket of strawberries, hulls on, that can be placed on the buffet along with the cake. Talk to your caterer about the options.

· 5 ·

THE BASICS

THE CAKES

POUND CAKE

When you are looking for a firm, closely textured, butter-laden cake, make a classic pound cake. Pound cakes are much firmer than butter cakes or génoise and have an incomparable, buttery aroma that emanates from the oven during baking. Pound cakes also keep very well at room temperature (about 5 days) and freeze very well, up to a month. Because the pound cake is so firm, it stands up well to a heavy covering, such as marzipan. The long, slow baking time is a factor of the formulation's denseness. You will need Magi-Cake Strips and a baking core for this recipe; see the Equipment chapter for details. Magi-Cake Strips really help this cake bake level, so use them.

FOR TWO 6 × 2-INCH CAKE LAYERS

2¹/₂ cups unsifted cake flour

1 teaspoon baking powder

¹/₄ teaspoon salt

12 ounces (3 sticks) unsalted butter, at room temperature

1¹/₂ cups sugar

2 teaspoons vanilla extract

6 large eggs

Preheat the oven to 325°F. Prepare two 6 × 2-inch cake pans with cooking spray and parchment paper.

Sift together the flour, baking powder, and salt. Set aside.

In the bowl of your mixer, beat the butter until creamy with the flat paddle on medium-high speed. Add the sugar gradually and continue to beat until light and fluffy. Beat in the vanilla. Add the eggs one at a time, beating well after each addition, scraping down the bowl once or twice.

Add the sifted dry ingredients in 3 batches, combining well each time. Scrape down the bowl after each addition. After all the dry ingredients are added, beat for about 2 minutes on medium speed to thoroughly combine.

Scrape the batter into prepared pans, smoothing tops with a small offset spatula. Bake about 60 to 70 minutes, or until a toothpick tests clean. The aroma will be very buttery and the cake will be golden. Cool, place on cardboards, and wrap with plastic wrap and foil.

FOR TWO 10 × 2-INCH CAKE LAYERS

6¹/₄ cups unsifted cake flour

2¹/₂ teaspoons baking powder

²/₃ teaspoon salt

1 pound, 14 ounces (7¹/₂ sticks) unsalted butter, at room temperature

3³/₄ cups sugar

1 tablespoon plus 2 teaspoons vanilla extract

15 large eggs

Prepare two 10 × 2-inch cake pans with cooking spray and parchment paper. Proceed as above for the 6-inch cakes.

This amount will just fit into your mixing bowl. Add the dry ingredients slowly and pulse the machine on and off to help incorporate the dry ingredients and to keep them in the bowl. If possible, use a splash guard attachment for the mixer. Proceed slowly and methodically. Use a baking core. Bake about 60 to 70 minutes. Cool, place on cardboards, and wrap with plastic wrap and foil.

FOR TWO 14 × 2-INCH CAKE LAYERS

Prepare two 14 × 2-inch cake pans with cooking spray and parchment paper. Make the 10-inch recipe twice, once for each layer. Do not double the recipe because it will not fit in your mixing bowl. Use a baking core. Bake about 70 to 80 minutes. Cool, place on cardboards, and wrap with plastic wrap and foil.

If you want 9- or 12-inch layers, proceed as follows: Double the 6-inch recipe for the 9-inch size. Double the 9-inch recipe for the 12-inch size. Adjust baking times accordingly. I did not test these sizes, but this gives you something to work from.

GÉNOISE

Génoise is the classic French sponge cake. It is the basis for many European gâteaux (cakes) and is meant to be torted or layered with any manner of fillings and buttercreams. It is a slightly dry cake that is to be moistened with a plain sugar or liqueur-flavored syrup. The texture is very different from an American butter cake or pound cake. Even after the syrup and fillings are added, some folks still perceive it as dry, which they don't like. It is best to try the small recipe out first so that you can see for yourself. Usually, Europeans are familiar with it and enjoy it, whereas some Americans may not have had anything like it before, and therefore, expect something denser and richer.

This génoise recipe is not a classic one; it has extra egg yolks in the batter to increase its richness. The batter is very thick, and you must follow the techniques, but it produces a very high, light, spongy cake that is a dream to work with. This cake can be frozen for one month, but I think it dries out in the freezer more easily than butter cakes do, so it is best to bake it three or four days before the event, wrap it well, and store it at room temperature.

FOR TWO 6 × 2-INCH CAKE LAYERS

3/4 cup cake flour, sifted

1/3 cup cornstarch, sifted

1/3 cup (2 2/3 ounces) warm clarified butter (page 4 in Getting Started chapter)

1 teaspoon vanilla extract

5 large eggs

2 large egg yolks (whole in their shells first for warming)

2/3 cup sugar

Preheat the oven to 350°F. Prepare two 6 × 2-inch cake pans with cooking spray and parchment paper. Resift together the flour and cornstarch and set aside.

Combine the clarified butter and vanilla in a small bowl and set aside. These should be warmed to room temperature.

For the batter to reach maximum volume, warm the eggs, shells intact, in a bowl filled with hot water for 10 minutes. Break the 5 whole eggs into the bowl of your mixer. Separate the other 2 eggs and add the yolks to the whole eggs. Reserve the whites for another use.

Add the sugar to the bowl and with the balloon whip, beat the mixture on medium-high speed until triple in volume, pale yellow, and light and fluffy.

Sprinkle 1/3 of the dry mixture over the eggs. Using a whisk, fold the dry ingredients into the eggs very gently. Proceed with the remaining dry mixture. By cutting down through the fluffy eggs with the whisk and folding the mixture over gently, the flour mixture will be well incorporated without deflating the eggs.

Add the butter mixture slowly, 1 tablespoon at a time, and whisk it in gently, but completely. Use the whisk, as above, to gently turn over the batter in broad strokes. Do not rush this step, because the butter, heavier than the fluffy batter, may sink to the bottom of the cake and create a rubbery layer. To avoid this, proceed slowly. The egg yolks make the batter very thick, so fold it gently until thoroughly combined.

Scrape the batter into the pans, smoothing tops with a small offset spatula. Bake for about 30 to 40 minutes or until a toothpick tests clean. The edges will just begin to shrink from the sides and the color will be pale gold. Cool, place on cardboards, and wrap with plastic wrap and foil.

FOR TWO 8 × 2-INCH CAKE LAYERS

1 cup cake flour, sifted

1/3 cup plus 1 tablespoon cornstarch, sifted

1/3 cup plus 1 tablespoon (generous 3 1/8 ounces) warm clarified butter (page 4 in Getting Started chapter)

1 1/4 teaspoons vanilla extract

6 large eggs

3 large egg yolks (whole in their shells first for warming)

3/4 cup plus 2 tablespoons sugar

Prepare two 8 × 2-inch cake pans with cooking spray and parchment. Proceed as above for the 6-inch cakes. Bake about 35 to 45 minutes. Cool, place on cardboards, and wrap with plastic wrap and foil.

FOR TWO 9 × 2-INCH CAKE LAYERS

1 1/2 cups cake flour, sifted

2/3 cup cornstarch, sifted

2/3 cup (5 1/3 ounces) warm clarified butter (page 4 in Getting Started chapter)

2 teaspoons vanilla extract

10 large eggs

4 large egg yolks (whole in the shells first for warming)

1 1/3 cups sugar

Prepare two 9 × 2-inch cake pans with cooking spray and parchment. Proceed as above for the 6-inch cakes. You will be able to whip the eggs and sugar together in your mixing bowl, but it will be quite full. Pour the egg-sugar mixture into a larger bowl before proceeding with the recipe. This will allow you to fold in the flour and butter more easily. Bake about 35 to 45 minutes. Cool, place on cardboards, and wrap with plastic wrap and foil.

FOR TWO 10 × 2-INCH CAKE LAYERS

1³⁄₄ cups plus 2 tablespoons cake flour, sifted

³⁄₄ cup plus 1 tablespoon cornstarch, sifted

³⁄₄ cup plus 1 tablespoon (6¹⁄₂ ounces) warm clarified butter (page 4 in Getting Started chapter)

2¹⁄₂ teaspoons vanilla extract

12 large eggs

6 large egg yolks (whole in their shells first for warming)

1²⁄₃ cups sugar

Prepare two 10 × 2-inch cake pans with cooking spray and parchment paper. Follow the directions for flour, cornstarch, clarified butter, and vanilla as above. The procedure for the remaining ingredients for this size cake differs. You need a large bowl ready for the entire batter. Whip 6 eggs and 3 yolks with ³⁄₄ cup plus 2 tablespoons of sugar in your mixer's bowl until light and fluffy. Pour this into the large bowl. Repeat with the remaining eggs, yolks, and sugar. Pour this on top of the first batch of eggs and sugar. Follow the directions for the 9-inch cake for the remainder of the recipe. Bake about 40 to 50 minutes. Cool, place on cardboards, and wrap with plastic wrap and foil.

FOR TWO 12 × 2-INCH CAKE LAYERS

Prepare two 12 × 2-inch cake pans with cooking spray and parchment paper. Make the 9-inch cake recipe twice, once for each layer. Bake about 45 to 55 minutes. Cool, place on cardboards, and wrap with plastic wrap and foil.

FOR TWO 14 × 2-INCH CAKE LAYERS

Prepare two 14 × 2-inch cake pans with cooking spray and parchment paper. Make the 8-inch cake recipe 4 times, twice for each layer. Bake about 45 to 55 minutes.

NUT GÉNOISE

As I explained in the master génoise recipe (page 131), a génoise is a light French sponge cake. The Nut Génoise uses finely ground nuts to replace some of the flour and these provide flavor and texture. The technique for this recipe is a bit different from the classic génoise. Here, the yolks and whites are whipped separately. The extra volume from the whites helps offset any potential heaviness from the nuts, and the thick batter suspends the nuts perfectly so that they do not sink to the bottom of the pan during baking. I first came across a recipe using this technique in Carole Walter's Great Cakes *book. It is an excellent reference book.*

Almonds, walnuts, pecans, and hazelnuts are all suitable for this recipe. The hazelnut version is used to great effect in the Hazelnut Dacquoise and Hazelnut Génoise Wedding Cake (page 91), which is a marvel of contrasts. Try all of the nut varieties; the diverse flavors will inspire you to create cakes just to showcase the recipe.

This cake does not dry out as quickly as the regular génoise. You may freeze the Nut Génoise for as long as a month, or you may make it a few days before serving. Whichever method you choose, wrap it well with plastic wrap and foil.

See the square variations that are featured in the Gâteau Opéra (page 109) at the end of the recipe.

FOR TWO 6 × 2-INCH CAKE LAYERS

2 tablespoons plus 2 teaspoons (1²⁄₃ ounces) warm clarified butter (page 4 in Getting Started chapter)

²⁄₃ teaspoon vanilla extract

4²⁄₃ ounces hazelnuts (about 1 cup), toasted and peeled (page 147 in Basics chapter)

¹⁄₂ cup unsifted cake flour

4 large eggs, separated

²⁄₃ cup sugar, divided into ¹⁄₂ cup and 2 tablespoons plus 2 teaspoons

Preheat the oven to 350°F. Prepare two 6 × 2-inch cake pans with cooking spray and parchment paper.

Combine the butter and vanilla in a small bowl and set aside at room temperature.

Place the nuts and flour in the container of a food processor fitted with the metal blade. Pulse on and off about 5 times. Let the processor run for about 10 seconds. Pulse again to fluff the mixture for finely ground nuts, not a paste.

Place the egg yolks in the bowl of your mixer, and with a balloon whip, beat the yolks with ½ cup sugar on medium-high speed until a thick ribbon forms.

In a clean, grease-free bowl, with a clean balloon whip, beat the whites until soft peaks form on low speed. Add the remaining 2 tablespoons plus 2 teaspoons sugar gradually and whip on medium-high speed until stiff, but not dry, peaks form.

In a large bowl, fold together the yolk and white mixtures. Divide the dry mixture into three portions and sprinkle over the batter, folding in with a large whisk. Cut the whisk down into the batter, bringing it up and folding it over. Retain the volume of the batter at all times.

Sprinkle the butter mixture, 1 tablespoon at a time, over the batter. Use the whisk to fold it in and finish the folding with a few broad strokes of a rubber spatula.

Pour the batter into the pans. Bake about 20 to 30 minutes, or until a toothpick tests clean. Depending on the variety of nuts used, the cake's color will be speckled brown and the sides will just be separating from the pan. Cool, place on cardboards, and wrap with plastic wrap and foil.

FOR TWO 9 × 2-INCH CAKE LAYERS

¹/₃ cup (2²/₃ ounces) warm clarified butter (page 4 in Getting Started chapter)

1¹/₃ teaspoons vanilla extract

9¹/₃ ounces hazelnuts (about 2¹/₂ cups), toasted and peeled (page 147)

1 cup unsifted cake flour

8 large eggs, separated

1¹/₃ cups sugar, divided into 1 cup and ¹/₃ cup

Prepare two 9 × 2-inch cake pans with cooking spray and parchment paper. Process as above for the 6-inch cakes. Bake about 30 to 40 minutes. Cool, place on cardboards, and wrap with plastic wrap and foil.

FOR TWO 10 × 2-INCH CAKE LAYERS

¹/₃ cup plus 1 tablespoon (hefty 3¹/₈ ounces) warm clarified butter (page 4 in Getting Started chapter)

1²/₃ teaspoons vanilla extract

11²/₃ ounces hazelnuts (about 3 cups), toasted and peeled (page 147)

1¹/₄ cups unsifted cake flour

10 large eggs, separated

1²/₃ cups sugar, divided into 1¹/₄ cups and ¹/₃ cup plus 1 tablespoon

Prepare two 10 × 2-inch cake pans with cooking spray and parchment paper. Proceed as above for the 9-inch cakes. Bake about 30 to 40 minutes. Cool, place on cardboards, and wrap with plastic wrap and foil.

FOR TWO 12 × 2-INCH CAKE LAYERS

²/₃ cup (5¹/₃ ounces) warm clarified butter (page 4 in Getting Started chapter)

2²/₃ teaspoons vanilla extract

1 pound plus ¹/₂ ounce hazelnuts (about 4 cups), toasted and peeled (page 147)

2 cups unsifted cake flour

16 large eggs, separated

2²/₃ cups sugar, divided into 2 cups and ²/₃ cup

Prepare two 12 × 2-inch cake pans with cooking spray and parchment paper. Proceed as above for the 6-inch cakes, with the following adjustments: Plan to process the nuts in batches. The amount of flour with each batch of nuts must be enough to keep the oil from the nuts turning the mixture into nut butter. Toss all the nuts and flour together before proceeding. Bake about 30 to 40 minutes. Cool, place on cardboards, and wrap with plastic wrap and foil.

FOR TWO 14 × 2-INCH CAKE LAYERS

Prepare two 14 × 2-inch cake pans with cooking spray and parchment paper. Make the 10-inch cake recipe twice, once for each 14-inch pan. Follow the directions for the 12-inch cakes. Bake about 35 to 45 minutes. Cool, place on cardboards, wrap with plastic wrap and foil.

SQUARE VARIATION

In general, square pans hold 25 percent more volume than round pans of equal size. You can simply increase any recipe in this book by 25 percent and bake the batter in a square pan. Baking temperatures remain the same but baking times often vary. The corners cook much faster than the center in a square pan. Rotating the pans frequently helps to control this. Use Magi-Cake Strips (see page 181), if you have sizes to fit the square pans. The Gâteau Opéra (page 109) uses this square variation with almonds as the nut. Use almond extract instead of vanilla in this case.

FOR TWO 6 × 6 × 2-INCH CAKE LAYERS

3 tablespoons plus 1 teaspoon (generous 1½ ounces) warm clarified butter (page 4 in Getting Started chapter)

Generous ¾ teaspoon vanilla extract

5½ ounces hazelnuts (about 1¼ cups), toasted and peeled (page 147)

⅔ cup unsifted cake flour

5 large eggs

¾ cup plus 1 tablespoon sugar (divided into ⅔ cup and 3 tablespoons plus 1 teaspoon)

Prepare two 6 × 6 × 2-inch cake pans with cooking spray and parchment paper. Proceed as above for the round cakes. Bake about 20 to 30 minutes. Cool, place on cardboards, and wrap with plastic wrap and foil.

FOR TWO 10 × 10 × 2-INCH CAKE LAYERS

½ cup (4 ounces) warm clarified butter (page 4 in Getting Started chapter)

2 teaspoons vanilla extract

13¾ ounces hazelnuts (about 3¾ cups), toasted and peeled (page 147)

1⅔ cups unsifted cake flour

12 large eggs

2 cups sugar (separated into 1½ cups and ½ cup)

Prepare two 10 × 10 × 2-inch cake pans with cooking spray and parchment paper. Proceed as above for the round cakes. Bake about 35 to 45 minutes. Cool, place on cardboards, and wrap with plastic wrap and foil.

FOR TWO 14 × 14 × 2-INCH CAKE LAYERS

Prepare two 14 × 14 × 2-inch cake pans with cooking spray and parchment paper. Make the 10-inch cake recipe twice. Use a baking core. Bake about 35 to 45 minutes. Cool, place on cardboards, and wrap with plastic wrap and foil.

SOUR CREAM CHOCOLATE CAKE

This is a very chocolatey, tender cake with a slightly mellow tang from the sour cream. It is also quite rich. It is the chocolate cake that I use when I want a good basic chocolate cake. It's not too heavy, not too light. To be precise, it should be called a "cocoa cake," but the flavor is so strong, true, and full of chocolate, I felt this name did it justice. Feel free to pair this cake with fillings and buttercreams of all complementary flavors: coffee, raspberry, orange, rum, and hazelnut, to name a few. This cake may be frozen for up to one month.

Note that the batter is quite thick and you must make sure the ingredients are blended homogeneously. One of my recipe testers, Mary McNamara, said she was sure that something was amiss, but when she was reassured by the directions that this texture was correct, she had the courage to continue.

FOR TWO 6 × 2-INCH CAKE LAYERS

1⅔ cups unsifted cake flour

⅓ cup unsifted Dutch-processed cocoa

¾ teaspoon baking soda

¾ teaspoon baking powder

¼ teaspoon salt

6 ounces (1½ sticks) unsalted butter, at room temperature

¾ cup sugar

⅓ cup packed light brown sugar

2 large eggs

1 cup sour cream

Preheat the oven to 350°F. Prepare two 6 × 2-inch cake pans with cooking spray and parchment paper.

Sift together the flour, cocoa, leaveners, and salt and set aside.

Place the butter in the bowl of your mixer, and with the flat paddle, cream butter on medium-high speed. Add the sugars gradually, and beat until light and fluffy. Add the eggs one at a time, beating well after each addition and scraping the bowl down once or twice.

Add the dry ingredients and the sour cream alternately, in 3 separate batches. To begin blending, turn the mixer on and off at low speed. Scrape down the bowl 2 or 3 times between mixing. When all the ingredients are added, beat well for 1 minute to blend thoroughly. Scrape the batter down once or twice during the final mixing. The batter will be a pale cocoa color.

Scrape the batter into the pans and smooth the tops with a small offset spatula. Bake for about 50 to 60 minutes, or until a toothpick tests clean. When the cake is done, it will have a very chocolatey aroma and the edges will be a slightly darker color. Cool, place on cardboards, and wrap with plastic wrap and foil.

FOR TWO 10 × 2-INCH CAKE LAYERS

4 cups plus 2 tablespoons unsifted cake flour
^{3}/$_4$ cup plus 1 tablespoon unsifted Dutch-processed cocoa
2 scant teaspoons baking soda
2 scant teaspoons baking powder
^{2}/$_3$ teaspoon salt
15 ounces (3^3/$_4$ sticks) unsalted butter, at room temperature
2 scant cups sugar
^{3}/$_4$ cup plus 2 tablespoons packed light brown sugar
5 large eggs
2^1/$_2$ cups sour cream

Prepare two 10 × 2-inch cake pans with cooking spray and parchment paper. Proceed as above for the 6-inch cakes. Add the dry ingredients and the sour cream alternately in 4 batches. Beat well after each addition and scrape down the bowl once or twice between additions. Bake about 55 to 70 minutes. Cool, place on cardboards, and wrap with plastic wrap and foil.

FOR TWO 14 × 2-INCH CAKE LAYERS

Prepare two 14 × 2-inch cake pans with cooking spray and parchment paper. Make the 10-inch cake recipe twice, once for each pan. Bake about 70 to 80 minutes. Cool, place on cardboards, and wrap with plastic wrap and foil.

DACQUOISE

A dacquoise is a nut-enriched meringue, usually baked into a disk and layered with buttercreams or mousses. Plain meringues are often sweet; it is the high sugar content that gives them their crunch. With a dacquoise, the nuts temper the sweetness, add a texture of their own, and when layered with fillings and cake into a towering creation, provide a contrast unattainable any other way. You may use almonds, walnuts, pecans, or hazelnuts—I have used hazelnuts as the example; the recipe is featured in the Hazelnut Dacquoise and Hazelnut Génoise Wedding Cake (page 91).

The extracts are optional; I usually do not add vanilla, but if I am using almonds, I do add the almond flavoring.

A successful dacquoise is dry and crispy. Do not attempt to make this on a humid day; the moisture in the air will work against you. These can be made a week ahead, but proper storage is critical. They must be stored flat, on cardboard rounds to prevent breakage, in an airtight container. I also use a Blue Magic insert (see page 178). Note that you will need several baking sheets to make this recipe.

FOR TWO 6-INCH ROUNDS, AND TWO 14-INCH ROUNDS PLUS EXTRA

10 ounces hazelnuts (about 2^1/$_2$ cups), toasted and peeled (page 147)
3 tablespoons plus 1 teaspoon unsifted all-purpose flour
12 large egg whites
1^1/$_2$ teaspoons cream of tartar
3 cups sugar
1 teaspoon vanilla extract or almond extract (optional)

Preheat the oven to 250°F. You will need three cookie sheets, which will fit in 2 ovens. If you have only 1 oven with 2 racks, then halve the recipe. These directions are for the whole recipe—prepare cookie sheets as follows: Cut a piece of parchment paper to fit each pan. Using the bottom of a 6-inch cake pan as a guide, trace two 6-inch circles onto 1 of the papers; they should not touch. Repeat with one 14-inch pan on the second sheet and draw a second 14-inch circle on the third. Flip the parchment papers over; the drawn circles should be visible. This prevents any ink or pencil lead from transferring to the dacquoise.

Place the nuts and flour in the container of a food processor fitted with the metal blade. Pulse on and off until the nuts are finely ground. The flour will prevent the nuts from becoming a nut butter. Set aside.

In a clean, grease-free bowl, with a clean balloon whip, beat the whites until frothy on low speed. Add the cream of tartar and beat on medium-high speed until soft peaks form. Add the sugar gradually and continue to beat, increasing speed, until stiff, but not dry, peaks form. Beat in the extract, if desired.

Scrape the meringue into a large bowl. Fold in the nut-flour mixture gently with a large rubber spatula. Place the meringue into a large pastry bag fitted with a large #6 tip (with ½-inch opening).

Starting in the center of the circle, pipe in a spiral pattern until the 6-inch and 14-inch circles are filled. Pipe out individual cookie shapes all around the circles, not allowing any of the dacquoise to touch. Use up all of the mixture.

Bake about 60 to 70 minutes. Turn off the oven and leave the dacquoise inside for another hour. The dacquoise must be completely dry and crisp, but barely colored. The low heat should do this easily. Test one of the cookies. They should be crackly and brittle. For maximum dryness, leave the sheet in the oven overnight with the oven turned off. Place disks on cardboard rounds and store in an airtight container, if possible, with a Blue Magic insert (page 178). If you do not have a large enough container, wrap the disks tightly with foil and leave them in an off oven. Whether you have a pilot light or not, this will be a dry haven. Dacquoise can be made up to 3 weeks ahead, but only if they can be stored in a place without any moisture.

FOR TWO 10-INCH ROUNDS, PLUS EXTRA

2½ ounces hazelnuts (about ¾ cup),
toasted and peeled (page 147)

2½ teaspoons unsifted all-purpose flour

5 large egg whites

⅔ teaspoon cream of tartar

1¼ cups sugar

Proceed as above, using 10-inch pans for tracing your circles. You will most likely need two cookie sheets. Bake about 70 minutes before turning the oven off. Leave in for at least one more hour before testing one of the cookies for dryness. Cool, wrap, and store.

Note: The extra "cookies" serve two purposes. First, you can actually try one to assess doneness. Second, these extras can be crumbled by hand and used as an attractive outer covering for cakes. See Hazelnut Dacquoise and Hazelnut Génoise Wedding Cake (page 91). They add a crunchy, textural element to your decoration. This type of side decor can also hide a not-so-smooth buttercream job—something all of us can use every now and then.

WHITE CAKE

When it comes to naming recipes, the accepted modus operandi is to call it what it is—nothing fancy or cute. The best names tell you what you are getting. Well, White Cake may not sound fancy, and this recipe isn't either, but that doesn't mean it isn't good or extremely versatile, which it is! The name says it all: This is a very basic white cake that is made with all egg whites and no yolks, hence the whiter color than a yellow butter cake has. It is a wonderful basic to have in one's repertoire and will mix and match with pretty much any filling or buttercream. The butter amount is a bit odd. Use your scale for accuracy. You will find this cake in the White Cake with Lemon Curd, Blackberry Curd, and Pressed Flowers (page 37).

This cake may be frozen for up to one month, but I prefer to bake it two days before the event.

FOR TWO 6 × 2-INCH CAKE LAYERS

2⅓ cups unsifted cake flour

1 tablespoon baking powder

⅓ teaspoon salt

4 large egg whites

1 cup whole milk

5⅓ ounces (slightly more than 1¼ sticks) unsalted butter,
at room temperature

1⅓ cups sugar

2 teaspoons vanilla extract

Preheat the oven to 350°F. Prepare two 6 × 2-inch cake pans with cooking spray and parchment paper.

Sift together the flour, baking powder, and salt and set aside. Whisk together the egg whites and milk in a small bowl and set aside.

Place the butter in the bowl of your mixer, and with the flat paddle attachment, cream butter on medium-high speed. Add the sugar gradually and beat until well blended. Scrape down the bowl once or twice and beat in the vanilla.

Add the dry ingredients and the egg white mixture alternately, scraping down the sides several times. Continue to beat on medium speed just until smooth.

Scrape the batter into the pans and bake about 40 to 50 minutes, or until a toothpick tests clean. The edges will be slightly brown and will begin to pull away from the sides of the pan. Cool, place on cardboards, and wrap with plastic wrap and foil.

FOR TWO 8 × 2-INCH CAKE LAYERS

3 1/2 cups unsifted cake flour

1 tablespoon plus 1 teaspoon baking powder

1/2 teaspoon salt

6 large egg whites

1 1/2 cups whole milk

8 ounces (2 sticks) unsalted butter, at room temperature

2 cups sugar

1 tablespoon vanilla extract

Prepare two 8 × 2-inch cake pans with cooking spray and parchment paper. Proceed as above for the 6-inch cake layers. Bake about 40 to 50 minutes. Cool, place on cardboards, and wrap with plastic wrap and foil.

FOR TWO 9 × 2-INCH CAKE LAYERS

4 2/3 cups unsifted cake flour

2 tablespoons baking powder

2/3 teaspoon salt

8 large egg whites

2 cups whole milk

10 2/3 ounces butter (slightly more than 2 1/2 sticks), at room temperature

2 2/3 cups sugar

1 tablespoon plus 1 teaspoon vanilla extract

Prepare two 9 × 2-inch cake pans with cooking spray and parchment paper. Proceed as above for the 6-inch cake layers. Bake about 45 to 55 minutes. Cool, place on cardboards, and wrap with plastic wrap and foil.

FOR TWO 10 × 2-INCH CAKE LAYERS

5 3/4 cups plus 1 tablespoon unsifted cake flour

2 tablespoons plus 2 teaspoons baking powder

3/4 teaspoon salt

10 large egg whites

2 1/2 cups whole milk

13 1/3 ounces unsalted butter, at room temperature

3 1/3 cups sugar

1 tablespoon plus 2 teaspoons vanilla extract

Prepare two 10 × 2-inch cake pans with cooking spray and parchment paper. Proceed as above for the 6-inch cake layers. Bake about 45 to 55 minutes. Cool, place on cardboards, and wrap with plastic wrap and foil.

FOR TWO 12 × 2-INCH CAKE LAYERS

Make the 9-inch cake recipe twice, once for each 12 × 2-inch cake pan. Bake about 50 to 60 minutes. Cool, place on cardboards, and wrap with plastic wrap and foil.

FOR TWO 14 × 2-INCH CAKE LAYERS

Make the 10-inch recipe twice, once for each 14 × 2-inch cake pan. Bake about 55 to 65 minutes. Cool, place on cardboards, and wrap with plastic wrap and foil.

WHITE CHOCOLATE CAKE

This is a fragrant, buttery white chocolate cake. The wonderful smell that emanates from the oven is due to the cocoa butter in the chocolate. To obtain this taste and aroma you must use a high-quality white chocolate that contains cocoa butter, such as Merckens' Ivory or Callebaut. Some white chocolates use oils, such as cottonseed and palm oils, for the fat component and these products will lack the nuances that you desire.

This cake is used as a building block for the White Chocolate Satin Apricot Cake with White Chocolate Flowers and Grapes. Feel free to use it as a component for any cake you can imagine. After baking, there may be a thin crispy crust on top of the cakes. Don't worry, it will come off during the leveling process. You may freeze this cake up to one month ahead, but I usually make it two days before the wedding.

FOR TWO 6 × 2-INCH CAKE LAYERS

8 ounces white chocolate, finely chopped

2 cups unsifted cake flour

1 tablespoon baking powder

1/2 teaspoon salt

4 ounces (1 stick) unsalted butter, at room temperature

3/4 cup sugar

1 teaspoon vanilla extract

2 large eggs

2/3 cup whole milk

Preheat the oven to 350°F. Prepare the pans with cooking spray and parchment paper.

Melt the chocolate in the top of a double boiler (*bain-marie*), stirring the chocolate frequently. Remove from the heat before the chocolate is completely melted. Stir until all the chocolate is melted and smooth. Cool to room temperature.

Meanwhile, sift together the flour, baking powder, and salt and set aside.

Place the butter in the bowl of your mixer, and with the flat paddle, cream butter. Add the sugar gradually and continue to beat until light and fluffy, about 1 to 2 minutes. Scrape down the bowl once or twice and beat in the vanilla. Add the eggs, one at a time, beating well after each addition. Scrape in the melted chocolate and beat until the batter is smooth.

Add the dry ingredients alternately with the milk in 3 separate batches. Scrape down the batter after each addition.

Scrape the batter into the pans. Bake about 30 to 40 minutes, or until a toothpick tests clean. The cake has a strong white-chocolate aroma and a mostly golden center and edges. Elsewhere the color will be ivory. Cool, place on cardboards, and wrap with plastic wrap and foil.

FOR TWO 9 × 2-INCH CAKE LAYERS
1 pound white chocolate, finely chopped
4 cups unsifted cake flour
1 tablespoon plus 1 teaspoon baking powder
1 teaspoon salt
8 ounces (2 sticks) unsalted butter, at room temperature
1 1/2 cups sugar
2 teaspoons vanilla extract
4 large eggs
1 1/3 cups whole milk

Prepare the pans with cooking spray and parchment paper. Proceed as above for the 6-inch cake layers. Scrape the batter down often for even mixing. Bake about 40 to 50 minutes. Cool, place on cardboards, and wrap with plastic wrap and foil.

FOR TWO 10 × 2-INCH CAKE LAYERS
20 ounces white chocolate, finely chopped
5 cups unsifted cake flour
1 tablespoon plus 2 teaspoons baking powder
1 1/4 teaspoons salt
10 ounces (2 1/2 sticks) unsalted butter, at room temperature
1 3/4 cups plus 2 tablespoons sugar
2 1/2 teaspoons vanilla extract
5 large eggs
1 2/3 cups whole milk

Prepare the pans with cooking spray and parchment paper. Proceed as above for the 6-inch cake layers. Scrape the batter down often for even mixing. Bake about 40 to 50 minutes. Cool, place on cardboards, and wrap with plastic wrap and foil.

FOR TWO 12 × 2-INCH CAKE LAYERS
Make the 9-inch cake recipe twice, once for each 12-inch pan. Bake about 45 to 55 minutes. Cool, place on cardboards, and wrap with plastic wrap and foil.

FOR TWO 14 × 2-INCH CAKE LAYERS
Make the 10-inch cake recipe twice, once for each 14-inch pan. Bake about 55 to 60 minutes. Cool, place on cardboards, and wrap with plastic wrap and foil.

BUTTERCREAMS, FROSTINGS, CURDS, AND FILLINGS

ITALIAN MERINGUE BUTTERCREAM

Bakers have many basic kinds of buttercream at their disposal. Confectioners' sugar–based buttercream is often used for wedding cakes, but I find it exceedingly sweet and grainy in texture. Its advantage is that it does not need refrigeration, but I do not believe in sacrificing taste for logistical needs. The advantages of Italian Meringue Buttercream are its sublime, silky texture and its not overly sweet taste. It is a very traditional preparation—an Italian meringue, by classic definition, is made up of whipped egg whites that are sweetened and stabilized with a cooked sugar syrup. For a buttercream, sweet, unsalted butter is added as well.

The first buttercream recipe I ever came across said that it had to be used fresh and could not be chilled for later use. Thankfully, I found this to be incorrect. This buttercream can be made ahead and refrigerated for almost one week, and can even be frozen for up to one month. I always make mine days before I need it, to free up the time closer to the wedding day for more ephemeral preparations. To transform this buttercream from a hardened chilled state to a fluffy, usable one does take some attention to technique, but the instructions are all here for you to follow.

You should use a candy thermometer, if possible. If not, the following clues help you judge when the syrup is done. As the syrup cooks at a rapid boil, it will be very liquid to start, with many small bubbles covering the surface. As it heats, the water evaporates and the mixture thickens. The bubbles get larger and thick and sticky. They also form and pop open more slowly. At this point, the syrup definitely looks thickened, but has not yet begun to turn color, which would result in caramel. Just before the caramelization stage—called the firm-ball stage—the syrup will be ready. If you drop some syrup into a glass of cold water, it will harden into a ball. When you squeeze the ball between your fingertips, it will seem firm. Once you make it a few times, you should have no problems assessing its temperature visually.

Temperature is everything with this buttercream. If ingredients are warm or hot when combined, the buttercream will become soupy and greasy. If they are cold, the mixture will be lumpy and too firm. Following the directions carefully should eliminate these problems. If you do end up with a loose buttercream, simply chill it slightly by placing the bottom of the bowl in a larger bowl filled with ice. Chill for a few minutes before proceeding. If the mixture is
too lumpy because cold butter has created pockets of solid fat, just keep whipping. It will smooth out.

This recipe will take advantage of the size of your 5-quart mixer's bowl. You will need to make more than one batch for most of the recipes in the book, and any extra can be frozen for later use. Or, store extras in a well-sealed, airtight container for four days in the refrigerator.

MAKES 7 CUPS

½ cup water

1¼ cups plus ⅓ cup sugar

8 large egg whites, room temperature

1 teaspoon cream of tartar

1½ pounds (6 sticks) unsalted butter, at room temperature

Place the water and 1¼ cups sugar in a saucepan over medium heat. Stir quickly to moisten all the sugar, but do not stir again during boiling because this encourages the formation of sugar crystals. As the mixture becomes hot, use a pastry brush dipped in cold water to brush any sugar crystals down from the sides of the pan. You may also cover the pan briefly at this point. Steam will develop and wash down the sides of the pans automatically. Bring to a boil.

Meanwhile, place the egg whites in a clean, grease-free mixing bowl, and with the balloon whip attachment beat the whites on low until frothy. Add the cream of tartar and turn the speed to medium-high. When soft peaks form, add the remaining ⅓ cup sugar gradually. Continue beating until stiff, but not dry, peaks form.

Raise the heat under the sugar mixture and bring it to a rapid boil. It must cook for about 5 minutes to reach the desired temperature, between 248° and 250°F. Try to have the syrup ready at the same time as the meringue. If the meringue is ready first, reduce the speed so that the whites move continuously, but slowly. If the syrup is done first, add a small quantity of hot water, not cold water, to lower the temperature and continue cooking until the meringue catches up.

When the syrup is ready, turn off the mixer briefly and quickly pour about ½ cup syrup onto the meringue. Immediately turn the mixer to high speed and continue to pour the syrup in a steady stream. Do not let the syrup get onto the beaters. Alternatively, turn off the mixer to add the syrup. Do not let the meringue sit motionless for longer than a few seconds.

Whip the meringue until it cools, about 15 minutes, depending on the room temperature. When the bowl is no longer warm, stop the mixer and touch the surface of the meringue to be sure it is cool. Do not add the butter while the meringue is warm, or the butter will melt and ruin the texture and decrease the volume. Turn the mixer down to medium speed and add the butter, 2 tablespoons at a time. The butter immediately becomes incorporated and the mixture becomes creamy. Continue to whip the buttercream and add the remaining butter. Keep mixing until the mixture is evenly blended and smooth. If at any time the mixture looks lumpy or separated, continue to beat until it smoothes out. Any flavorings may be added at this point. See below for variations.

Store in an airtight container in the refrigerator or freezer.

TO RECONSTITUTE:

Because of the high butter content in this buttercream, it becomes very firm when chilled. Follow the same instructions for reconstituting the buttercream if you have frozen and thawed it overnight in the refrigerator.

You may use one of three different methods, but in all cases, heat it slowly so the butter does not melt. If its storage container is microwaveable, place it in the microwave on very low power and heat it in 15-second spurts, checking for softness each time. It should be uniformly warmed to room temperature, but not melted. To use this technique, you must be familiar with your microwave and know how to control its temperature and defrosting times.

The technique I usually use is to place a quantity of cold buttercream in the stainless steel bowl of my mixer and place it over extremely low heat on top of the stove; use a flame tamer (page 180), if possible. Hold the bowl with one hand and constantly stir the chunks of buttercream, folding the pieces over each other so that no one piece is constantly on the bottom receiving too much heat. You want to warm the buttercream, but not melt the butter out.

Another technique is to place a quantity of buttercream in the mixing bowl and heat it with a warm hair dryer, by blowing hot air across and around the buttercream.

When the buttercream is warm, use a balloon whip to beat it until smooth, creamy, and homogenous. Heat again if it is still lumpy; chill it if it is too soft.

The buttercream is now ready to use.

VARIATIONS:

These options are formulated as small tasting batches. They scale up directly for your wedding cake needs. Remember that a total volume of about 8 cups is all that you should attempt to handle at once in your mixer. Individual yields are noted.

VANILLA BUTTERCREAM

The basic recipe can be used as is for a sweet cream taste, but for a vanilla taste, you must use pure vanilla extract. Its dark brown color will slightly tint the buttercream, adding a subtle warm golden tone. I do not mind this and prefer it to using artificial clear vanilla extract. Alternatively, use the powdered natural vanilla that is a very pale light beige. It will color your buttercream less than the liquid. Use it in equal proportions to the liquid.

MAKES 2 CUPS

Add 1 teaspoon vanilla extract to every 2 cups buttercream. Beat in with balloon whip until well blended.

LIQUEUR-ACCENTED BUTTERCREAM

Here the varieties are virtually endless. Some of the flavors used in the book are peach schnapps, dark rum, Kahlúa, and Amaretto. Try your favorites and even combine flavors such as an orange liqueur with a coffee-flavored one.

Add approximately 2 tablespoons of liqueur to every 2 cups of buttercream. Adjust tastes, as needed. Some of the more potent liqueurs will require less and some more. The texture of the buttercream will guide you; it should not be too liquid. Beat in with balloon whip until well blended.

MAKES 2 CUPS

WHITE OR DARK CHOCOLATE BUTTERCREAM

This version adds a healthy dose of melted and cooled chocolate. With the white chocolate, the buttercream will be decidedly off-white, so make sure that the bride knows this when offering the suggestion. Semisweet or bittersweet chocolate buttercream will be a milk chocolate color. If you want a darker color and more assertive chocolate flavor, refer to the recipe for Bittersweet Chocolate Ganache (page 145).

To 2 cups buttercream, add 4 ounces of melted white, semisweet, or bittersweet chocolate that has cooled to room temperature. If the chocolate is too warm, it will melt the butter. Beat in with balloon whip until well blended.

MAKES 2 1/8 CUPS

MARMALADE BUTTERCREAM

This is a very flavorful, chunky buttercream used as a filling. Its texture is unsuitable for piping or for use as an exterior buttercream.

Combine 1 cup marmalade with 2 cups buttercream. Beat well with flat paddle attachment to incorporate.

MAKES 3 CUPS

ESPRESSO BUTTERCREAM

Coffee-flavored buttercreams are a gorgeous café au lait *color. An unexpected wedding cake frosting, this can be quite sophisticated, especially when paired with a white or dark chocolate accent applied for borders. See Double Espresso Wedding Cake (page 43) and Gâteau Opéra (page 109). The bitterness of the coffee tempers the sweetness of the buttercream, which I like.*

Dissolve 1 tablespoon instant espresso coffee powder in 2 teaspoons boiling water or warmed Kahlúa. Add to 2 cups buttercream, beating well with balloon whip to incorporate. The coffee flavor can be adjusted up or down according to your preference.

MAKES 2 CUPS

COCONUT BUTTERCREAM

This is a flavorful buttercream, a bit sweeter than the basic recipe, but full of coconut essence. I use the Coco Goya brand of cream of coconut, but whatever brand you use, make sure to shake or stir it well first. One-quarter teaspoon of vanilla powder or extract can really accentuate the coconut flavor here, but it is not necessary.

Add 2 tablespoons cream of coconut to every 2 cups buttercream. Beat in with balloon whip until well blended.

MAKES 2 1/8 CUPS

RASPBERRY BUTTERCREAM

This buttercream is an outrageously bright pink color so it is best to keep it safely ensconced between the cake layers. Raspberries frozen without sugar work perfectly. Fresh raspberries are expensive, quite seasonal, and often a bit moldy. Make a purée in the food processor from the defrosted berries. I leave the seeds in, but you may strain them out, if you wish. The buttercream may appear soupy, but with continued beating, it will absorb the purée eventually.

Add 1/3 cup purée to 2 cups buttercream. For best results when making larger amounts, add the purée a little at a time, beating well after each addition. Beat in with balloon whip until well blended.

MAKES 2 1/4 CUPS

LEMON CURD BUTTERCREAM

This is featured in the White Cake with Lemon Curd, Blackberry Curd, and Pressed Flowers (page 37), but I offer it, and the blackberry variation, in the Basics chapter hoping you will use it in other ways as well. I wish lemon curd had a more appealing name, but lemon curd has its devotees and when incorporated with buttercream, the result is a gorgeous, creamy, pale yellow, lemony icing. See below for the Lemon Curd recipe.

Add 1/3 cup lemon curd to 2 cups of buttercream, beating well to incorporate. Use curd made with rind for the most intense flavor, but use curd without rind if you will be using this buttercream for piped decorations. Beat in with balloon whip until well blended.

MAKES 2 1/4 CUPS

BLACKBERRY CURD BUTTERCREAM

I came up with the idea for a blackberry buttercream when I was making a cake for my great aunt's 95th birthday. I wanted a pretty color to complement her demeanor, and I made this gorgeous lilac curd. See below for Blackberry Curd recipe.

Add ⅔ cup blackberry curd to 2 cups buttercream. Beat in with balloon whip until well blended.

MAKES 2½ CUPS

LEMON CURD

Lemon Curd is rich and intense in flavor and tastes like the filling of a lemon meringue pie. You may use the curd as is and spread between cake layers or combined with buttercream as explained in the variation for Lemon Curd Buttercream (page 141).

After filling your cake layers, store extra curd in the refrigerator and use it as a filling for tarts or for spreading on toast. You can double the recipe, or halve it if you want to try a small sampling first. Make this at least one day before you use it; it should chill overnight to firm. Store it for up to one week in an airtight container in the refrigerator.

MAKES 4 CUPS

⅔ cup freshly squeezed lemon juice
6 large eggs
2 large egg yolks
2 cups sugar
8 ounces (2 sticks) unsalted butter, room temperature
Finely grated zest of 3 lemons, yellow part only (optional)

Place all ingredients, except the rind and butter, in a heat-proof bowl, or top of a double boiler (*bain-marie*). Whisk together, just enough to break up the eggs and begin to combine the mixture. Cut the butter into chunks and add. Place the top over and just touching hot water. Cook over medium heat and bring the water to a simmer.

Cook for about 40 to 50 minutes, whisking frequently, or until the mixture reaches 180°F on an instant read thermometer. The mixture becomes thick and forms a soft shape when dropped by spoonfuls on top of the remaining curd. Remove from the heat and stir in the rind, if desired. Let cool to room temperature, scrape into an airtight container, and refrigerate until needed.

BLACKBERRY CURD

This delicious, concentrated fruit curd is a gorgeous lilac color. You may use the curd as is, spread between cake layers or combined with buttercream as explained in the variation for Blackberry Curd Buttercream (this page). Make the curd up to three days ahead and refrigerate in an airtight container.

MAKES 3 CUPS

4 cups blackberries, fresh or frozen, unsweetened
½ cup sugar
3 large eggs
2 large egg yolks
1 tablespoon freshly squeezed lemon juice
4 ounces (1 stick) unsalted butter, at room temperature

If using fresh berries, rinse briefly, if necessary, just before using. For frozen berries, defrost in the refrigerator overnight, and discard or reserve the juice for another use. Place the blackberries in the container of a food processor fitted with the metal blade and process until the purée is smooth and uniform.

Scrape the purée into a heat-proof bowl or top of a double boiler (*bain-marie*). Add the remaining ingredients, except the butter, and whisk together just enough to break up the eggs. Cut the butter into chunks and add. Place the bowl or pot over and just touching hot water. Cook over medium heat and bring the water to a simmer.

Cook, whisking frequently, for approximately 20 to 30 minutes, or until the mixture reaches 180°F with an instant read thermometer. The mixture becomes thick and forms a soft shape when dropped by spoonfuls on top of the remaining curd. Remove from the heat. Cool to room temperature, scrape into an airtight container, and refrigerate until needed.

EGG YOLK BUTTERCREAM

This is similar to the Italian Meringue Buttercream recipe (page 139) with yolks replacing the whites. It is far richer and it doesn't hold up quite as well unrefrigerated. When I don't mind adding another component to my list, I make this for the filling, using up the yolks set aside from the Italian Meringue Buttercream.

The syrup is the proper temperature when the surface is covered with tiny bubbles and several large 1-inch bubbles surface and pop. The mixture will have thickened a bit as well. Storage is the same as for Italian Meringue Buttercream.

MAKES 9 CUPS

2¼ cups sugar

1 cup water

16 large egg yolks

2 pounds (8 sticks) unsalted butter, at room temperature

Place sugar and water in a small saucepan and stir to combine. Cook over medium and bring to a boil. Do not stir again to avoid formation of sugar crystals. If sugar crystals stick to the sides of the pan, wash them down with a pastry brush dipped in water. Or, cover the pan briefly to encourage steam, which will wash away any sugar crystals automatically.

Meanwhile, with a balloon whip, beat the yolks until thick, light, and creamy.

When the sugar syrup reaches 240°F, remove the pan from the heat and pour the syrup in a slow, steady stream over the yolks with the machine on low. Turn the machine on high and continue to pour in the syrup in a steady stream, avoiding the beaters. Alternatively, turn off the mixer to add the syrup.

Beat on high until cool, or about 15 minutes. Touch the bottom of the bowl to test the temperature. When the bowl is cool, stop the machine and test the surface of the buttercream. It should be cool to the touch. Do not add the butter while the mixture is warm, or the butter will melt and ruin the texture. Add the butter several tablespoonfuls at a time. Continue to whip until the buttercream becomes well blended, pale yellow, and fluffy. Scrape into an airtight container, and store in the refrigerator or freezer.

VARIATIONS:

Add any of the flavorings suggested for Italian Meringue Buttercream (page 139) in the same proportions of buttercream to flavoring.

HONEY OR MAPLE SYRUP BUTTERCREAM

This resembles an Italian Meringue Buttercream (page 139), but calls for liquid sweeteners instead of granulated sugar. The lighter the honey or maple syrup, the more delicate the flavor; the darker it is, the stronger the flavor. To measure honey or maple syrup easily, use a large liquid measuring cup (mine is a two-cup Pyrex measurer with a pouring spout) and spray it lightly with cooking spray. The sticky sweetener will slip right out. For simplicity, I refer to the sweetener as honey throughout. For the Honey Lavender Cake (page 97) look for lavender honey, made from bees that feed on lavender flowers, for a faint lavender aroma. (See Resource section, La Cuisine, page 188.) Take care when making this: If you add the butter while the meringue is warm, the butter will melt and ruin the texture. It will also decrease the volume of the final product. You can make this four days before use and store it in an airtight container in the refrigerator, or freeze for one month.

MAKES 8 CUPS

1 cup honey or maple syrup, or a combination

8 large egg whites, at room temperature

2 pounds (8 sticks) unsalted butter, at room temperature

Place the honey in a saucepan and heat it to simmer.

Meanwhile, place the egg whites in a clean, grease-free bowl. Using the balloon whip attachment, whip until soft peaks form using a medium-high speed. Turn the beaters up to high speed and beat until stiff, but not dry, peaks form. At the same time, raise the heat and bring the honey to a rolling boil, about 1 to 2 minutes. When the egg whites are stiff and the honey is boiling, remove the honey from the heat, turn off the mixer briefly, and add some honey. Immediately turn the mixer on and continue to pour the honey in a steady stream, avoiding the beaters. Use a rubber spatula to scrape the honey from the pan.

Beat the mixture on high until cool, or about 15 minutes, depending on the room temperature. Touch the bottom of the bowl to test the temperature. When the bowl is cool, stop the machine and test the surface of the meringue. It should be cool to the touch. Turn the mixer on medium speed and add the butter, 2 tablespoons at a time. The butter immediately becomes incorporated and the mixture turns creamy. Continue to whip the buttercream and add the remaining butter. Keep beating until the mixture is homogenous and smooth. If at any time the mixture looks lumpy or separates, just continue to beat; it will come together. Scrape into an airtight container and store in the refrigerator. Or, freeze for one month.

Note: For instructions on reconstituting cold buttercream, refer to Italian Meringue Buttercream (page 139). The techniques are the same.

WHITE CHOCOLATE CREAM CHEESE FROSTING

This frosting is used for cheesecake as well as for the Pumpkin Cake with Crystallized Ginger, Walnuts, and Dried Cranberries (page 25). The optional citrus oil in the frosting does not discolor it as it does cheesecake batter. When I tried to add the oils, regardless of flavor, to my cheesecake batters, they turned greenish. My guess is that there is a chemical reaction with the eggs in the batter that does it.

For smooth-flowing buttercream, strain the chocolate before piping it because any chunks of chocolate will clog the decorating tip. You can make this up to two days before use; refrigerate, but do not freeze.

MAKES 10 CUPS

30 ounces white chocolate, finely chopped

36 ounces cream cheese, at room temperature

15 ounces (3³/4 sticks) unsalted butter, at room temperature

1 tablespoon vanilla extract

1¹/2 teaspoons lemon or orange oil (optional)

Melt the chocolate in the top of a double boiler (*bain-marie*). Stir frequently until the chocolate is almost completely melted. Remove from the heat and continue to stir until all the chocolate melts.

Meanwhile, place the cream cheese and butter in the bowl of your mixer and with the flat paddle, beat on medium-high speed until smooth, about 2 to 4 minutes. When chocolate is barely warm to the touch, place a strainer over the mixing bowl and press the white chocolate through the strainer, eliminating any solids. Beat chocolate into the cream cheese mixture. Add vanilla and beat until smooth. Add lemon or orange oil, if desired. Scrape the cream cheese into an airtight container and refrigerate.

ROYAL ICING

Many wedding cake designers use royal icing to make flowers, leaves, and other decorations. Since it is made with egg whites and sugar, it is edible but I do not find it particularly palatable and I truly dislike cakes that are so covered with royal icing ornamentation that you cannot even see the cake! However, royal icing does make certain decorations that no other formulation can duplicate. You can find it used in this book in the English-Style Fruitcake with a Twist recipe (page 79) and for the monogram on the Honey Lavender Cake (page 97).

Royal icing is quick to make and I prefer to use it immediately after preparation. It may be made one week ahead if you store it in an airtight container; however, it will become spongy and will need rebeating. For success, your mixing bowl, balloon whip, and storage container must be totally free of any grease or oils. I even reserve a rubber spatula exclusively for this preparation because rubber spatulas are made of a material that tends to hold grease easily.

I always weigh confectioners' sugar because, depending on whether you sift it or not, measuring it by volume can give such varying results.

MAKES 1 ¹/2 CUPS

10 to 12 ounces confectioners' sugar (about 1¹/3 cups), sifted

2 large egg whites

¹/4 teaspoon cream of tartar

Place 10 ounces of sifted confectioners' sugar in your mixer's bowl and add the whites and cream of tartar. With the balloon whip, beat the mixture on medium-high until it is smooth and fluffy; about 3–5 minutes. For a stiffer consistency, add the remaining sugar. Or if it is too stiff, add water drop by drop until it is the right consistency. To prevent a crust forming, cover the bowl with a damp towel after beating.

If a crust or lumps do form and you cannot pipe them through decorating tips, strain the icing by forcing it through a fine mesh sieve with a rubber spatula. Store in a clean, airtight container or use immediately.

BITTERSWEET CHOCOLATE GANACHE

This exceedingly simple recipe is one of my favorites because it is so delicious and so versatile. By combining the two ingredients in the basic recipe, you can make a dark, gorgeous glaze to pour over cakes while warm, or use to pipe decorations when chilled. It belongs in all bakers' repertoires, professional and otherwise, as you will refer to it again and again. The chilled version can even be rolled into balls for truffles. A basic ganache has equal weights of chocolate and cream. This one has a slightly larger proportion of chocolate, which I feel gives a better texture. The recipe can be scaled up or down directly. If the metal blade stops during processing, a large hunk of chocolate is probably caught under the blade. To avoid this, make sure to cut your chocolate into small pieces before starting. Follow the manufacturer's guidelines for determining the capacity of your food processor.

Bittersweet Chocolate Ganache may be frozen for one month. I usually make it four days before I need it, store it in an airtight container, and refrigerate it.

MAKES 2½ CUPS

12 ounces bittersweet or semisweet chocolate
(or use a combination of 1 ounce unsweetened chocolate
and 11 ounces semisweet), finely chopped
1¼ cups (10 ounces) heavy cream

Place the chocolate(s) in the bowl of a food processor fitted with the metal blade. Process the chocolate by pulsing on and off until it is the texture of coarsely ground nuts.

Meanwhile, heat the cream in a heavy-bottomed saucepan until it comes to a simmer. Immediately pour the hot cream down the feed tube while the machine is running. The hot cream will melt the chocolate and the processor will turn these two ingredients into a shiny, homogenous mixture. This will take approximately 10 seconds.

For pourable ganache, use it immediately, or cool slightly. A temperature of 90°F is perfect for glazing.

For piping ganache, cool the mixture, at room temperature, until thick enough to pipe, or stir over a bowl of ice water until thick.

Store ganache in an airtight container in the refrigerator or freezer.

To melt chilled ganache, place it in the microwave at low power, checking and stirring frequently. Or melt it in the top of a double boiler (*bain-marie*) over warm water.

Note: I like my ganache to be bittersweet. As I suggested in the ingredients list, you can improve many semisweet chocolates by adding a small amount of unsweetened chocolate, or you may choose to start with a bittersweet chocolate.

WHIPPED GANACHE

A whipped ganache is a mixture of chocolate and heavy cream, with a larger proportion of cream than pourable ganache. It is really like a very rich chocolate whipped cream and is very simple to make. Whip the chilled mixture of chocolate and cream just before use. The trick here is to not overwhip the ganache, or it will become grainy. It that happens, gently remelt the ganache and chill and rewhip it. Notice that the recipe is twice the amount of cream to chocolate, by weight. You can scale it up or down accordingly.

MAKES 8 CUPS

1 pound semisweet or bittersweet chocolate, finely chopped
4 cups (2 pounds) heavy cream

Place the chocolate in a large bowl. Heat the cream in a medium saucepan to a boil and pour over the chocolate. Stir until the chocolate melts and the mixture is well blended. If any unmelted chocolate remains, set the pan aside for 10 to 15 minutes, stirring occasionally until the chocolate completely melts. Or, use a food processor with a large capacity. See directions for Bittersweet Chocolate Ganache.

Pour ganache into the bowl of your mixer. Cover with plastic wrap, pressing the wrap onto the ganache's surface to prevent a skin from forming. Refrigerate at least 6 hours, or overnight.

With a clean balloon whip, beat the chilled ganache on medium-high speed until the mixture starts to thicken. Watch the ganache closely at this point and whip just until soft peaks form. If you prefer, stop beating as soon as the mixture thickens and finish beating by hand with a large whisk. Do not overbeat.

The ganache is now ready to use. It firms up quickly, so have your cakes and other components prepared and ready.

VANILLA PASTRY CREAM

Pastry Cream is traditionally used in eclairs and napoleons. In this book, you will find it in the Croquembouche (page 101) and the Tahitian Vanilla Bean Pound Cake with Orchids and Fruit (page 69). As it cooks, the mixture will look and feel thicker. When it is done, tiny bubbles will appear around the edges of the pan if you stop whisking for a moment. If you pull your whisk across the pastry cream, you should be able to see the bottom of the pan. This is the time to take it off the heat. Any extra pastry cream can be refrigerated for up to four days and used in tarts or other desserts. Store it in an airtight container or it will pick up flavors from other foods. Vanilla beans of all types can be purchased at most specialty food stores or mail-ordered through La Cuisine (see Resources, page 188). You may make this up to four days ahead.

MAKES 6 CUPS

4 cups whole milk

2 vanilla beans, preferably Tahitian, split lengthwise

14 large egg yolks

1 cup sugar

pinch salt

$^1/_2$ cup cornstarch, sifted

Place the milk and the vanilla beans in a medium, nonreactive saucepan and heat to a scald. Reduce the heat to low.

Meanwhile, in a nonreactive bowl combine the yolks and sugar. Add the salt and sifted cornstarch and whisk until smooth.

Remove the vanilla beans from the milk and with a blunt knife or spoon tip scrape the seeds into the milk. Whisk to break up the sticky clumps of vanilla beans. Pour about ¼ of the warm liquid over the egg yolk mixture, whisking constantly. This will temper the eggs. Then, add the remaining liquid and stir to combine. Immediately pour mixture back into the pot and cook over a low-medium heat. Whisk continuously, continuing to cook, but do not let it boil.

Pour the pastry cream, including the vanilla seeds, through a strainer into a clean, nonreactive bowl to remove any uncooked egg. If seeds don't go through, simply stir them in.

Press plastic wrap directly onto the surface of the pastry cream to prevent a skin from forming. Refrigerate at least 3 hours or until thoroughly chilled. Store in an airtight container in the refrigerator.

VARIATION:

For a variation using liqueur, such as Grand Marnier, omit the vanilla beans and add 2 to 4 tablespoons of the selected liqueur, which you whisk in when the pastry cream has chilled slightly. The amount you use depends on the taste and the consistency you want for the final pastry cream.

NECESSARY ADDITIONS

SUGAR SYRUP

Cookbooks often refer to this as "simple syrup," a combination of sugar and water used to moisten cakes—I suggest this throughout the book—and to sweeten sorbets and buttercreams. You can also use this as a medium for liqueurs for flavor enhancement. Depending on its application, you need to vary the ratio between the sugar and the water. For our purposes, I find a medium-weight syrup is best, which you make with two parts water and one part sugar.

I came across one variation of the syrup in an unusual way. On my last visit to Paris, I had wandered into Hediard, the large and upscale specialty-food store on the Place de la Madeleine. *In its liquor section, I noticed a bottle of clear liquid with a vanilla bean suspended in it. It was labeled* Syrop de Sucre de Canne *and consisted of a sugar syrup (65 percent sugar) and a vanilla bean. The sales clerk told me it was for sweetening tropical drinks, such as Planter's Punch, but of course I immediately saw its other applications! As soon as I returned home, I made up a sugar syrup, poured it into a beautiful glass bottle, and added a plump vanilla bean. I store it in the refrigerator and use it whenever I want the extra boost from the vanilla essence.*

The recipe may be scaled up directly. You may make it a month ahead and store it in an airtight container in the refrigerator.

MAKES 1 ¼ CUPS

1 cup water
½ cup sugar

Combine both ingredients in a small saucepan, stirring to moisten the sugar thoroughly. Heat over medium-high heat and bring to a simmer. Boil for 30 seconds. Remove from the heat, cool to room temperature. Chill and store it in an airtight container in the refrigerator until needed.

VARIATIONS:

LIQUEUR-FLAVORED SYRUP

The amount of liqueur you add depends on the strength of the alcohol and the taste you want. When the syrup has cooled to room temperature, start by adding ¼ cup liqueur to the basic mixture (1¼ cups syrup). Stir to combine well. Store as suggested above.

VANILLA SYRUP

Simply add a vanilla bean slit lengthwise to the warm syrup and store it in an airtight container in the refrigerator. I add one bean to at least 4 or 5 cups of syrup; the vanilla flavor goes a long way. Steep the vanilla bean in the syrup for at least one week before using.

NUTS: PEELING AND TOASTING

Nuts add flavor and texture to cakes. For best results, buy them fresh because they contain perishable oils that turn rancid. The best way to test for rancidity is by taste. Nuts should have a distinct flavor, unique to the particular nut, without any musty aftertaste. The aroma can offer clues as well. They should not smell moldy. Buy only the quantity of nuts that you need, from a reputable vendor who has a high turnover. After you toast or peel the nuts, if you have any extras left over, store them in an airtight container in the freezer. If you toast them before freezing, you will want to refresh them briefly in the oven before use.

TO PEEL

I suggest and assume that you buy your nuts already shelled. (Let's not carry the term "from scratch" too far!)

Sometimes hazelnuts come already peeled, but otherwise you must peel off their papery skin. To do this, spread the nuts out in a single layer on a rimmed baking sheet and roast them in a 350°F oven for 5 to 10 minutes, shaking the pan once or twice for even browning. The nuts are done when they become fragrant and turn golden brown. Remove them from the oven and cool. Using clean kitchen towels, rub the nuts vigorously. With a little effort, the skins will come off. My hazelnuts usually retain a tiny bit of skin and that's fine. You have both toasted and peeled hazelnuts in one fell swoop.

Almonds are sold whole, sliced, and slivered, either blanched (peeled) or natural (unpeeled). You cannot peel sliced or slivered nuts, so buy these almonds the way you need them. If you care to spend the extra money on whole blanched nuts, go ahead. It will save you time. If you need to peel whole ones yourself, drop them in boiling water and blanch them for 1 minute and drain. You should be able to slip the skins right off with your fingers. Walnuts and pecans do not need any peeling. Macadamias usually come ready to use. If your macadamias are salted, rinse before toasting.

TO TOAST

Your hazelnuts will probably be toasted enough during the peeling process. Place walnuts, pecans, almonds, or macadamias in a single layer in a large roasting pan. Toast them for 5 to 10 minutes in a 350°F oven or until golden brown and fragrant. Shake the pan once or twice during toasting for even browning.

MARZIPAN

Marzipan has its roots in the ancient Middle East and in Italy, possibly predating the 1300s. A sweetened almond paste mixture with a decidedly almond flavor, marzipan can greatly accent sweets with its moist, chewy texture. You can make marzipan from scratch, grinding the almonds and adding the remaining ingredients. I prefer to start with prepared almond paste, because I like the extra-smooth results better. It is also easier for the home cook to do. You can buy almond paste from cake-decorating stores, specialty food stores, and even your supermarket. Because some marzipan contains raw egg white, for health reasons, I offer a version moistened with corn syrup. You must let the marzipan rest for several hours to allow time for the oils to become evenly distributed. This makes the marzipan easier to work with.

Marzipan is sometimes used beneath a final coating of ganache or icing, but sometimes it is used as the final coating of a cake itself. Any extra marzipan can be rolled into balls, dipped in melted semisweet chocolate, and rolled in cocoa for a delicious candy. Marzipan will keep in the refrigerator for months if stored in an airtight container, but I prefer to use it within the month.

See individual recipes for the amounts needed for particular cakes.

MAKES APPROXIMATELY 2 POUNDS

1 pound almond paste
1 pound unsifted confectioners' sugar
¹/₃ cup light corn syrup

Place the almond paste, broken up by hand into large pieces, and the confectioners' sugar into the container of a food processor fitted with the metal blade. Pulse on and off until mixture resembles coarse sand and the almond paste and sugar are evenly distributed.

Pour light corn syrup through feed tube, with machine running, and process for approximately 10 seconds. The marzipan will look like wet, coarse sand. Stop the machine, open the top, and grab a handful. When you press your hands together, the marzipan should compress and yield a smooth ball. If it does not, process a bit longer.

Dump the marzipan out onto a clean work surface and knead it until it comes together. Dust surface with confectioners' sugar, if necessary, to prevent sticking. I often knead two or three portions together instead of trying to knead the entire batch. Keep kneading until you have a smooth ball.

Wrap marzipan in plastic wrap, then place in a resealable plastic bag. Let sit at room temperature at least 2 hours before using to allow oils to distribute evenly. Then store in refrigerator until needed. Knead again before using to ensure smoothness.

CHOCOLATE PLASTIC

Chocolate plastic, or modeling chocolate, is a combination of melted chocolate and light corn syrup. But the sum is greater than its parts because these two ingredients make a wonderful, malleable chocolate clay that can be rolled out and molded into a variety of shapes. I first saw a recipe for chocolate plastic in Cook's *magazine in the mid-'80s in an article featuring Albert Kumin, the revered former White House pastry chef. He had created a wedding cake covered with broad chocolate ribbons and curls, all made out of this wonderful substance. It piqued my interest immediately and I have enjoyed using this material ever since. I have come across many different proportion suggestions, and some work better than others. This recipe is the one I use and it gives reliable results.*

You may make the plastic out of semisweet, milk, or white chocolate. Or, you can make all three and marbleize them together, or roll them out side by side to make broad stripes. Your imagination is the limit. When you combine the corn syrup with the chocolate, the chocolate may look grainy and about to seize. Keep stirring, but don't worry if it doesn't look completely smooth. When you pour it out, the chocolate will resemble a large, thick puddle.

The white chocolate plastic can be tinted with paste colors and/or brushed with powdered colors (see page 169). Use the paste colors judiciously as they are quite potent; a toothpick can be used to add color a tiny bit at a time. The powders are applied after whatever you are molding is done. Powders can also be used on top of paste dyed plastic for a custom look.

Chocolate plastic may be made one week ahead if wrapped tightly with several layers of plastic wrap and then placed in an airtight container. Just make sure it does not dry out. It will harden as it sits regardless and will require kneading before use.

This recipe works with real chocolate or chocolate coating. Real chocolate, with cocoa butter, will be a little harder to work with than coatings made with vegetable oils. For making leaves, either is fine, but when making roses and other shapes that require a lot of manipulation, the chocolate coating is easier to work with and doesn't get as greasy as with the real chocolate. The cocoa butter in real chocolate has a low melting point, so the warmth of your hands tends to melt it out quickly.

Chocolate plastic shapes can be made weeks ahead if you store them in an airtight container. Stored leaves that are then draped over cakes have a tendency to crack. If they are very fresh, this problem is minimized. If they have been made way ahead, just make sure to bring them to a warm room temperature before manipulating. The recipe can be doubled or halved.

MAKES 2¼ POUNDS

28 ounces semisweet, milk or white chocolate
or chocolate coating, finely chopped

1 cup light corn syrup

Melt the chocolate in the top of a double boiler (*bain-marie*) over but not touching hot water or in the microwave. Stir the corn syrup into the melted chocolate until the mixture becomes homogenous. Scrape this out onto a large piece of plastic wrap and wrap it up well.

Set aside for at least 1 hour to cool at room temperature, or until it is completely firm. Divide the chocolate with a bench scraper into several manageable pieces. Knead each piece before use with warm hands to soften. It is now ready to roll out and be made into flowers, leaves, grapes, or other shapes.

CARAMELIZED NUTS

Nuts add flavor, texture, and color to baked goods. They also can accent the other flavors in the recipe or be a major component of the recipe. Caramelized nuts add sweetness as well as a shiny luster that decorates the exterior of certain cakes perfectly. Look at the Chocolate Almond Torte with Sugared Nuts (page 21) as an example of sliced, sugared nuts and the Caramel Rum Cake with Caramelized Walnuts as an example of using whole caramelized nuts.

I caramelize sliced natural or blanched almonds, whole pecans and walnuts, and whole, peeled hazelnuts most often. But feel free to experiment with other nuts and shapes as well. The techniques of coating the sliced and whole nuts are different, so I have given directions for both.

Sugaring the sliced nuts is a breeze. On the other hand, coating the whole nuts is a tedious procedure, but not difficult; just set aside enough time.

I usually make these a day or two before I need them, but they may be stored in an airtight container for up to two weeks. A Blue Magic insert (see Equipment chapter, page 178) is put to good use here.

SLICED SUGARED NUTS
MAKES 4 CUPS SLICED NUTS

1¾ cups sugar

⅔ cup warm water

4 cups untoasted, sliced almonds, or other nuts
raw or blanched

Preheat the oven to 350°F. Line a baking sheet with parchment paper and lightly spray it with cooking spray.

Combine the sugar and water in a bowl and stir until the sugar dissolves. Add the almonds and toss to coat evenly. Spread the almonds out in a single layer on the baking sheet.

Bake for about 20 minutes. Check once during baking to make sure the nuts are browning evenly; stir several times for even browning, if necessary. Let the nuts cool in the pan. Store in an airtight container with a Blue Magic insert.

WHOLE CARAMELIZED NUTS

You need to skewer whole nuts before dipping them into hot caramel, and if you gently insert the tip of the toothpick into the nut just enough to stick, you will greatly lessen the chances of cracking the nut. Dry the nuts and let the caramel harden by sticking them onto a piece of foil-covered Styrofoam. Make sure your saucepan is large enough to hold the ingredients and tall enough for the depth you need for dipping the nuts. Note that the color of your pan will affect your ability to assess doneness. You want the caramel to be golden brown, but if your pan is dark, you may not be able to tell. Take care not to let any hot caramel drip on your fingers because it will result in a bad burn. Make sure you have a bowl of ice water ready that is large enough to hold the saucepan. The ice will keep the caramel from overcooking.

MAKES 24 CARAMELIZED NUTS

24 nuts

toothpicks

1/2 cup sugar

1/4 cup water

1/4 teaspoon lemon juice

Skewer each individual nut with a toothpick and set aside.

Place the sugar, water, and lemon juice in a 1½-quart saucepan. Stir to moisten the sugar. Heat to a simmer, without stirring, washing down the sides of the pan once or twice with a wet pastry brush. You may cover the pan briefly at this point. Steam will develop and wash down the sides of the pan. Continue to cook until the caramel begins to color, about 10 minutes; it will darken quickly, so be prepared to work efficiently. To test the color, drip some caramel onto a white plate. Depending on the darkness you prefer, the temperature should measure between 330° and 360°F with an instant-read thermometer. When done, remove the caramel from the heat and immediately plunge the saucepan into the ice water.

Immediately, dip the nuts one at a time into the dipping caramel, letting the excess drip back into the pan. Stick the free end of the toothpick in the styrofoam; do not let the nuts touch. Repeat with the remaining nuts. If the dipping caramel begins to firm, place it over a low heat to soften.

Let all the nuts harden. Snip off any strands of caramel with kitchen shears. Store the nuts in an airtight container with a Blue Magic insert (see Equipment chapter, page 178).

· 6 ·

FINISHING TOUCHES

Cardboard Rounds

I mention cardboard rounds for placing under baked cake layers first in this chapter because most of the following techniques depend on their use. Buy precut cardboard rounds instead of trying to cut your own to size. The edges of homemade rounds will not be as straight nor as smooth as the manufactured ones, and this affects how your finished cake looks, because the board's edges act as your guide when you are applying the buttercream. See the Equipment chapter, page 178, and the information on Covering a Cake with Buttercream, page 154, for further details.

Cardboard rounds should be the same size as each individual layer. Occasionally, you will bake a 6-inch-round cake intending to place it on a 6-inch cardboard round. But after baking, you notice that the cake has shrunk and is really more like 5¾ inches round. In these cases, I still use the 6-inch rounds and use them as a guide to build up the buttercream on the sides.

With your cakes on cardboard rounds, you can pick up each layer or tier to transfer it from your turntable to the work space or into the refrigerator without cracking the cake.

Masonite Boards and Cake Drums

Unless you have a very large, strong, flat decorative platter, you will want to use Masonite boards or cake drums to support the bottom layer of your cakes. These are available wherever cake-decorating products are sold. To cover them with foils, papers, or fabrics, cut a piece of the material large enough to cover the top of the board with a wide enough border to fold under the board. I usually leave about 3 inches for folding. No one will ever see the bottom of the board; simply tape down whichever covering you select with a strong tape, such as duct or masking tape. Make sure the top is smooth; that's the only necessity. ·

In the Equipment chapter, page 181, I mention the use of cake drums as well. These are ½-inch thick and come already covered with gold or silver foil. Use these if desired, especially for extra-heavy cakes like cheesecakes, fruitcakes, and truffle cakes.

I don't coat my boards with icing very often, but they may be covered with a flood of thinned Royal Icing (see English-Style Fruitcake with a Twist, page 79). Simply thin a batch of Royal Icing with water to a pourable consistency. Pour it over the center of the board and let it flow out to the edges—like glazing a cake with ganache. When the icing is completely dry, at least overnight, you can cover the edges with a ribbon or other material to conceal the seam between the icing and the board. You can do this easily by cutting a ribbon to fit the circumference and "gluing" the ends together with a dab of royal icing. A pin can hold the ribbon in place until the icing dries, or you can use a glue gun.

Remember that these bases will be the widest measurement of your cake. Make sure that they fit in your refrigerator, with some room for sliding in and out.

To affix the bottom cake tiers on their cardboards to a covered board, spread some softened buttercream on the center of the covered board. Center the bottom tier on the buttercream "glue" and chill to firm the buttercream so the cake will stick.

Leveling

One important process in readying your cake for decoration is leveling. After your cakes have baked and cooled, you will notice that some layers are taller than others; some are almost level; some are peaked in the center; and some may be a tad lopsided (it happens to the best of us). You must decide how tall they should be. If two of the tiers measure 3½ inches each, but the third tier measures only 3 inches, then each must be 3 inches tall or the finished tiers will not be even or symmetrical. Of course, if you want your tiers to vary to achieve a certain visual impact, then proceed accordingly. But in general, the tiers should be uniformly level horizontally and the same height.

I must tell you a funny anecdote here. Although I am very good at eyeballing volumes of ingredients,

I am terrible at leveling the tops of cakes. Or so I thought. For years I went to work on my wedding cakes on my wooden butcher-block baking table and often had problems with uneven layers or tiers. Well, I finally took a carpenter's level and placed it on my table only to find that I had been working on an unlevel surface the whole time! What can I say? Make sure your table is level, from one side to the other and from front to back. Check your oven, too.

To level a cake layer, place it on your turntable and kneel down so you can see the top of the cake at eye level. The bottom of the cake should be sitting on a cardboard round. To slice off any area on the surface that is protruding, use a gentle sawing motion. This will not damage the cake. In most cases, a long slicing knife or serrated bread knife—ideally, one that is longer than the diameter of the cake—is the tool of choice. Invest in a knife that measures at least 14 inches long, though that may not be large enough for very large tiers. Check that the surface is level—I actually have a very small, light level that I place on top of my trimmed cake for a final judgment of evenness. When you are sure the surface is level, place another cardboard on top of the cake, flip it over, and remove the cardboard from the new top, which is the former cake bottom. This gives you a perfectly flat surface for the top of your cake. You may also use this technique for 3-inch-deep tiers that you may be torting (see below). Save the cake scraps for snacks or for a dessert trifle.

Torting

Torting is the process of taking a solid layer of cake and splitting it into several even layers before spreading them with fillings and reassembling them. The reason for torting is that you can easily split the cake into two, three, four, or even more layers. Also, because the cake started out as a solid tier, it will have nice straight sides when reassembled (see Sachertorte, page 117, for example).

To torte, place the single cake tier on a cardboard round and set this on your turntable. Take a small,

sharp knife and cut a vertical line, big enough to be visible, from top to bottom. I usually make one the width of a toothpick. This line will help you realign the layers later. Decide how many layers you want to make. I keep a ruler in the kitchen for techniques like this, right next to my calculator. Divide the height of the cake by the number of layers that you would like. If you have a 2-inch cake layer and would like to slice this into four layers, then each layer will measure ½ inch thick. Make sure that you place the ruler on top of the cardboard round so that you are measuring from the bottom of the cake. The cardboard round can add up to ¼ inch and will throw off your measurements. Mark off your layers in ½-inch increments up the side of the cake, all around its circumference. Do this by making small horizontal cuts. To make the final horizontal cuts level, place a few toothpicks into the cake at the increments you have marked off (see picture). These will help you guide the knife evenly through the cake.

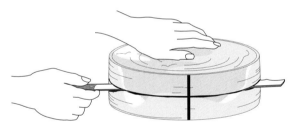

Cut vertical line into cake. This cake is being torted into two halves.

Three cuts will make four layers. If the cake is to have three layers (two cuts), then slice through the top layer first. Lift it off gently without cracking and breaking the layer, by sliding a cardboard round beneath it. Move the layer away and set it aside. You may also use the removable inserts from metal tart pans. These are very thin and have a sharper edge than the cardboard rounds. Some of the cakes, such as the pound cake, will be sturdy enough for you to lift with your hands without causing any damage. Proceed until you have completed the three layers.

This is where that initial vertical cut comes in. You will have the bottom layer on the turntable in front of you. Spread whichever filling you have chosen on it. Take the next layer, find the small incision on its side, and line it up with the cut on the bottom layer. Repeat the process with any remaining filling and cake layers. This way the filled layers rest on top of one another in their original position. This will create the most even shape.

Adding Sugar Syrup to a Cake

Whether a sugar syrup is liqueur-flavored or not, it accomplishes the same objective—it adds moisture to the cake. There are many ways to apply syrup to a cake layer, but you always want to have an even application. Many recipes will suggest using a pastry brush. Dip it in the syrup, brush off the excess, and then literally brush this over the top of the cake. But this technique can bring up a lot of crumbs and make a mess. Another brush technique is to dip the brush into the syrup and dab the brush repeatedly on top of the cake. This works a little better. You can also dip the brush in the syrup and drizzle the syrup onto the cake. Regardless of the technique, you can see where you have applied the syrup because the syrup makes the surface of the cake a bit darker.

One of my favorite techniques doesn't call for a brush at all. I use a squeeze bottle with a long, thin, cone-shaped top. These are sold in drugstores for hair-color application or in cake- and candy-decorating supply stores where they are sold for squeezing chocolate and coatings into small molds. I fill the bottles with syrup and cut a very small opening in the tip. If the tip opening is too large, you will have no control over the flow, but you can enlarge the hole, if needed. Squeeze the syrup very gently onto the cake, keeping a careful eye on the surface of the cake to see where you need to apply syrup for an even application. You can also shake the bottle up and down to sprinkle the syrup over the cake. Many cooks find this less labor-intensive than using a brush, and you can store the bottle in the refrigerator.

Filling Techniques

In general, buttercreams used as fillings are firm enough to stay where you put them. And, in general, the cakes tested were made with from ¼- to ½-inch filling on each layer. The amount you use will depend on your penchant for fillings and on the particular recipes used. Some of the fillings, such as the fruit curds, are softer and may need encouragement to stay between the cake layers and not seep out onto the sides of the cake. To do this, take some of the buttercream for the outside coating and place it in a pastry bag with a plain round tip—a ½-inch opening works well. Pipe a border of buttercream all around the top surface perimeter of each bottom layer, regardless of the layer's shape. The buttercream forms a barrier that keeps in the filling. Then, using a small offset spatula, spread the filling inside the border. Place the next cake layer on top and proceed as directed in the individual recipe.

Covering a Cake with Buttercream

Most of the cakes in this book call for a coating of buttercream. Making a buttercream-covered cake for a two-year-old's birthday party may be done fairly quickly and swiftly. But large celebration cakes such as these demand a bit more attention, time, and care. And a turntable. I suggest that you use a turntable for all of the cakes in this book. Your ability to smoothly turn your tiers around greatly facilitates the decorating process.

The best thing to do is to think of a three-tiered wedding cake as three small, separate cakes. In other words, take it one step at a time, and proceed slowly and carefully. Start with the largest tier, and while you are working on it, put all your focus there. When it is done, proceed to the next smaller tier, until you have finished the cake. As far as the order of tiers is concerned, I usually start with the largest tier, because psychologically, I like getting the largest tier over with first because it is often the most difficult to work with. Also, the larger tiers take longer to chill between steps, so by starting with the largest, you'll be proceeding in a logistically suitable way as well.

To get a smooth, professional look, there are a few tips to follow. First, make sure your buttercream is at the right temperature. If it is too cold, it will be stiff and have a lumpy texture. If it is too warm, it will not stay where you spread it. The buttercream should be light, fluffy, and absolutely smooth. Also, make sure that you have enough buttercream to make both the crumb coat—that is, the first layer of buttercream you apply—and the final coat or coats. If you have a colored buttercream, such as a coffee hue, two separate batches will most likely look different, so make enough in the beginning to eliminate this problem. I have suggested generous quantities in the individual recipes.

Remember that if you are covering a dark chocolate cake with a light buttercream frosting, it does need a more thorough, accurate technique. The dark cake may show through the light-colored buttercreams, resulting in an unattractive appearance. You just need to be quite thorough in your buttercream application. You might need to do a crumb coat first and then two top coats. Make extra buttercream accordingly. Also, it is easier to cover a cake top than its sides. Consider covering the top of the dark cake with a few coats of a light-colored buttercream and covering the sides with shaved chocolate, nuts, crushed nougatine, or dacquoise to help cover up any shortcomings in your frosting-application abilities.

The crumb coat consists of a very thin veneer of buttercream that seals in any crumbs that remain on the cake's surface. To do this, set your cake tier (filled, if required) in front of you on your turntable. Place a generous amount of buttercream on top of the cake and smooth it over the top of the tier, spreading out the excess towards the sides. Don't worry if the buttercream catches up some crumbs. They will not mar the texture or appearance of the final coating. Spread the buttercream over onto the sides of the cake. Now

hold the spatula vertically with the tip of the spatula facing straight down, resting against the outside of the cardboard for guidance. The flat part of the spatula should rest almost flat against the cake; just angle it out slightly. Rotate the turntable and smooth the buttercream along the sides. Some chefs find using a straight-edge spatula is easier to work with, but others prefer an offset spatula. I use my trusty straight 8-inch spatula for almost everything, but switch to a larger 14-inch offset spatula when working with the tops of the largest tiers. Use whichever is better for you to create a smooth, even crumb coat. You will see much of the cake through this thin layer and this is fine. Even the top and square the edges of the tier, and chill it thoroughly, for about two to four hours. To test for firmness, touch the buttercream lightly; your finger should come away from the surface clean.

Smooth buttercream on top of cake, then spread it onto sides as you rotate turntable.

When the crumb coat is firm, you are ready to proceed with the final coat. Set the tier on the turntable and have your final-coat buttercream ready—soft, whipped, and in sufficient quantity. Place a generous amount on top of the tier. Using the spatula, spread a somewhat thick layer over the top. Manipulate your spatula so that it glides over the coat of new buttercream, pushing it out from the center. Do not let your spatula touch the crumb coat. This prevents the spatula from scraping the cake's surface and catching up any crumbs. The final coat goes on more smoothly than the first coat because the crumb coat provides an easier surface to work on. Follow the above suggestions for using your spatula and smoothing the sides with the perfect shape of the cardboard guiding your spatula. Feel your way along the edge of the cardboard, bridging your spatula vertically between it and the upper edge of the cake. By keeping the spatula perfectly vertical, and rotating the turntable simultaneously, you will be able to create smooth sides. No matter how much decorating you are planning to do, a smooth, final buttercream coating will present the best canvas.

Follow some professional tips to achieve a super-smooth look: Run your spatula under the hottest tap water. Wipe it dry and then use the warmed tool to smooth the final coat of buttercream. The warmth of the spatula will slightly melt the uppermost layer of buttercream, creating an ultra-smooth texture. I use this technique for practically every cake I make. Some pastry chefs use a clean spray bottle to apply a fine mist of warm water to the cake's surface and smooth out any imperfections with a spatula. Some bakers and food stylists use large palette knives instead of icing spatulas. You can buy them in hardware stores; they are used for applying spackle. Bench scrapers can also be used. They all feel a little different; see which is easier for you and which gives you the best results.

To cover the sides, parts of the sides, or entire cakes with dacquoise, cake crumbs, chopped nuts, coconut, or anything similar, use the instructions that follow. I use nuts as the example.

Fill, crumb coat, and spread the final coat of buttercream (ganache or other coating) on the tiers. While the buttercream is still soft—that is, before you have refrigerated the cakes—apply the nuts. Hold one tier on its cardboard round in your left hand—reverse hands for lefties. Scoop up the nuts with your right hand and press them to the sides of the cake. Rotate the cake in your left palm by rotating your wrist as you go along. The nuts that do not stick will fall back down on your work surface. It is best to do this over a piece of

Applying nuts.

parchment so that you can keep scooping up the nuts easily as you need them. If you are covering a ganache-coated cake with nuts, some of the nuts that fall may be so covered with wet ganache that they are not attractive anymore. Keep using fresh nuts to coat the cake, if needed, and reserve the chocolatey nuts for folding into melted chocolate to make chocolate bark or just to eat. Repeat procedure until the entire surface to be covered is done.

A combing tool (decorator's comb) (see Equipment, page 178) can be used to make straight lines or a wavy pattern on the sides of your cake by dragging the comb along the sides of the cake over the buttercream. The comb will remove excess buttercream as it leaves its pattern. You can keep adding more buttercream and re-doing the pattern until it looks right. (See Hazelnut Dacquoise and Hazelnut Génoise Wedding Cake, page 91, and White Chocolate Lemon Buttermilk Cake with Sugar Sea Shells, page 105.)

Glazing with Ganache

You may never have seen a wedding cake covered with satiny, shiny chocolate glaze before, but why not? For the chocolate lover, nothing could be better. Sometimes a ganache formula will include corn syrup for shine, butter for richness, or a liqueur for flavor. But a cream-based ganache is a ganache at

Using a combing tool (decorator's comb).

its simplest, nothing more than a combination of chocolate and heavy cream. The chocolate provides most of the body, taste, and color, and the cream tempers that texture so that the ganache can be poured, spread, and piped.

Ganache has a wonderfully smooth texture, but it does not hide imperfections as well as buttercream does. Therefore, you must make sure that your cake surface is smooth and free of crumbs. If the cake is covered with a buttercream crumb coat first, your problem is solved; if it is not, use a soft brush to flick off any loose cake crumbs before applying the glaze.

Set your cake tier (filled if required) on a cardboard round on a large cooling rack that is set over a clean pan, or a large piece of aluminum foil or parchment paper. The ganache should be warm. If it is too hot, it will be loose and runny. If it is too cold, it will be stiff. Your trusty instant read thermometer will come in handy here. A temperature of 90° to 100°F usually works well. Your sense of feel is important and it is easy to manipulate the ganache's temperature quickly by stirring it over a bowl of hot or ice water.

Pour a quantity of ganache on top of the cake and aim for the center—it will spread out towards the sides by itself. Keep pouring so that a generous amount reaches the outer edge and begins to flow down the sides. Stop pouring at this point and use a spatula to gently cover any gaps on the sides of the cake. The top will already be covered and will

need little or no touch up. One key to a smooth, mirror-like finish is to touch the ganache as little as possible. Any swipe of the spatula is likely to leave a mark, so use restraint. If you need to touch up the ganache, pick up the cake and tilt it from side to side to encourage the ganache to cover the entire top surface. If any large gaps remain on the sides, pour more ganache right at the top edge above the bare spot so the ganache can drip down to cover it. If you are going to cover the sides later, as in the Chocolate Almond Torte with Sugared Nuts (see page 21), you can be a little less careful touching up the sides.

Covering a Cake with Marzipan

For a smooth coating of marzipan, ready your cake tier by setting it on a cardboard round and slightly beveling the top edge of the cake. This allows the marzipan to drape smoothly and helps keep it from tearing. To do this, take a sharp paring knife, holding it at a 45° angle, and trim off a ¼-inch thick strip. Then, spread a crumb coat over the cake. This gives a slightly tacky surface for the marzipan to adhere to. Note that the cakes in this book covered with marzipan are fairly firm cakes, such as a fruitcake. Do not attempt to drape a light, spongy génoise with marzipan. The cake will buckle beneath its weight and the cake's heavenly texture will be compressed.

Next, prepare a clean, smooth surface large enough to roll out the entire piece of marzipan and dust it liberally with confectioner's sugar. Use a dusting bag (see Equipment chapter, page 179) or dredger as you go along. Have a well-kneaded piece of marzipan ready to go. For a 14-inch-by-4-inch-round-tier, for example, you will need to roll out a piece that is a least 24 inches in diameter. This will allow enough to trim and give you enough extra so that you will not have to stretch it too much. Or, in certain instances where the seams will be hidden, you may roll out a circle the same diameter as the top of the cake first and then a strip or two to go around the side.

For one large piece, roll it out with a rolling pin to the required size, making sure that the piece is no thinner than ¼ inch thick. My first few attempts to use marzipan as a covering resulted in a poor finished product because I mistakenly thought a thinner layer would be better. But a layer that is too thin permits tears to form and shows up any imperfections on the cake. Have your ruler handy for measuring. Make sure that the piece of marzipan does not adhere to the work surface. Stop a few times during the rolling process to move the marzipan around, sprinkling a little extra confectioners' sugar beneath it, if necessary. This is just like rolling out pie crust dough. As with pie crust, roll from the center out to the edges.

When you are ready to pick it up and drape it over the cake, set your cake right next to you on a turntable—the shorter the distance you have to move the marzipan, the better. To move larger sizes, use the rolling pin and roll up half of the marzipan so that when you lift the rolling pin, the marzipan will be draped over it. The wider the rolling pin, the better its support. For smaller tiers, it is easy enough to lift the marzipan by hand— drape it over your hands, palms up, and use your forearms for added support, if necessary. Then center it and drape it over the cake as follows.

To smooth the marzipan on the cake, center it over the top of the cake so that the far edge of the marzipan is slightly overlapping the base of the cake. Then drawing your hands towards you, ease the marzipan over the top, always taking care not to pull, which would encourage tearing. Remove your right hand from underneath the marzipan and use it to smooth the marzipan down over the cake top as you continue to ease it down the near side with the left hand. Continue moving your left hand under and finally out. Reverse these instructions for lefties.

The sides will drape down with some overlap. Smooth the marzipan so that it lies flat against the cake sides. You want to eliminate any folds and you can do this by gently pulling the last inch or two out and away from the base of the cake while

Drape marzipan over cake.   Smooth marzipan with hands.

smoothing it down with the other hand at the same time. You may have to repeat this procedure several times with the larger sizes. The constant smoothing of the marzipan prevents the trapping of any air bubbles beneath it. But if an air bubble is trapped, simply prick it with a pin held at an angle and then, again pressing with the hands, gently expel the air, smoothing the marzipan flat. After smoothing, you can trim the bottom with a sharp pairing knife or a pizza cutter, using the cardboard round as a guide. You will not be able to see the cardboard, but you will be able to feel it with your knife tip. Some scraps will have a bit of buttercream or jam adhering to them and these cannot be used again but you may reuse very clean scraps.

An easier way to cover a cake with marzipan is to make a top disc and side strips separately. Measure the diameter of your cake top and roll out a piece of marzipan slightly larger than the measurement. Use the cake pan as a guide and cut a perfect circle to fit. You can easily pick this up and place it on top of the cake. Then, measure the height of the sides of the cake which will now include the ¼ inch added by cardboard and ¼ inch for the piece of marzipan on top. Also measure around the circumference of the cake to determine the length you need for the sides. You will be quite surprised how large a number this is. For instance, to go around a 10-inch cake, you will need 32 inches worth of side strips! Roll out a long piece of marzipan and cut pieces to fit. Try to cut the side strips in one or two pieces. The length will equal the circumference, the width will equal the height of the cake plus cardboard plus top marzipan disc.

Pick up the strips and stick them to the sides of the cake, gently pressing them against the cake and the marzipan top so that all components adhere to one another.

You can also roll marzipan out with a textured rolling pin to achieve a different look, as I did with the Marzipan Chocolate Cake with Apricot Filling and Cognac on page 83. You can buy these from cake-decorating supply stores such as Sweet Celebrations (see Resources, page 189).

Stacking Cake Tiers

A "stacked cake" means that a cake's tiers are not separated by columns but are assembled instead to rest directly on top of one another. This may look easy to do, and it is, but you must put some care, thought, and planning into the logistics.

One-quarter-inch wooden dowels provide internal support within the tiers and prevent the tiers from sinking into one another. The cardboard rounds that each tier sits on act as hidden separator plates and are supported by the dowels. I use four or five dowels for 14-inch-round bottom tiers, and one less for each successively smaller tier.

Stack tiers after the final outer coating of buttercream or covering of your choice is chilled and firm. Place the bottom tier upon the prepared Masonite board. For a center-stacked cake, insert the dowels near the center of the tier and within the space that the next, smaller tier will cover. Insert the dowel into the tier and mark it at the surface of the cake for the correct height. Remove the dowel and cut it to that size; use this dowel for measuring the other dowels for this tier. I use a serrated knife for cutting the dowels, but you may use a small saw instead. Re-insert the dowel and it should be flush with the top of the tier; repeat with the remaining dowels. Spread some softened buttercream over the dowels. Place the next tier over the area and repeat the sequence for that and any remaining tiers. The buttercream will glue the tiers together. Obviously, you do not need to insert dowels in the top tier unless you need them to support something substantial, such as a ceramic vase.

For offset-stacked cakes, insert the dowels within the space that the next upper tier will cover.

Assembling Cakes with Pillars

Some cakes call for columns, or pillars, to separate the tiers. You will find three types of columns on the market. The basic type is usually referred to simply as "pillars" or "regular pillars." Another type is the "spiked" pillar, which goes through the cake tier beneath it all the way through to the cardboard below. This is the kind I use most often. A third type works like the spiked pillars and is referred to

Insert dowel and mark flush with top of cake.

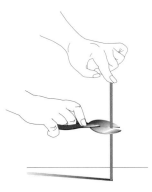

Remove dowel and cut at mark.

Re-insert dowel.

as "hidden" or "trimmable" pillars. These are simply spiked pillars you can trim to create custom-height separations between the tiers. This creates the illusion that the tiers are floating above one another. Because these pillars are completely round, they are perfect for wrapping with ribbons or covering with frosting. There is also the Bellini Cake (see page 55) that calls for something other than the standard columns. The instructions for the creative use of glasses or other objects are given in the individual recipe. Think about suitable objects in your house that could be used effectively as columns.

Regular Pillars

The regular pillars come in many styles, from the most common Grecian and Roman ones to the more ornate pillars—which I do not use—decorated with swans and dancing cherubs. The classic-looking Grecian and Roman pillars are made of white plastic. When I use them, I usually paint them first. These pillars work with plastic separator plates that go below and above each cake tier. The ones that must sit on top of each tier, to provide support for the pillars coming down from the tier above, are out in plain sight. This is why I do not like using them, unless they are integrated into the design somehow.

Columns are available in many different heights, allowing you to leave very small or very large distances between cake tiers. In general, cakes with separated tiers present a more formal look than stacked cakes. You can also mix and match distances between tiers. For example, use a shorter distance between the smaller top tiers and larger ones for the bottom tiers. Or, you can have just one separation for a many-tiered cake. Columns are sold in sets of four.

You may use separator plates the same size as, or slightly larger than, the cake tiers. If you are doing an elaborate bottom border or treatment with flowers, then use the larger plates.

After you have selected the sizes of the separator plates, affix the cake tiers, which are already on cardboard rounds, to the plates using some soft buttercream. You can now apply any final decorations, including your borders. Chill to firm. You will use the same size plate to attach the bottom of the columns to. This plate will rest, knob side up, on top of the tier below. Internal dowels, cut to size, will support the weight of this plate that is supporting the columns and cake above.

To paint separator plates and columns, use spray or brush-on paint. If you need an unusual color, good acrylic paints (including metallic ones), can be found in artists' supply stores. I often use the

Put separator plate, knobs up, on cake.

Attach pillars.

Set second separator plate on top of pillars.

Mark cake with separator plate, knobs down.

Lift off plate; marks will remain.

Insert columns using marks as guides.

Liquitex and the Golden brands. Paint all visible surfaces.

Spiked Pillars

These are the pillars I prefer to use because they are simple, good looking, and stable. They also offer great stability because the pillars are "spiked," or pressed right down into the cake. The selection is more limited than that of the regular pillars, but I think these are more attractive. The selection includes clear acrylic almost cylindrical pillars with a tight spiral design. These are a good choice for wrapping with ribbon. Another acrylic type has a more open spiral shape with very contemporary look. There are also some that are white or clear plastic with a Grecian column top and a bottom that tapers out, allowing you to press them into the cake easily. Spiked pillars have separator plates, but they are used a bit differently. Plates support each cake tier, which the pillars will attach to. But then, the pillars will go down through the cake below, instead of connecting with another separator plate. Some are available with a loose plastic piece that looks like the top of the column. It slides onto the column like a ring and then, after the pillar is put into place, settles on the cake surface at the visual bottom of the pillar. It makes it look like the column has a top and a base, instead of the bottom just disappearing into the cake.

You may also paint spiked pillars, but using a slightly different technique. You should paint all surfaces of the separator plates. But since some sections of the spiked pillars get inserted in the tiers, these sections should be left unpainted. (This limits the paint's contact with the food.) For example, measure the final height of the tiers. If each is 3 inches tall, then leave the 3 inches at the bottom of the pillar unpainted; it will not be visible when you insert it into the cake.

You may use separator plates the same size as, or slightly larger than, the cake tiers. If you are doing an elaborate bottom border or treatment with flowers, then use the larger plates. After you have selected the sizes of the separator plates, you need to mark the tiers for placement of the columns. Marking the tiers sounds more difficult than it is. If you have three tiers, you will be using two sets of columns and two separator plates. Begin by placing the largest bottom tier in front of you. It should already be mounted on its cardboard round and affixed to a covered board. Take the separator plate that will support the middle tier and center it over

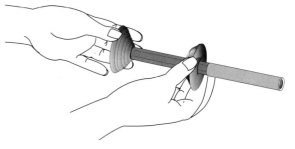

This is a spiked pillar with additional, loose column base.

Insert spiked pillar (here with loose column base).

Slide base down to rest on cake.

Repeat with other pillars and set separator plate and cake on top. Repeat with remaining tiers.

the bottom tier. The separator plates have knobs on their undersides and the pillars click onto the knobs. Lightly press the knobs onto the surface of the tier, just enough to leave a mark—you will use the marks as guides when you insert the columns into the cake tiers. Remove the plate. Repeat this step with the remaining tiers, using the separator plate from the tier above to mark it.

The next step is to affix all the cake tiers to their plates. Use some buttercream to stick the cakes and their cardboards to the separator plates. Now you are ready to apply your final decorations. Chill the cake well and transport the tiers separately, assembling them with their columns at the reception.

Trimmable or Hidden Pillars

These are cylindrical pillars that you can custom cut to size. They sink into the bottom tiers like other spiked pillars do. Their round shape makes them perfect for wrapping with ribbon.

They are also perfect to use when you want "hidden" pillars that create the impression that the tiers are floating above one another. Simply cut the pillar to the desired height.

Flowers: Edible, Crystallized, Pressed, and Otherwise

The following is a list of flowers that are edible—that is, if they are free of pesticides, herbicides, and fungicides. But it does not mean that they all taste great! Even the ones that are quite palatable, like roses, will not please some people. I think it is as much the unusual floral taste as the thought of eating flowers that turns some folks off.

Many flowers are so beautiful that you may want to use them even though they do not taste good. That's fine, so long as you present them as a removable decoration, not an integral part of the cake. If they are going on your cake, they should be organically grown. Commercial florists should be able to tell you the status of their blooms. Green markets, and your own or a friend's garden, are the most reliable sources. When foraging through gardens or green markets, what you find depends on the season and, of course, on where you live. However, since most weddings take place in the warmer months, which corresponds to flower season, this is not usually a problem.

I like to use fresh, crystallized, and pressed flowers on cakes, because, frankly, I do not think that even hand-crafted replicas can come close to those produced in nature. I use the occasional handmade flower of marzipan or chocolate, but real flowers, to me, are far more beautiful. Why use a replica when the real thing is available? Just to show off expert technique at the cost of flavor, texture, and overall effect is not my style. Anyway, once you have chosen the edible flowers, you can proceed with decorating.

Popular Edible Flowers

Remember, not all parts of each plant are edible. For instance, a tulip blossom is edible, but steer clear of the bulb! Please read up on this subject before embarking on an edible-flower project of your own.

Apple blossoms	*Malus genus*
Tuberous begonias	*Begonia tuberosa*
Borage	*Borago officinalis*
Calendula	*Calendula officinalis*
Carnations	*Dianthus caryophyllis*
Chive blossoms	*Allium schoenoprasum*
Chrysanthemums	*Chrysanthemum cultivars*
Cymbidiums	*Cymbidium genus*
Citrus blossoms	*Citrus genus*
Cornflower	*Centaurea cyanus*
Daylily	*Hemerocallis species and cultivars*
Dianthus	*Dianthus species and cultivars*
Elderflower	*Sambucus nigra*
English daisies	*Bellis perennis*
Fuchsia	*Fuchsia hybrida*
Gardenia	*Gardenia jasminoides*
Geraniums	*Pelargonium cultivars*
Hibiscus	*Hibiscus rosa-sinensis cultivars*
Hollyhock	*Alcea rosea*
Honeysuckle	*Lonicera genus*
Hyssop	*Hyssop officinalis*
Iceland poppy	*Papaver nudicaule*
Lavender	*Lavendula officinalis*
Lilac	*Syringa genus, S. vulgaris*
Lemon verbena	*Aloysia triphylla*
Marigold	*Calendula officinalis*
Nasturtiums	*Tropaeolum majus*
Passion flowers	*Passiflora species and cultivars*
Roses	*Rosa genus*
Petunias	*Petunis hybrida*
Safflower	*Carthamus tinctorius*
Sunflowers	*Helianthus annuus*
Tulip	*Tulipa species and cultivars*
Pansies	*Viola tricolor*
Violets	*Viola odorata*
Yucca	*Yucca elephantipes*
Zucchini blossoms	*Curcurbita pepo species and cultivars*

Crystallized Flowers

To crystallize flowers, make sure that the blooms are dry and free of any loose pollen or dust. Fill a shallow bowl with superfine sugar—sold in supermarkets—with a teaspoon set at its side. (The small-grained sugar coats flowers more evenly and prettily than granulated sugar. Do not try to make your own superfine sugar by whizzing granulated sugar in a food processor. I tried this and the grains are uneven. This ruins the look.)

The bowl needs to be wide enough to accommodate the flower with the largest diameter. You will also need a small bowl with a lightly whisked egg white and two small, soft paintbrushes; stiff ones will bruise and tear the petals. One paintbrush remains dry to help separate petals, and one is used for painting on the egg white. Also ready a rack with a small-holed grid set over a pan, parchment paper, or aluminum foil to catch any sugar that falls off. Tweezers help pick up and hold some flowers, while your fingers will be fine for others.

Set up your work space as follows: On the left, arrange your flowers, then moving to the right, set out the bowl of egg whites, the sugar, spoon, and rack. Pick up one of the flowers at its base. Spread the petals apart gently with your fingers or the dry brush to expose all surfaces. Dip the other paintbrush in egg white and paint all of the surfaces and coat them evenly. Now, holding the flower above the sugar bowl, scoop up some sugar with the spoon and begin to sprinkle it over the flower. Keep rotating the flower so that the sugar reaches all surfaces. If any large unsugared petals flop over and stick to one another, use the tweezers or a toothpick to gently pry them apart. Tweezers can harm the petals, so be careful. When the flower is completely covered with sugar, place it on the rack to dry. If the sugar does not adhere to a part of the flower, it may not have been coated with any egg white. You can patch this with more egg white and sugar, but if you get egg white on already sugared petals, they will become thick and unsightly. Practice on a few imperfect blooms until you get the hang of it. You may crystallize edible leaves, such as mint leaves, as well.

Dry the flowers completely. And I mean totally. Many recipes tell you to dry them for a day or two at room temperature in a dry environment. This can work, if conditions are optimal, but humidity is hard to control. While researching recipes and techniques for this book, I found myself making crystallized flowers on a particularly damp day. No room in the house qualified as low in humidity. So, I placed the rack with its pan in my gas oven. The pilot light was on and it provided a nice dry, warm environment. I left the flowers in there overnight. They were beautiful in the morning, but some of the larger, more intricate flowers needed more time. I left them in there for another day and night. Forty-eight hours did the trick and they were dry as a bone—crisp, beautiful, and elegant.

To store them, I place my crystallized flowers— a single layer is best—on top of parchment paper inside a large, flat airtight container with a Blue Magic device (page 178). I then seal the top and the flowers last for months.

If you prefer to purchase flowers already crystallized, call Meadowsweets (see Resources section, page 188). This company offers an exceptional product.

Wrapping and Wiring Stems and Flower Spikes

Other flowers are not edible, yet can lend that special touch. Or, perhaps, the "edible" flowers that you find are not organically grown. In either case, you can take certain steps that will still allow you to use them. The stems, which will be the only parts that come in major contact with your cake, can be wrapped with floral tape. Another technique is to wire the flowers. Both of these techniques are easy to do, and you can find directions in books on flower arranging.

You can also insert the stems into flower spikes, small elongated, plastic cups that can be inserted into cakes below the frosting's surface. This way the stems do not come in contact with the cake at all. Fill the cups with a tiny amount of water or a piece of damp sponge before inserting the flower stems.

Pressed Flowers

One of the most innovative ideas I came up with while working on this book was using pressed flowers for cake decoration. Most of you are probably familiar with what a dried and pressed flower looks like. You take a flower, press it in a flower press or between two pages of a heavy book, and leave it there until it becomes dried and brittle. Both result in a flower that can be glued onto a card or bookmark, or arranged in a picture frame. But they do not belong on a cake. The dry, crumbly texture would be most unpleasant. What I do is press flowers for one to two weeks until they are completely flattened, but still keep some of their flexibility, resiliency, and color. They can be placed onto the sides and tops of cakes for a unique look.

Flat flowers work the best for drying. Simply pick your edible flowers, place them between two sheets of parchment paper to keep them from sticking to anything, and press them in a flower press or large book. Leave them undisturbed for a week, then carefully check them. Some of the flowers might be ready; others will need more time, but no more than two weeks. Beyond that time the flowers begin to dry out too much. Pansies are not only one of my favorite flowers, because of their color variety and shape, but they are particularly wonderful for pressing. See the White Cake with Lemon Curd, Blackberry Curd, and Pressed Flowers, page 37, for the results. I have also placed them on the tops of cheesecakes under a pale, almost-clear apple jelly glaze. They look like flowers under glass.

Purchasing and Arranging Fresh Flowers and Greenery

Retail florists abound and may be a good resource for you. But also look to local farmer's markets and wholesale florists for supplies. If you or a friend are lucky enough to have a garden abundant with blooms, don't overlook this resource. When purchasing flowers, I always plan ahead, call around, and order what I need so that I can be assured of getting what I want, when I want it. I suggest you do the same.

The photos in this book show several different ways of arranging flowers and greenery, but by no means are these the definitive styles. I have never arranged flowers the same way twice. I just start and assess as I go along, making changes where necessary.

But there are some tips to consider. In general, flowers should be fresh, fresh, fresh. Not only will they look better and brighter, but they will last longer once placed on or around the cake. There are exceptions, of course. If you want full-blown roses or open tulips, proceed accordingly. If you buy tight buds and want a more open look, place the stems in warm water. This will hasten the blooming process. Store flowers overnight in water in the refrigerator to keep them looking their best.

Flowers and greenery can be draped on the table, either along the top edges or in swags around the sides. Garlands can also be arranged around the base of the covered Masonite boards or whichever platter you are using.

I love to scatter petals around the cake onto the tablecloth. Rose petals work well for this. Ask your florist about "seconds," or flowers that are a bit past their prime. These are fine for this purpose and will be less expensive.

Crystallized and Fresh Fruit Decoration

For some cakes, like the Poppyseed Cake with Orange Marmalade Filling and Grand Marnier Buttercream (see page 63), fresh fruit—either as is or crystallized—can be used to great effect.

For fruit, such as strawberries and blueberries, buy nice, firm clean berries. Rinse and dry them, if necessary, just before use. If you select raspberries, do not rinse them but use them as is.

There are two ways to crystallize fruits. For the first method, follow the directions for crystallized flowers, but let the fruit sit only for a few hours—it

is best to make them the morning of the event and dry them at a cool room temperature. This develops a hard, sugary crust, giving the fruit a frosted look.

The other way to crystallize fruit produces a clear, hard, crunchy sugar coat. Whole fruit, such as strawberries, grapes, and miniature Lady Apples, work best. To do this, combine 2 cups sugar and 1 cup water in a saucepan and heat it until it reaches 310°F. The amount of sugar and water will vary with the amount of fruit to be dipped; just keep the proportions the same. Dip your fruit into the sugar syrup, let the excess drip back into the pan, and dry the fruit on a rack. This produces more of a candied fruit than a crystallized one, but you may like the effect and want to use it in certain instances.

For any of these fresh-fruit preparations, you must buy the fruit as fresh as possible, without blemishes or any signs of mold. If the fruit is the least bit soft and exuding juice, your results will be inferior.

Working with Chocolate

Chocolate is an emulsion of chocolate solids, cocoa butter (a fat), and other ingredients. When melted simply in the top of a double boiler (*bain-marie*) or microwave, this delicate balance may be altered; fat crystals become unstable and when the chocolate dries, it develops greyish steaks. Basically, tempering chocolate, which is the controlled lowering and raising of the chocolate's temperature, stabilizes the fat crystals in the cocoa butter; this produces a shiny, beautiful chocolate once it hardens. This is why it is good to temper chocolate when making curls, fans, cigarettes, filigree, or other pure chocolate decorations for the top of the cake. Tempered chocolate also shrinks slightly when cooled so it is ideal for chocolate molding because it unmolds easily. It is not necessary to temper chocolate for a batter or when making chocolate plastic.

You have all seen chocolate "in good temper." It is shiny and snaps when broken or bitten into. Chocolate that is "out of temper" will be dry, chalky, and dull, with grey streaks on its surface. This discoloration is called "bloom" and although it does not affect the taste of the chocolate, it certainly affects its appearance. It is the by-product of cocoa butter separating and rising to the surface of the chocolate. Usually chocolate is in good temper when it is purchased. Once it is melted, however, it loses its temper. Chocolate that has a bloom on it can be melted and restored to a proper state. *Couverture,* a chocolate with a high cocoa butter content—at least 32 percent—is the best chocolate to temper. Individual recipes will tell you whether or not the chocolate has to be tempered.

You can temper chocolate by hand or by machine. By hand, you need a chocolate thermometer with a range of 40° to 130°F in one-degree increments, necessary for assessing the chocolate's progress. You also need a marble slab and a long offset spatula. If you temper chocolate often, you may want to buy a small, home chocolate-tempering machine. Although these units are expensive, they temper chocolate automatically. The Sinsation machine by Chandre is a wonderful tool and useful to own; refer to the Resources section, page 186.

TEMPERING CHOCOLATE
1 pound chocolate, finely chopped

Place the chocolate in the top of a double boiler (*bain-marie*) over, but not touching, hot, not boiling, water. Stir constantly until the chocolate is melted. Insert the thermometer into the center of the chocolate; do not let its temperature rise above 120°F.

Remove the top of the double boiler and wipe the bottom dry so that no water can drip into the chocolate. Begin to cool the chocolate by stirring it gently. When the temperature has dropped to 100°F, pour about two-thirds of the chocolate onto the marble slab. Begin to work it back and forth with the offset spatula—spread it thin, gather it up, and spread it out again. Work the chocolate until it begins to thicken. The thermometer should register about 75° to 80°F.

Scrape the chocolate into the top of the double boiler, but do not set it over hot water. Stir it together with the remaining melted chocolate to blend. Test with the thermometer: The temperature should be 88° to 91°F for bitter and semisweet chocolates; 85° to 88°F for milk chocolate; and 84° to 87°F for white chocolate. If the temperature is lower, place the chocolate over the hot water. Stir continuously until the proper temperatures are reached, but do not let the chocolate overheat, or it will lose its temper. To retain the correct temperature, place the pot on a warming tray or over the warm water. Another trick is to place it on a plastic-covered heating pad. Keep track of the temperature and maintain it within the proper ranges while working with it. The chocolate will have a tendency to firm up and harden around the edges of the pan where it cools first. Stir constantly to prevent this from happening. The chocolate is now ready to use. After you have made your shapes, store them in an airtight container in the refrigerator or freezer.

Solid Chocolate Molding
Both flexible and rigid plastic or silicone molds are readily available on the market. Tempered chocolate can be used in these molds to create a variety of shapes. The flexible molds, which are the ones used in this book, usually consist of a shape that has been imprinted onto a piece of soft plastic or silicone; you fill up the imprint with tempered chocolate and level it with a straight-edge spatula. After that, you set the mold aside until the chocolate firms at room temperature or in the refrigerator. To unmold the chocolate, turn the mold over, placing its open side on a piece of parchment paper. Peel back the flexible mold to reveal the chocolate piece. When handling finished pieces, it is a good idea to wear soft cotton or smooth plastic gloves so you do not transfer fingerprints onto your gorgeous creations.

Clean all molds gently with soapy water. Never use anything that would scratch or mar the inner surface of the mold.

Chocolate Curls, Leaves, and Filigree
When making any of these chocolate decorations, pay close attention to the temperature of the chocolate, the room, your hands, and the utensils—all

make a difference. If the chocolate is too cold, the shapes will splinter and crack. If it is too warm, the shapes will fold over on themselves and you'll have soft, dull piles of chocolate.

Experiment with different techniques for varying the temperature of the chocolate. For blocks of chocolate, try holding them between your palms to allow your body heat to do the work, or place them in a microwave and heat on lowest power, checking every 10 seconds.

The material of the surface onto which you place melted chocolate can affect the outcome. A marble slab is excellent, and you can also use your Formica countertop. Many recipes suggest that you use cookie sheets; a stainless steel cookie sheet is excellent, but do not use aluminum ones. This metal is soft and you may inadvertently scrape some up with the chocolate. Flexible plastic acetate, purchased at an art supply store, is an excellent surface for piped decorations.

When spreading melted chocolate onto a surface, the longer you wait, the firmer the chocolate will become. If it has hardened too much, place it under a warm lamp or gently wave a hair dryer blowing warm air over the surface. Chocolate is forgiving because you can always remelt it and begin again.

Start with chocolate that is in good temper and, when melting, temper it first before using. Make sure that your utensils are clean and use *couverture* chocolate for best results.

You can make chocolate shapes one month ahead and store them in airtight containers in the refrigerator or freezer. Store them at room temperature if you will be using within one week. Apply the shapes by spoon or other utensil right before setting the cakes out for display. The heat of your fingers can melt and distort the shapes. Or, run your hands under ice cold water, dry them thoroughly, and work quickly.

Chocolate Curls

Curls can be made from any type of chocolate, except unsweetened chocolate, and can add drama

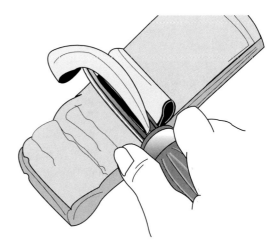

Making simple chocolate curls.

and great taste and texture to many cakes. The first and easiest way to make them is to wrap a block of chocolate in parchment paper and hold it in your hand. Take a sharp vegetable peeler and make long strokes down the length of the chocolate. Work over a piece of parchment paper to catch the curls as they fall. Experiment with pressure to make curls thicker or thinner, and tighter or looser. If the chocolate splinters, it is too cold; if the curls are soft and do not hold their shape, the chocolate is too warm. Adjust the temperature accordingly. A hair dryer works wonders here for gentle warmth.

Alternatively, use an offset spatula to spread tempered chocolate on your work surface (see suggestions). Let the chocolate set, then holding a triangular scraper at a 45° angle to the surface, begin to scrape the chocolate away from you. Or, use a long icing spatula, holding the handle end in one hand and the tip end in the other hand, and scrape the long edge of the spatula over the chocolate towards you. The chocolate should roll over itself and form curls. If it cracks and splinters, it is too cold; if the chocolate is too soft, curls will not form.

You may use other tools for a different look. Alice Medrich, pastry chef and author of *Cocolat*, one of my favorite books, suggests using a round cookie cutter with a very sharp edge. She explains that by pulling the cookie cutter towards you over the surface of the chocolate, you will make rounded curls. Vary your pressure for different results. Curls by nature are free form, so a variety of shapes is desirable.

When you have made the amount that you want, pick up the piece of parchment and pour the curls into a flat plastic container. Do not touch them with your hands because your body warmth may melt them. Store them in an airtight container in the refrigerator or freezer. Room temperature will suffice if the curls will be used within the week.

Chocolate Leaves

You can make chocolate leaves using real leaves as models and tempered chocolate. Because these take time to make, I usually set aside some time when I have nothing else pressing to do. Then I make a large quantity of them and store them in an airtight container in the refrigerator or freezer until needed.

The amount of chocolate varies depending on the number and size of leaves but I suggest using at least one pound because if you are going to set aside the time to make the leaves, you might as well make plenty. You may use dark, milk, or white chocolate. Dark chocolate leaves are showcased nicely on the Sachertorte on page 117.

I wear plastic gloves while making leaves to avoid leaving any fingerprints on the chocolate and minimizing any heat transference from my hands. These inexpensive gloves are sold in cake decorating supply stores specifically for use when making chocolates. Or you can purchase gloves from a medical supply house. You will also need a small, soft artist's brush and many whole, unblemished leaves, free from rot, rust spots, or cuts. Wash and dry the leaves. Line a cookie sheet with parchment paper. Temper and ready the chocolate. Pick up a leaf and hold it by the stem. Brush the melted chocolate over the underside of the leaf. This side has the pronounced veins that you want to imprint onto your leaves. Cover the entire surface thinly and evenly. Make sure not to brush any of the chocolate around the edges and onto the top side of the leaf or you will find it nearly impossible to peel the leaf away from the firm chocolate.

Place the leaves on the cookie sheet and refrigerate them briefly. The chocolate will become dull and dry to the touch. For larger leaves, or leaves with an intricate shape, at this point you may want to apply another coat of melted chocolate for added stability. When chilled, gently hold the edges of the leaf with one hand and with the other pick up the stem and peel off the leaf in an even motion. The leaf should come off in one piece. If it

Paint chocolate onto real leaves.

Let chocolate harden, than peel real leaf away.

doesn't, simply pick off the remaining pieces carefully. The chocolate leaf will still be fine. Temperature, again, is the defining factor. If the chocolate is not chilled enough, the green leaf will not come free. If the chocolate is too cold, it will have a tendency to crack. Place the chocolate leaf in a chilled airtight container and touch it as little as possible or the chocolate leaf may begin to melt. You may reuse the green leaves if they are intact.

For a variation, try the following. Cookbook author Marlene Sorosky has written many books, and her book *Entertaining on the Run* has a marvelous variation for chocolate leaves. By using melted white chocolate and butterscotch chips and painting them both on each leaf, you can achieve an incredibly beautiful, mottled look.

Simply melt white chocolate and butterscotch chips separately. Brush the butterscotch on the leaves, leaving some green parts unpainted. Chill them, then paint them completely with white chocolate. Chill thoroughly. When you peel the green leaves away, the chocolate leaves will be a gorgeous combination of both colors and flavors. The look is very autumnal.

Chocolate Filigree

This looks like chocolate lace and is easy to make. Trace the outline of the desired shape (fan, heart, or other shape) on parchment paper. Place a piece of clear, flexible acetate over the parchment paper and place both on a cookie sheet. Pour tempered chocolate into a parchment cone, snip a small opening for the tip, and pipe the chocolate along the outline of the shapes. Let them set a few minutes until the chocolate is dull. Then fill in the shapes with lacy filigree patterns of chocolate. Make sure the chocolate lines touch in several places or the pattern will not be strong enough. These are delicate, so make extra.

Place the cookie sheet in the refrigerator and let them chill until completely firm. For larger shapes, and even some smaller ones, removing them from the acetate is the hardest part. Ready a container with an airtight lid to hold the shapes in a single layer. Then remove the chocolate shapes by peeling the chocolate from the acetate with a tiny offset spatula or your fingers. Gently pry up a corner and lift it away from the acetate; place the chocolate in container immediately. Alternatively, peel the acetate away from the chocolate by cutting it so that each shape is on its own little piece of plastic. Hold the edges of the chocolate shape gently and peel the acetate away from it with your other hand. Try both to see which works for you and the specific shapes. Store in the refrigerator or freezer. The Gâteau Opéra, page 110, shows some filigree.

Chocolate Plastic or Marzipan Flowers, Grapes, and Leaves

Flowers made out of a delicious sweet such as chocolate or marzipan are exquisite to look at and to eat. Clients cannot believe that these are not genuine, particularly the realistically colored ones. Making roses and other types of flowers does demand a lot of handiwork and I prefer to use chocolate plastic made with chocolate coating as it is easier to work with. You can use chocolate plastic made with real chocolate or marzipan, but it takes a little more finesse to get the results you want. The directions are the same, regardless of which you use.

Using a few specific tools will make your job easier. Small, nonstick rolling pins and rolling boards specifically made for gum paste work wonderfully with all of the food materials here. These are sold at cake-decorating supply houses. Purchased cutters, gum paste tools, an X-acto knife, a small offset spatula, and a dusting bag also come in handy.

For coloring white chocolate plastic or marzipan, knead some paste color into the "clay." Start out with tiny bits of color applied with a toothpick; the color is potent. You can also brush powdered colors onto the flowers after they are made.

Store the prepared chocolate plastic and marzipan items in an airtight container at cool room temperature or in the refrigerator for up to one month. Empty egg cartons are perfect for holding individual flowers in each cup.

Note: If chocolate plastic or marzipan becomes overly soft while you are working with it, simply let the "clay" rest for a few minutes, then resume. The warmth of your hands and a warm room can play havoc with these materials.

Chocolate Plastic Grapes

Tint white chocolate plastic with paste colors to mimic green and red grapes. For the green grapes, a combination of moss green and leaf green is good. For red grapes, use burgundy paste color and brush after molding with a purple powder color.

For each grape, you will need one florist wire (26 gauge) and dark green florist tape. Bend the end of each wire into a small hook. Roll small, slightly elongated balls to resemble grapes (the size of large raisins). Insert the hook end of a wire into each grape. Repeat until all grapes are suspended on wires.

To make grape clusters, take several grapes (6 to 8) and arrange them in a bunch with one grape hanging down on the bottom and the cluster getting wider with more grapes towards the top. Wrap the wires with florist tape; you may cut the wire bunch through the tape when it comes time to assemble your cake. You will probably want the wires to be about 3 inches long for inserting into the cake during decorating.

Sculpting Roses

Before you begin to sculpt roses, I strongly recommend that you study a live rose, including the petals, calyx, and leaves, and its general shape, construction, and color. This will help you create more realistic flowers. You can shape the petals by hand or with rose petal cutters of varying sizes. I find cutters are easier to work with.

Start with a quantity of material, which for simplicity's sake, I will refer to as "chocolate plastic," although you may use marzipan, gum paste, or fondant as well. Dust the work surface liberally with confectioners' sugar. Roll out the chocolate

Cut out petals.

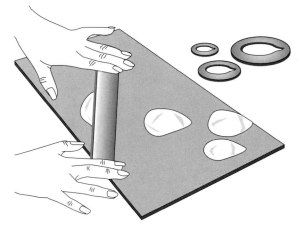

Thin edges with rolling pin.

plastic very thin, about ⅛ inch thick. Cut out the petals with the cutters. You will need between 3 and 7 petals of the same size for most individual roses, depending on whether you are making rosebuds (3 petals), or fully opened blooms (7 petals). Remove excess chocolate plastic from around the petals, wrap it in plastic wrap, and store it for later use. This process is just like cutting out cookies.

Loosen the petals from the board with a spatula. Dust the board with more confectioners' sugar, if needed. Using the rolling pin, thin out the broad edges of the petals; these should be thin and delicate for a realistic look.

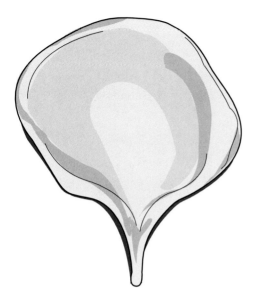

Using point of petal as a guide, pinch bottom part of petal together.

You also need to mold a center for each rose. Roll a piece of chocolate plastic into a cone with the broad end down and the point of the cone up. The cone should be the same height as the petals are and the width of its own base should be half that of its own height.

Take one of the petals and, using the point on the narrow end as a guide, fold the leaf in half lengthwise while still keeping the top of the petal open. Pinch the bottom together. Gently flare out the top edge in a tight outward furl. Some asymmetry is permissible and even desired. Real roses are not perfect. Real petals have tiny cuts and a combination of loosely curled and tightly curled shapes.

Place this first petal against the cone base with the pinched end down. Flatten one broad side of the petal against the cone, leaving the other side open and away from the cone. This will allow another petal to be tucked beneath it in an overlapping manner, just like a real rose. Repeat with a second petal, starting in the middle of the first petal applied. Your third petal will be tucked under the first. These 3 petals create a rosebud. You may add additional petals, each beginning in the middle of the one underneath. As you add more petals on outer layers, they should be more and more open and not as tightly fixed as the initial rows.

The base at this point may be quite wide and clunky. Loosen the entire rose from your work surface by sliding an offset spatula or thin, sharp knife beneath the flower. Trim away any excess chocolate with a sharp paring knife. Roll the bottom back and forth between your fingers to create a rounded shape. Again, you are trying to recreate what a real rose looks like. When you are done, use a broad, soft brush to dust off any extra confectioners' sugar.

Other Flowers
To make stephanotis-like blossoms, you need a gum paste tool with a cone-shaped tip. Roll a round ball of chocolate plastic the size of a small walnut between your palms; then elongate one end, and gently flatten the bottom of the other. It will look like a large chocolate kiss. Insert the tool

Place first petal on center cone. Subsequent petals are placed so they overlap half of the preceeding petal. Use three petals for a small bud, more for a full flower.

in the center of the flat end about halfway down; this is the center of the flower, rotating it gently; this will begin to thin out the flower's edges. Remove the tool and make five evenly spaced cuts around the rim of the hole; these are the petals. Using your thumb and forefinger, flatten and thin out the petals, rounding their petal shape.

To make daisies, use a daisy cutter, available in many sizes. Roll out enough chocolate plastic to cut out two daisies for every flower; plastic should be ⅛ inch thick. Use a gum paste boning tool, if desired, to make long vertical marks on the petals. Using some water or a soft piece of plastic, affix one daisy on top of the other, placing the petals offset. Roll a tiny ball for the center and press a piece of tulle into the center to create texture. Or dip chocolate plastic ball in tiny dragées, which are tiny gold or silver sugar balls. They can be purchased at cake-decorating stores. Affix ball to center of flower, pressing gently. To make daisy buds, simply cut out one daisy and roll a fairly large ball of plastic for each flower. Place the ball on the daisy and fold the daisy petals up and around the ball, pressing until they adhere.

Calyx

The calyx is the part of the flower below the petals where the bud attaches to the stem and its addition makes a more realistic look. Calyx cutters are available for specific flowers.

Roll out the plastic about ⅛ inch thick and cut out a calyx of the appropriate size. Thin out the edges gently. Attach to the bottom of each flower. For buds, the calyx should be tightly formed around the flower. For open blooms, the calyx can be looser.

Leaves

I love making leaves out of marzipan and chocolate because they are easy to do and appeal to my desire to decorate cakes using nature as a guide. I color white chocolate plastic in a range of greens and sometimes leave the plastic or marzipan its natural color. Look through the book for ideas.

I use purchased leaf cutters because I find making templates tedious. Leaf veiners are plastic-and-silicon mats that come in almost as many shapes as do cutters. They are patterned with raised veins so you can easily transfer their designs to your cut leaves. The mats create realistic veins that will bring the leaves to life. You can also make veins by hand using the blunt edge of a knife, but this will take a long time, especially if you are making many leaves at once. I suggest buying veining mats to match your assortment of cutters.

Roll out your chocolate plastic ⅛ inch thick and cut out the number of leaves desired. Trim away any excess chocolate with a sharp paring knife and loosen the leaves from the board with an icing spatula.

Press them against the appropriate veining mat. To give the leaves a curved shape, drape them over curved objects of varying widths.

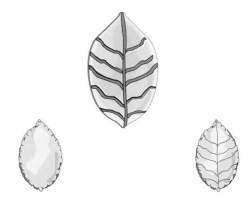

Cut leaf out of chocolate plastic or marzipan. Then use leaf veiner (center) to imprint veins on edible leaf.

For example, wine bottles will give a nice gentle curve and small objects, such as paper towel cardboard tubes, will bend the leaves dramatically. I often leave the leaves flat and then drape them directly onto the cake, using the angles of the tiers to dictate the shape (see Almond Banana Cake with Amaretto Buttercream and Marzipan Leaves, page 73). Regardless of their shape, leaves should be covered well in plastic wrap until needed.

Chocolate or marzipan leaves dry out slightly during storage and become difficult to bend or manipulate into the shapes you need. You will frequently want to make last-minute adjustments and the leaf may crack. Thus, these should be made close to the time you will be applying them to the cake—I usually make them the day before.

You can also use metal leaf forms (see Matfer in the Resources section, page 188) that both make veins and shape the leaf for a 3-dimensional look, but these leaves are thicker than rolled leaves. To use the rigid metal form, dust the form with confectioners' sugar. Take a piece of chocolate or marzipan and press it onto the form evenly. Trim away any excess chocolate with a sharp paring knife. Then gently peel off the leaf, which will already be imprinted and curved. Set it aside and cover it well with plastic wrap until needed.

Sugar Molding

Molding sugar is very easy and the results make impressive decorations. With just two ingredients, superfine sugar and water, you can make cherubs, flowers, leaves, vases, and various shapes that can add drama to your cakes. You can buy very inexpensive, flexible molds (many cost under $5) from cake-decorating suppliers, or use molds that you have around the house. Just make sure that the open end of the mold is wider than, or the same size as, the bottom.

The simple recipe calls for combining 1 cup superfine sugar and 1 tablespoon water in a bowl. Stir with a fork to distribute water evenly. This proportion can be scaled up or down as needed. If you want to add color, stir coloring into the water before blending.

Pack the wet sugar into the mold and press it down firmly with your fingers. Level off excess with an icing spatula using the edges of the mold as a guide. Quickly invert the mold onto a piece of parchment paper laid on a flat surface. The sugar form should pop out. If it doesn't succeed and the shape either crumbles or cracks, just scoop up the wet sugar and try again.

Set the unmolded sugar aside at room temperature, and leave it undisturbed overnight. The water evaporates and the molded sugar hardens. If it is an extremely large or thick shape, the center may still be damp. These larger sizes can benefit from being hollowed out. If the edges are dry, scoop out the still-damp sugar from the center, being careful not to make the mold too thin. Let the shape dry overnight again, or until completely hardened.

Dry sugar pieces can be painted with gold or silver powder dissolved in vodka, or these can be covered with gold or silver leaf for a truly extravagant look.

MARZIPAN SWEETS

These miniature replicas of fruits, vegetables, and figures are a tribute to the Europeans who raised this humble mixture of ground almonds and sugar to an art form.

For more ideas on how to mold marzipan into animals and other shapes, refer to the book Decorations, Borders, Letters, Marzipan and Modern Desserts *by Roland Bilheux and Alain Escoffier.*

You may store these at a cool room temperature for up to one month. Some of the colors may fade or brighten.

**MAKES DOZENS OF ITEMS,
DEPENDING ON SIZE**

About 3 pounds marzipan (see page 148)
Dusting bag filled with confectioners' sugar
Gum paste tools

Making marzipan fruits, leaves and vegetables is time consuming, but not that difficult. I have broken it down into manageable steps. Take one step at a time, and the process will go smoothly.

COLORING

The first step is to dye your marzipan the colors that you'll need. Tint small pieces of marzipan in various colors. Leave some marzipan uncolored in case you need more of one color.

Use paste color applied with a toothpick. Be judicious, because you can always add color. Blend colors for custom hues. For example, if you are going to make pumpkins, combine colors for an orange pumpkin hue. Keep each individually colored piece of marzipan well wrapped in plastic while you work on the rest.

For leaves, a variety of greens is best. Or, for fall leaves, a marbleized effect can be quite lifelike. To do this, tint some marzipan reddish-brown, another piece yellowish-brown, a third piece orangey-brown and individual balls of each main color. Knead the various combinations together just enough for them to adhere to one another. Roll out on a surface, preferably marble, dusted with confectioners' sugar. The marzipan should be no thicker than ⅛ inch. The marbleized effect will become more pronounced as you roll.

CUT AND ROLL FOR LEAVES

Follow detailed instructions for marzipan leaves, page 169.

MODELING

To roll by hand, make the shapes that you need: rounds for apples and oranges, long banana shapes, acorn shapes, pear shapes, or whatever else you want. You can fine-tune the individual pieces as you go along. You can add texture to oranges and strawberries by rolling the marzipan over a fine grater. You can make details such as the cleft in the top of a peach with gum paste tools. You can also use machine rollers, called Marzipan Rollerboards. One type makes lemons and strawberries and the other makes pears and a ball shape that can be used for apples, oranges, and similar shapes. Follow the manufacturer's instructions. Looking at photos of real or marzipan shapes really helps.

DECORATION

Use powdered colors to highlight fruit. For instance, a burgundy color on an orange will give it the look of a blood orange. Some dark brown or black can accent bananas. Cloves make perfect little stem accents.

Gold and Silver Leaf, Powder, and Skewings

You may be shocked at the idea of eating gold, but it is tasteless, harmless, and unlike any other embellishment. Gold and silver leaf may be used for a dramatic and elegant look. If you want impact, this is the way to go. Gold and silver leaf, powder, and skewings can be purchased from a variety of sources (see Resources, page 185). Your local art store will most likely sell leaf, but there are more economical sources. I buy mine from a local sign painter, and his costs, because he purchases them in bulk, are about ⅓ lower than retail. Store all types in a cool, dry place. They will last indefinitely.

When purchasing gold leaf, you will find it in all grades, but only use 22, 23, and 24 karats for use in food. It is available as "loose" and "patent," and depending on which applications you intend to use, one will suit you better than the other.

Gold leaf comes in booklets of 25 sheets that measure 3½ inches square. The loose leaves are separated by a type of parchment paper; the patent leaves adhere to the paper. When using loose leaves, be careful not to open the book of leaves unnecessarily because the metal will crumple with the slightest exposure to air movement. Even your breath can cause it to fly away or become irrevocably mangled. To use loose leaf, gently slide the leaf and its separator paper about ⅓ of the way out of the glassine envelope. Slowly peel back one of the parchment papers, exposing the leaf. You now have access to the metal and can proceed with the directions given below and in the individual recipes.

To be edible, silver leaf must be made from pure silver; make sure that it does not contain aluminum or other lesser metals. This also comes in packages of 25, but these sheets are 3¾ inches square.

Depending on the use of the metal, you will need different tools and have to vary your procedure.

There are many good books on gilding and the use of gold and silver leaf. Although these books suggest the use of true sizing, which is inedible, several of the techniques described will be of enormous help to you in your endeavors.

APPLYING LOOSE GOLD OR SILVER ON GANACHE OR OTHER STICKY SURFACES

On sticky surfaces, I limit my designs to scattered pieces of metal, not whole sheets. You will need a soft, dry sable brush and/or tweezers and loose gold or silver leaf. Peel back the parchment to expose a leaf or sheet of gold or silver. Use the dry brush or tweezers to lift up bits of metal and transfer them directly to the cake (see Chocolate Raspberry Truffle Cake, page 93). The leaf is quite light and the static electricity on the brush will make the leaf adhere to it very easily. As you bring the leaf to the surface of the cake, allow only the far edge of the leaf to touch down on the surface of the cake, then release the tweezers or remove the brush. Do not let the brush come into contact with the cake surface or it will become moist and sticky and you will have to change to a dry brush for use with the leaf. It may also mar the cake.

APPLYING LOOSE GOLD OR SILVER LEAF ON A DRY SURFACE

You can cover the entire surface of a cake or monogram using this technique. You will need two soft sable brushes, a pair of straight-edge tweezers, and some egg white. Use one brush for applying the egg white. This will act as the sizing, the substance that helps the gold or silver leaf adhere to the dry surface. Use the other brush and the tweezers to transfer the metal onto the item to be covered. Apply some of the beaten egg white to the desired surface (marzipan, royal icing, or other). Pick up the loose metal as described above and lay it down over the sized area. It will stick immediately. Repeat the process until you have covered the entire area you want to cover. Use an X-acto knife to trim away any excess metal. Polish with a ball of cotton.

APPLYING PATENT LEAF ON A DRY SURFACE

You may apply patent leaf to any dry surface, such as chocolate plastic, marzipan, royal icing, or other. Place the metal side down on the surface. Using your finger or a gum paste tool, rub the outside of the parchment to transfer the metal to the surface. Experiment with the pad of your finger, your fingernail, and various tools. Each gives different results. You will be able to see through the parchment paper where the metal has transferred and where you need to rub some more. When you are done, peel the parchment paper off. Your surface should be covered with the metal.

Silver and Gold Powder

Silver and gold powder can be sprinkled over cake surfaces for an ethereal effect. (See Gianduja Truffle Cake, page 75.) Look for powders through mail-order sources and at specialty purveyors and cake decorating stores.

Silver and Gold Skewings

Skewings are basically scrap pieces of loose gold or silver leaf and may be less expensive than sheets. If you are scattering bits of gold or silver over a cake, then this can be an economical choice.

Tabletop Decorations

Attractive tablecloths and table coverings will show your cakes off to their greatest advantage. Look through the book for ideas. A cake with many fresh flowers often looks good on a dark green cloth that harmonizes with the greens of the blooms. Maybe the wedding has a theme or color scheme, which can suggest colors or types of fabrics. A very old-fashioned looking cake might showcase well on a table covered in damask or tapestry. Experiment and use your intuition. If you are making cakes professionally, it pays to amass a collection of cloths to draw from.

A pretty new or antique cake knife and cake server will not only accent the cake, but be put to good use. The servers can be left plain if they are elegant or decorative in their own right, or they may be tied with pretty ribbons with or without flowers or sprigs of greenery.

How to Cut and Serve a Tiered Cake

Whether your cake has columns or is stacked, treat them similarly. You basically deal with each tier one at a time. For a cake separated by columns, remove the top tier and set it aside, remove the columns, and repeat with the remaining tiers and columns. You will now have a few or several single-tiered cakes set out in front of you.

For stacked cakes, insert a sharp paring knife or icing spatula beneath the cardboard round of the top tier. It should lift up easily from the tier below. Repeat with the remaining tiers. You will now have separate cakes. Remember to remove the wooden support dowels before serving. These will be easy to locate.

Cake Cutting Diagram

In general, a sharp, straight-edged slicing knife works best to cut cakes. Dipping the blade into hot water (and then wiping dry and clean) between cuts will ensure the neatest slices.

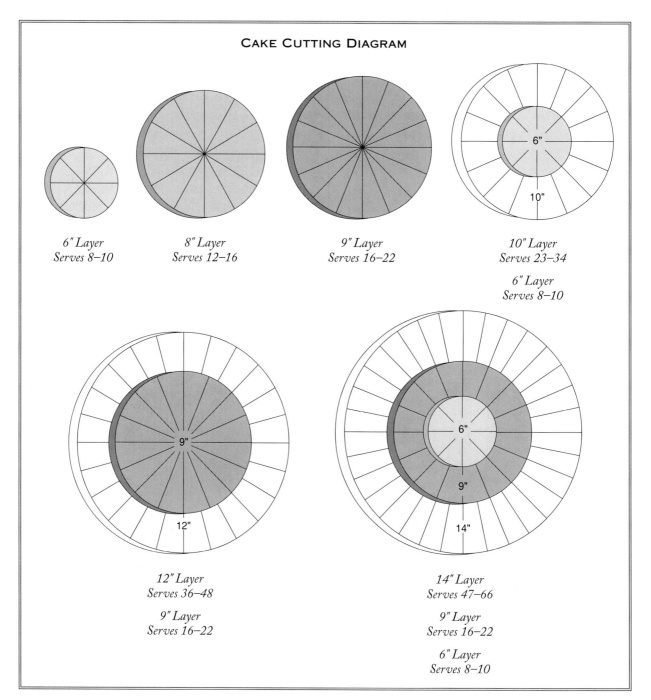

CAKE CUTTING DIAGRAM

6" Layer
Serves 8–10

8" Layer
Serves 12–16

9" Layer
Serves 16–22

10" Layer
Serves 23–34

6" Layer
Serves 8–10

12" Layer
Serves 36–48

9" Layer
Serves 16–22

14" Layer
Serves 47–66

9" Layer
Serves 16–22

6" Layer
Serves 8–10

·7·

EQUIPMENT

Baking Core

A baking, or heating, core is a small, hollow, blunt-top metal cone that attracts heat to the cake's center. This results in the cake baking more evenly. I only recently tried one and it made the difference between some of my larger tiers being merely fine and being great.

To use it, fill up your cake pan with the batter, but set some aside. Press the baking core down into the center of the batter, with the wide opening facing up. Fill up the cone with the extra batter. After the cake has baked and cooled, remove the core, pop out the little cakelet inside, and use it as a plug for the hole the core made in your cake. After filling and covering the cake with buttercream, no one will know the difference.

Bench Scraper

If you have not been in a professional bakery, you may never have seen one of these useful tools. It is a rectangular piece of stainless steel with a wooden or hard-plastic handle. Bread bakers use it to divide dough and to help scrape up and loosen dough from the work surface. In my kitchen, I use it to gather ingredients together, scrape up bits of dry ingredients, spread batter in large pans, and scrape my work surface clean. If you don't own one, you don't know what you are missing. Once you have one, you'll wonder how you baked without it.

Blue Magic

Blue Magic is a small glass bubble device with a solid bottom and a perforated top. The device contains alumina, which absorbs moisture when the glass bubble is placed in an airtight container with whatever it is protecting. It changes color from blue to lavender when it has absorbed its maximum amount of moisture. Then, you just heat it up in the oven or microwave to dry it out and use it again! It is manufactured by the Luce Corporation of Connecticut, and I was reminded of its existence by Flo Braker, a revered colleague (I later remembered that my Nana used it at her beach house). Braker uses it to help keep baked goods moisture free. The best part is that Blue Magic is inexpensive.

I place it in airtight containers with my dacquoise, crystallized flowers, and gum paste designs. And I also use it to keep crackers and pretzels crisp.

Cake Bases

You can use any sturdy, appropriate platter to support your cakes. If you have silver, fine china, pottery, or glass platters that are large enough, by all means use them. If not, Masonite boards or cake drums are always available and can be covered decoratively.

Cake Leveler

These items are usually comprised of a long, metal serrated blade attached to some kind of contraption that can be set to help you slice cake layers into specific thicknesses. They can be expensive, but if you will be baking often, order one from a cake-decorating supply source. Just make sure that you get one with a blade that is longer than the width of the largest tiers you will be working with.

Cardboard Rounds

I cannot stress enough the importance of purchased and sized cardboard rounds. They come in sizes from 4 to 18 inches round and can be obtained from cake-decorating stores and mail-ordered from Wilton or N.Y. Cake and Baking Distributors. As described in the Finishing Touches chapter, page 152, the cardboards are used as guides for your icing spatula to help make a smooth, clean buttercream coating. They are available in square shapes as well.

Combing Tool

Often called a decorator's comb or cake comb, this tool has serrated edges, which are used for making different patterns in the buttercream. Drag it along the cake's surface to make straight lines or swirl it to make wavy lines. I use a triangular comb manufactured by Wilton. Each side makes a different pattern.

Cookie Cutters and Gum Paste Cutters

Everyone knows what cookie cutters look like and how to use them. Usually cookie cutters are shaped for a specific design—that is, a leaf-shaped cookie cutter will look like a leaf. On the other hand, gum paste cutters sometimes come in parts, so to make a daffodil, you may need two or three different cutters to make up the various parts of the flower. Gum paste cutters are made the same way as cookie cutters, although usually without seams, and are used similarly. With the assortment of cookie and gum paste cutters available, you will find practically any shape you desire.

Cooling Racks

Properly cooled cakes will have the best texture and cooling racks are necessary for cakes to defuse heat efficiently. Invest in heavy-duty cooling racks that are large enough to support the largest cake you will bake. Racks with wires set close together offer the best support.

Decorating Tips

Tips are quite inexpensive—most cost less than one dollar—and owning a variety will allow you to experiment with different looks. Equip yourself with a basic set, which should include a range of round tips, closed and open star tips, leaf tips, petal tips, and one for basket-weave designs. Specialty tips for drop flowers, ruffles, fantasy shapes, and multi-openings can be purchased as you expand your collection.

Although certain American-made tips are ordered by number, some import lines will have numbers that do not correspond to ours. Know what you want when you shop. And not all tips are created equal. Some nickel-plated ones have heavy seams which make less delicate shapes. Others are seamless and often more expensive.

Clear plastic tips are available also. Try out a variety of types to see which you like working with. The imported clear plastic ones are actually of very high quality and do not break easily at all.

Decorating Turntable

You can frost a cake without using a turntable, but it will not look as good as a cake frosted with one. A free-turning turntable will aid in creating ultra-smooth coatings of buttercream or glaze. I do not suggest attempting any of these cakes without one. You can purchase an inexpensive plastic lazy Susan, or if you plan to decorate cakes often, invest in a heavy-duty turntable with a cast-iron bottom and a stainless steel top.

Dredger

A dredger is a small metal container, often sold in eight-ounce sizes. It has a perforated top made either of mesh or pierced metal. Perforation holes vary in size to allow more or less of the contents to flow out.

Filled with flour, confectioners' sugar, cornstarch, powdered cocoa, or cinnamon, a dredger can be used to give a dusting of the desired ingredient. I use them most often to shake sweet ingredients over desserts and plates for decoration or fill them with flour, cornstarch, or confectioners' sugar to dust my work surface.

Dusting Bag

This is a tool you make rather than buy. You will need a square of cheesecloth—I usually use an eight-inch-square piece—and fill this with confectioners' sugar. Use a rubber band to close up the top; this way you can easily open and refill the bag, as needed.

Use the bag to shake out sugar over the ingredients you are working with. Many of the cake components need to be rolled out and manipulated and the dry contents of the dusting bag will help reduce the chances of your material sticking to your work surface, cutters, or molds. You can also use the dusting bag to pat the insides of gum paste molds and other items, something you cannot do with a rigid dredger.

Flame Tamer

This is a heat-proof tool that can go directly over your gas or electric burner; it is usually round and a dimension similar to standard burners. Its purpose is to insulate whatever you are cooking from direct heat. The King Arthur Flour Baker's Catalog (see Resources, page 187) has a beautiful one and it can come in handy when you need to keep something warm, like cream when making caramel, or caramel itself during the assembly of a Croquembouche.

Food Processor

The recipes were tested with a Cuisinart DLC-7 model, but any food processor with a metal blade and shredding attachments will work. I use my processor for grinding nuts, shredding carrots, and making purées. Like mixers, motor powers vary with make and model. Always follow your manufacturer's instructions.

Heavy-Duty Mixers

In my wedding cake business, I depend on my mixers. I have a 20-quart Hobart, which is a commercial machine, and a tabletop KitchenAid model K5, which has a five-quart capacity. I tested all of the recipes with the KitchenAid and suggest that you use the same or a similar stationary machine. The KitchenAid not only has a large capacity, it also has the power. If you have a five-quart machine without the same strength, mixing times may be different; proceed cautiously and follow the manufacturer's instructions.

The KitchenAid comes with a stainless steel bowl, and balloon whip, flat paddle, and dough hook attachments. The balloon whip incorporates air into cream, buttercream, and eggs; the flat paddle creams butter, cream cheese, and most cake batters. The dough hook doesn't figure into any of the recipes in this book.

It is handy to have an extra stainless steel bowl, which can be purchased separately, especially when a recipe calls for creaming butter and the yolks and then calls for a clean, grease-free bowl for whipping egg whites. There is also an optional splash guard attachment that will keep dry ingredients from flying out onto your counter. It's not necessary by any means, but very nice to have.

Icing Spatula

Believe it or not, my favorite icing spatula is my most important tool. Using the correct spatula makes it much easier to achieve a professional finish on your cakes. Whether you are using buttercream, jam, fruit curd, whipped ganache, or a glaze, an icing spatula will help you do the job. I have several straight and offset spatulas, but the one I use most often is an 8-inch-straight spatula stamped with "Russell, Green River Works, Stainless." I haven't the faintest idea where I got it. It's just one of those tools that I have had for years, never realizing how important it was to me until decorating cakes became a regular activity for me. For some reason, it is better than any other I own.

What do I mean by better? Well, for the size of my hand, and the amount of flexibility I find most helpful, it fits the bill perfectly. The point is that you may buy one that feels stiff in action and you may find it difficult for frosting a cake smoothly—your technique may not be at fault. Try a more flexible or a longer spatula and see what happens. You can assess the flexibility of a spatula by gently flexing it back an forth against your palm. Be careful though, because some salespeople may frown at this. But you wouldn't buy a car without driving it, would you? This is a very subjective purchase and must be assessed individually. An icing spatula that fits your individual needs and style will make all the difference in the world. Some pastry chefs even like using broad spackling-type spatulas from hardware stores or bench scrapers.

Make sure that your icing spatula has perfectly smooth edges and a nicely rounded tip. Any nicks, ripples, or dents will show up as patterns in your frosting. Always wash and dry your spatula immediately after use. Leaving it hanging around in the dish rack is asking for trouble. I tuck it into my apron string when I begin a day of cooking. I feel like I am wearing a sword, but I can draw it out whenever I need it.

Leaf Veiners
These are soft, flexible mats (often silicone or other plastic) that come in various leaf shapes. The vein pattern particular to that leaf appears as raised lines on the mat. Soft chocolate plastic, marzipan, gum paste, or fondant is pressed onto the mats and the vein pattern is transferred.

Magi-Cake Strips
I am not a paid spokesperson for this product (although I could be!). However, there is simply nothing else on the market that accomplishes what Magi-Cake Strips do. They are fabric strips, lined on one side with an aluminum material, that are soaked in water and wrapped around the sides of cake pans before placing them in the oven. They are fixed in place with a "T"-headed pin and are a snap to use. What they do is keep the edges of your cakes moist by helping them bake more slowly than the center, yielding a more evenly baked cake. Just as importantly, the cakes will rise evenly without peaking in the center. This makes your job easier when it comes time to level your layers and tiers. One box has strips to fit 8- and 9-inch cakes; the other size has strips to fit 10-, 12-, 14-, and 16-inch cakes. They can be found in cake-decorating stores and through certain mail-order sources.

The cakes in this book were tested with Magi-Cake Strips, except where they were not necessary or not sized to use, such as the cheesecakes or truffle cakes. Substitutes can be made by using long strips of wet paper towels folded in aluminum foil.

Masonite Boards and Cake Drums
Masonite boards are stiff, strong particle boards that can be customized with foils, decorative papers, icing, or fabrics. They are thin, usually ¼ inch thick, but will hold the weight of most cakes. They can be purchased in cake-decorating supply stores.

Cake drums are ½ inch thick and come already covered with gold or silver foil. Since they will hold the heaviest cakes, I use them often; the downside is that they are more expensive than the Masonite boards.

Both Masonite boards and cake drums can be used as bases for any of the cakes in this book.

Measuring Cups and Spoons
For dry ingredients, I use high-quality stainless steel cups, sturdy enough not to dent. Dents make for inaccurate measurements. A good set is more expensive, but will last for years. Most cup sets have ¼-cup, ⅓-cup, ½-cup and 1-cup sizes. Some also have an ⅛-cup size, which may be helpful. The same goes for measuring spoons. Flimsy aluminum ones are not worth purchasing. Measuring spoon sets have ¼-teaspoon, ½-teaspoon, 1-teaspoon, and 1-tablespoon sizes (which is equivalent to 3 teaspoons). Some also have a ⅛-teaspoon size. A pinch is generally considered to be equal to ⅛ teaspoon, and a dash half of that. Foley makes reliable measuring equipment. Inexpensive lesser-known brands can, unfortunately, be quite inaccurate. Steer clear of them.

For liquid measurements, I use the standard Pyrex measuring cups available at most supermarkets and kitchenware stores. For the most accurate measurements, use a measuring cup closest to the size of what you are measuring. For instance, if you need ½ cup of liquid, use a 1-cup, not a 4-cup, measurer. Always set your cup on a flat surface, fill it with the liquid, and assess the amount at eye level. The surface of the ingredient should be level with the line marking on the cup denoting the desired amount. For the recipes in this book, it is handy to have 1-cup, 2-cup, and 4-cup sizes.

Microwave Oven
It is hard to standardize recipes using microwave ovens, because they come equipped with various wattages. My Sharp oven has 900 watts, which is considered a powerful oven. I have given approximate levels of power for microwave usage in the

recipes. I use my microwave for melting dark chocolates, defrosting cakes and frozen ingredients, and most often, for softening buttercream and butter, readying them for creaming.

Nonreactive Saucepans

Aluminum saucepans are found in many kitchens, but this metal reacts with acidic foods. For instance, if you cook lemon curd in aluminum, the curd may develop a metallic taste. Certain delicate foods, like dairy-based sauces, can discolor from a reactive pot. Some nonreactive materials are stainless steel, glass, and enamel. If I question the acidity of an ingredient, I use stainless steel pans.

Ovens and Oven Thermometers

Most professional kitchens have gas stoves and ovens and occasionally even convection ovens. Home bakers usually have gas or electric ranges. These recipes were tested on both home gas and electric ranges and the baking times have taken this into consideration. Internal oven temperatures can vary from the dial settings by as much as 25 to 50°. Because of this, I strongly suggest using an oven thermometer and adjusting your oven accordingly.

Also, one very important factor that is not often mentioned in baking books is the necessity of a level oven. Your floor may not be perfectly level, and if it is not, your cakes may always bake lopsided. Use a carpenter's level to assess the situation and prop up oven legs, if necessary.

Pans

I have used pans of varying qualities over the years. I suggest heavy aluminum baking pans, such as Magic Line, that are sold in cake decorating stores or through catalogs such as Wilton, Beryl's, or N.Y. Cake and Baking Distributors. The thinner gauge ones do not hold up and are not a worthwhile investment.

I'd like to say something here about dents. If you are starting out with new pans and equipment, I cannot stress strongly enough that you should take good care of them. Sometimes, if a cake is stubborn, refusing to come out of the pan, it is tempting to turn the cake upside down and rap the edges of the pan on the counter. Don't do it. The rapping can dent your pan and that will ruin your chances of making a beautiful, symmetrical cake in the future. (To release cakes perfectly, run an icing spatula around the sides of the cakes, pressing out towards the pan and away from the cake. Otherwise, you may unknowingly shear off some of the cake's sides. The cakes should release easily.) When you wash the pans, let them drain briefly, then wipe and put them away immediately. If they sit in a drain rack, heavier pots and pans may be placed on top of them and make dents. Trying to frost a cake that starts out with uneven, dented sides is no fun and puts you at a disadvantage.

Also, make sure that the larger-sized pans fit in your oven before you start! (See page 183 for more information on pan sizes.)

Parchment Paper

Parchment paper is available in rolls, like aluminum foil, from kitchenware stores and mail-order sources. Most professional chefs use parchment paper to provide a nonstick surface for baking. Cut out circles to fit pan bottoms, and use it to line baking sheets. When used with a greased pan, your cakes will come free effortlessly.

Parchment paper can also be cut into triangles to make paper cones. I use these for writing or decorating on cakes with melted chocolate.

Baking suppliers sell extra-large sheets that measure 16½ × 24 inches. These fit perfectly into full size sheet pans, which pastry chefs often use. I buy these in bulk and cut them to fit my needs, such as a parchment cone for decorating. A local bakery will probably sell you some, if you ask.

Pastry Bags

These recipes require pastry bags, coupled with various tips, for applying decorative buttercreams and frostings. Fabric ones are available, but I prefer the polyester type made by Wilton. They are called

---

PAN SIZES: 2-INCH VS. 3-INCH PANS AND LARGER DIAMETERS

Some of the cake tiers in the book are baked in two individual 2-inch-high pans. This is because these particular recipes work better this way. The individual shorter layers bake more evenly and quickly and yield a tender cake. The cakes for which I use 3-inch-deep pans do not suffer, in my opinion, from this method. Either because of their structural make-up, or because of the shorter baking time, the single deep tier works fine. It allows you to torte the cake after baking to create your layers. The advantage here is that because the torted layers originally came from one tier, they will be quite even when re-assembled. Of course, some cakes, like the cheesecakes and the coffeecake, are baked in 3-inch-deep pans because they will not be split after baking and you want a deep tier as an end result. Follow the advice for the sizes suggested and the recipes will work as tested.

As for the larger diameter layers, these are a fact of life when baking wedding cakes or other large special-occasion cakes. Measure your oven. The largest tiers suggested in this book are 14-inch squares and rounds. You should have at least two spare inches on all sides in your oven for air and heat circulation. If your oven is smaller than this, you can still proceed with the recipes by using half-pans. Many baking supply houses, such as N.Y. Cake and Baking Distributors, carry half-pans. For larger sizes such as 14-inch rounds or more, you can purchase these pans in the shape of a half circle. They will fit in your oven on the diagonal. Simply make and pour half the amount of batter (per round) into one of the half-pans and bake. Repeat with the second half batch. After the two half circles are baked, place the two halves together on a cardboard to make one whole layer. After the buttercream is applied, no one will know the difference.

Featherweight Decorating Bags and come in sizes ranging from 8 to 18 inches (in 2-inch increments). The openings are trimmed to allow a large decorating tube or coupler to fit. The coupler allows you to change small tips easily. I use the 14-inch size most often.

As with the rubber spatulas, if you do a lot of work with royal icing, it is best to keep a few pastry bags set aside specifically for this icing. Although the bags can be boiled clean, traces of grease may remain, which would break down your royal icing.

To clean, they may be boiled or simply washed well with hot, soapy water. Be sure to wash and dry them carefully or leftover foodstuffs will be left to ferment and ruin your bag. Do not store in a drawer with loose tips or other sharp objects. These can pierce the bags and ruin them for future use.

Plastic Squeeze Bottles with Needle-Nosed Tops

As described in the section on Adding Sugar Syrup to a Cake, page 154, these bottles can be purchased in drug stores or from cake-decorating supply stores. Fill them with sugar syrup, cut a small hole in the tip, and use to apply syrup to cake layers.

Rubber Spatulas

The standard rubber spatula sold in supermarkets is too small to be effective for some techniques. Kitchenware stores and restaurant supply houses stock extra-large ones that make it easy to gently fold ingredients together. This is crucial when you are handling light génoise batters and meringues where retaining volume is mandatory.

If you do a lot of work with royal icing, set aside a rubber spatula specifically for this purpose. The grease from buttercreams and other sources that collects on most rubber spatulas will break down even a well-made royal icing.

Another type of plastic spatula comes shaped like a rectangle without a handle. Approximately 4 × 6 inches, these are flexible and can be used for scraping up batter from bowls and spreading batter in pans.

Sheet Pans and Cookie Sheets

In the professional kitchen, there are usually two types of flat baking pans: a full sheet pan and a half sheet pan. A full sheet pan measures 18 × 26 inches and is much too large for a home oven. A standard half sheet pan measures 13 × 18 inches and may come in handy for certain recipes, such as the dacquoise, or for spreading chocolate for making large curls. For the larger tiers of the dacquoise, you will need a sheet pan or cookie sheet with a larger interior area. Or, you can use a roasting pan, if it is large enough.

Slicing Knife

Although a serrated knife will work well for torting and leveling cakes, it does create crumbs. Excess crumbs will only complicate your decorating attempts and should be avoided at all costs. I do keep a serrated knife handy for some jobs, but I prefer a slicing knife. This has a very thin, flexible blade with a straight edge. Needless to say, either knife should be razor sharp for best results, and preferably should be longer than the cake you are cutting. This may not be possible for the largest tiers, but the knife blade should be at least 14, preferably 16 or more, inches long.

Strainer and *Tamis*

A *tamis* is the French name for a professional sieve, as well as the word describing the action of sifting. A wide band of thin, flexible wood holds a round of wire mesh through which you sift dry ingredients. These are quick and efficient to use and can sift large quantities of dry goods. Purchase them in restaurant supply stores.

A standard bowl-shaped wire-mesh strainer with a long handle that fits over a bowl is fine for sifting dry ingredients as well. I prefer not to use a traditional flour sifter. They are small and not efficient for the amounts of ingredients used in this book.

Thermometers

I constantly use my Taylor Instant Read Thermometer to test the temperature of buttercreams, glazes, butter, and caramel. These types of thermometers come with a protective sheath attached to a clip. Restaurant chefs often clip them onto an arm pocket on the sleeve of their chef's coats. I clip mine to my apron string to always have it handy.

A chocolate thermometer is necessary to use during tempering and has one-degree increments. These allow you to accurately judge the temperature of the chocolate, which is crucial during this procedure.

Tip Saver

This tool, manufactured by Wilton, will reshape bent tips of many sizes. It is an inexpensive and very useful tool to have.

Triangular Scraper

This is made for pastry and chocolate work, but it is identical to the type of spatula used for applying spackle to a dry-wall. It consists of a handle with a metal bottom shaped like a blunt-topped triangle. The broad side of the triangle is the working edge and is quite sharp. Triangular scrapers are used to make chocolate curls and other shapes. Purchase in hardware stores.

Whisks

I use whisks constantly to finish off whipped ganaches and meringues and to "fold" ingredients together. Whisks come in all lengths and diameters, and with varying rigidity. Like with an icing spatula, your individual feel will determine which are right for you. Most likely, you will want to have an assortment handy.

RESOURCES

This section is meant to be comprehensive. Since I have designed this book to be used as a source book, I have included a detailed list of companies that can provide you with what you need to custom-design your cake. Most resources provide mail-order catalogs. The first listing is not a supplier, but a cake society that may be of interest.

For flowers and greens in general, you can use a retail florist, but if you live near a flower wholesaler, or even a whole district in larger metropolitan areas, do not hesitate to shop them. Announce yourself as a cake designer shopping for wedding cake flowers, and you should have no problem.

I. C. E. S. (INTERNATIONAL CAKE EXPLORATION SOCIETY)
3087 30th Street
Grandville, MI 49418
Marsha Winbeckler (206) 631-1937

I. C. E. S. MEMBERSHIP
1740 44th Street S. W.
Wyoming, MI 49509

This organization is geared specifically to the cake decorator, not the baker. Since 1976 they have provided members with a network of like-minded individuals, both professional and of the avid-home decorator persuasion. Members reside throughout the United States as well as South America, Australia, the Philippines, Japan, England, India, and beyond.

There is an annual fee for membership, which entitles you to a newsletter and access to scholarships for study and networking with members. There is also an annual 4-day convention, held in a different city every year, where you can learn about the latest in cake decorating technology and styles. Classes are offered: everything from learning about the business end of opening a bakery to marzipan work, how to expertly photograph your creations, and working with sugar.

ALBERT USTER IMPORTS, INC.
9211 Gaither Road
Gaithersburg, MD 20877
(800) 231-8154
FAX (301) 948-2601

Albert Uster offers a large selection of imported equipment and ingredients through mail order. They offer a great selection of candy-making equipment, molds, spatulas, pans, knives, and wedding cake stands, much of it from Switzerland.

BERYL'S CAKE DECORATING EQUIPMENT
P.O. Box 1584
North Springfield, VA 22151
(703) 256-6951
(800) 488-2749
FAX (703) 750-3779
E-MAIL Beryls@internext.com

Beryl herself will most likely be the one to answer the phone and help you with any cake-decorating question you may have. Her mail-order company offers gum paste cutters, colors, gold dust, pastes and powders, gum paste tools, ready-made rolled fondant, cake drums, cake pans, tips, books, videos, and more. Her large catalog will inspire ideas and designs. Excellent service.

THE BRIDGE CO.
214 East 52nd Street
New York, NY 10022
(800) 274-3435
FAX (212) 758-4387

This New York City institution has almost everything you need to bake a cake, including pans, tubes, molds, and decorating equipment. Many French imports.

BROADWAY PANHANDLER
477 Broome Street
New York, NY 10012
(212) 966-3434
FAX (212) 966-9017

This store has an entire section devoted to cake baking and decorating equipment, including tips, pans, parchment paper, and much more.

CHANDRÉ
14 Catharine Street
Poughkeepsie, NY 12601
(800) 3-CHOCLA
FAX (914) 473-8004

This mail-order company manufactures and sells the Sinsation, a small chocolate tempering machine that is perfect for home use. It is compact, hundreds of dollars less than any other on the market, and turns out perfectly tempered chocolate, dark, milk or white, every time. If you work with tempered chocolate a lot, this machine is a godsend. They even have a technical support line answered by knowledgeable staff. I use it when I need tempered chocolate for curls, filigree, or molds.

THE CHEF'S CATALOG
3215 Commercial Avenue
Northbrook, IL 60062-1900
(800) 338-3232

A great mail-order catalog from which you can buy KitchenAid mixers, Cuisinart food processors, large professional-sized rubber spatulas, bench scrapers, tart pans, extra-long hot mitts, parchment paper, pasta machines for rolling out chocolate plastic, and more, and all at very competitive prices.

THE CHOCOLATE GALLERY/
N.Y. CAKE AND BAKING DISTRIBUTORS

56 West 22nd Street
New York, NY 10010
(212) 675-CAKE
(800) 94-CAKE-9
FAX (212) 675-7099

At this store, you'll find chocolates, including Valrhona, ready-made gum paste flowers, silver and gold dragées, silver and gold dust, gold Jordan almonds, tips, molds, cutters, Masonite boards, cardboard rounds, cake pans, Magi-Cake Strips, paste and powdered colors of all kinds, professional baking sheets, books, magazines devoted to decorating, videos, and more. Visiting the store is a must. Unfortunately some employees seem uninformed about the products. Ask for owner Joan Mansour for very personalized service. This business also offers cake decorating classes through its School of Confectionary Arts. Request a catalog.

COUNTRY KITCHEN

3225 Wells Street
Fort Wayne, IN 46808
(219) 482-4835
(800) 497-3927
FAX (219) 483-4091

You'll find pans, colors, cutters, molds, tips, some ingredients, thermometers, squeeze bottles, and more. Catalog available.

EASY-LEAF

947 N. Cole Avenue
Los Angeles, CA 90038
(213) 469-0856

This operation is primarily wholesale, but management will address the needs of the home cook. The entire company is devoted to gold products—gold leaf, skewings, gold powder, brushes, and related equipment. Call for prices.

GREEN VALLEY GROWERS

10450 Cherry Ridge Road
Sebastopol, CA 95472
(707) 823-5583

This company specializes in flowering herbs, garden roses, fruit on the branch, and some of the most beautiful unsprayed hydrangeas you have ever seen. You can obtain many unsprayed greens from them too. Jerry Bolduan typically sells wholesale, but will be happy to quote a market price. You'll find kumquats, lemons, persimmons, wild rose hips, and more. They will also search for and buy for you things that they do not grow. I used many of their items on the Gianduja Truffle Cake (page 75).

J.B. PRINCE CO.

36 E. 31st Street
11th floor
New York, NY 10018
(212) 683-3533
FAX (212) 683-4488

Another New York supply house specializing in professional equipment. Great resource for pans, knives, spatulas, racks, and books.

KING ARTHUR FLOUR BAKER'S CATALOG

P.O. Box 876
U.S. Route 5 South
Norwich, VT 05055
(800) 827-6836
FAX (802) 649-5359

This wonderful, low-key catalog has flours of all description, vanillas, dried fruit, Merckens chocolates, some equipment, diced lemon and orange peels, flame tamers, and more. They also carry the Monin brand of flavored syrups. The retail store is located on Route 5 South.

LA CUISINE
323 Cameron Street
Alexandria, VA 22314
(703) 836-4435
(800) 521-1176
FAX (703) 836-8925

This very comprehensive supply house has excellent equipment, such as cake pans and baking cores; high-quality ingredients, such as Valrhona chocolates, Tahitian vanilla beans and lavender honey; and personalized service. Call for a catalog and to ask any questions you may have about a product you are looking for. Visit the store when in Virginia.

LUCE CORPORATION
P.O. Box 4124
Hamden, CT 06514
(203) 787-0281

This company manufactures Blue Magic, that wonderful product that removes moisture from enclosed containers. Use it for preserving crystallized flowers, pralines, cookies, crackers, pretzels, chips, and more.

MATFER KITCHEN AND BAKERY EQUIPMENT
16249 Stagg Street
Van Nuys, CA 91406
(818) 782-0792
(800) 766-0333
FAX (818) 782-0799

When I was in Paris, I bought some beautiful metal leaf forms that I use with chocolate and marzipan. When I came back home, I found out that I could have just ordered them through this French equipment distributor. It also carries copper, whisks, icing spatulas, cake pans and molds, and a large selection of French pastry books that are hard to find elsewhere in the States. Catalog available.

MAXI FLOWERS À LA CARTE
1015 Martin Lane
Sebastopol, CA 95472
(707) 829-0592

This mail order company has a wonderful selection of organically grown edible flowers.

MEADOWSWEETS
Box 371
Middleburgh, NY 12122
(518) 827-6477

This mail-order company makes the most exquisite crystallized flowers. If you do not want to make your own, this is the source to use. Owner Toni Elling offers cheerful, personalized service.

PARRISH'S CAKE DECORATING SUPPLIES, INC.
225 West 146th Street
Gardena, CA 90248
(213) 324-2253
(800) 736-8443
FAX (213) 324-8277

Cake pans made by them; custom chocolate molds; decorating equipment; heavy-duty turntables; and the most beautiful, clear acrylic columns and separator plates are available from this mail-order company and retail store. Call for catalog.

SUR LA TABLE
Pike Place Farmers Market
84 Pine Street
Seattle, WA 98101
(206) 448-2244
(800) 243-0852

They have a general catalog and a catalog devoted to baking. You will find pans, tips, truffle shaver (good for chocolate), and more. They also carry sterling silver "pudding charms" to bake into your cakes as in the English-Style Fruitcake with a Twist (page 79). Call for store locations in Washington and California.

SWEET CELEBRATIONS/MAID OF SCANDINAVIA

P. O. Box 39426

Edina, MN 55439

(612) 943-1508

(800) 328-6722

Maid of Scandinavia was a wonderful company now called Sweet Celebrations. The catalog is much smaller now, but just ask for what you want. They have an extensive line of decorator equipment including tips, pans, columns and separators, some ingredients, including Merckens chocolates, and more.

THE VERMONT COUNTRY STORE

Mail Order Office

P.O. Box 3000

Manchester Center, VT 05255-3000

(802) 362-2400

FAX (802) 362-0285

Customer Service (802) 362-4647

This company is a walk-in retail store as well as a mail-order business. They sell quince jelly, which can be hard to find. They also carry wonderfully, thirsty, and inexpensive kitchen towels, something I never have enough of, and a hand-crank apple peeler that I would not be without.

WILLIAMS-SONOMA

P.O. Box 7456

San Francisco, CA 94120

(415) 421-4242

(800) 541-2233

FAX (415) 421-5253

Famous for its mail-order catalog, Williams-Sonoma also has retail stores nationwide. You will find great measuring tools, Boyajian oils, vanilla, some chocolate and cocoa, and equipment.

WILTON INDUSTRIES, INC.

2240 West 75th Street

Woodbridge, IL 60517

(630) 963-7100

(800) 772-7111

Their great catalog offers heavy-duty cake pans, tips, colors, plastic molds, cardboard rounds, and much more. The catalog functions as an idea book as well.

BIBLIOGRAPHY

Amendola, Joseph. *The Baker's Manual.* Rochelle Park, N.J.: Hayden Book Company, 1972.

Amendola, Joseph, and Donald Lundberg. *Understanding Baking.* New York: Van Nostrand Reinhold, 1970.

Beranbaum, Rose Levy. *The Cake Bible.* New York: William Morrow, 1988.

——— *A Passion for Chocolate.* New York: William Morrow, 1989.

Bilheaux, Roland. *Decorations, Borders and Letters, Marzipan and Modern Desserts.* New York: Van Nostrand Reinhold, 1987.

Bloom, Carole. *The International Dictionary of Desserts, Pastries, Confections.* New York: Hearst Books, 1995.

Boyle, Tish, and Timothy Moriarty. *Grand Finales.* New York: Van Nostrand Reinhold, 1997.

Braker, Flo. *The Simple Art of Perfect Baking.* New York: William Morrow, 1985.

Careme, Antoine. *Le Patissier Royal Parisien.* 10th ed., vol. 1 and 2. Paris, 1828.

Clifton, Claire. *Edible Flowers.* New York: McGraw Hill Book Co., 1984.

Dannenberg, Linda. *Paris Boulangerie Patisserie.* New York: Clarkson Potter, 1994.

Desaulniers, Marcel. *Death by Chocolate.* New York: Rizzoli, 1992.

Dubois, Urbain. *Grand Livre des Patissiers et des Confiseurs.* 2 vols. Paris: Librarie E. Dentu, Galerie d'Orléans, Palais-Royal, 1883.

Facciola, Stephen. *Cornucopia: A Sourcebook of Edible Plants.* Vista, Calif.: Kampong Publications, 1990.

Ford, Mary. *Decorative Sugar Flowers for Cakes.* Dorsett, England: Mary Ford Publications Ltd., 1991.

Friberg, Bo. *The Professional Pastry Chef.* New York: Van Nostrand Reinhold, 1996.

Gonzalez, Elaine. *Chocolate Artistry.* Chicago: Contemporary Books, 1983.

Goodbody, Mary, and Jane Stacey. *Pretty Cakes.* New York: Harper and Row, 1986.

Hannemann, L. J. *Patisserie, Professional Pastry and Dessert Preparation.* New York: Van Nostrand Reinhold, 1971.

Healy, Bruce, and Paul Bugat. *Mastering the Art of French Pastry.* New York: Barrons, 1984.

Heatter, Maida. *American Desserts.* New York: Alfred A. Knopf, 1985.

———*Best Dessert Book Ever.* New York: Random House, 1990.

———*New Book of Great Desserts.* New York: Alfred A. Knopf, 1982.

———*Book of Great Chocolate Desserts.* New York: Alfred A. Knopf, 1983.

Lang, Jenifer Harvey. *Tastings.* New York: Crown Publishers, 1986.

Lenotre, Gaston. *Faites Votre Patisserie comme Lenotre.* Paris: Flammarion, 1975.

Lewis, T. Percy, and A. G. Bromley. *The Victorian Book of Cakes, Recipes, Techniques and Decorations from the Golden Age of Cake-Making.* New York: Portland House, 1991.

Linx, Robert. *La Maison du Chocolat.* Paris: Robert Laffont, 1992.

Lodge, Nicholas. *The International School of Sugarcraft.* Vol. 1 and 2. London: Merehurst, 1988.

Malgieri, Nick. *How To Bake.* New York: HarperCollins, 1995.

Medrich, Alice. *Cocolat.* New York: Warner Books, 1990.

———*Chocolate and the Art of Low-Fat Desserts.* New York: Warner Books, 1994.

Montagne, Prosper. *The New Larousse Gastronomique.* New York: Crown Publishers, 1977.

Morse, Kitty. *Edible Flowers, a Kitchen Companion with Recipes.* California: Ten Speed Press, 1995.

Murfitt, Janice. *The Essential Cake Decorator.* London: Anness Publishing, 1995.

Peters, Colette. *Colette's Wedding Cakes.* Boston: Little, Brown and Co., 1995.

———*Colette's Cakes.* Boston: Little, Brown and Co., 1991.

Purdy, Susan. *Have Your Cake and Eat it Too.* New York: William Morrow, 1993.

———*Piece of Cake.* New York: Atheneum, 1989.

Rosbottom, Betty. *First Impressions.* New York: William Morrow, 1992.

Roux, Michel. *Finest Desserts.* New York: Rizzoli, 1995.

Sax, Richard. *Classic Home Desserts.* Vermont: Chapters Publishing, 1993.

Silverton, Nancy. *Desserts.* New York: Harper and Row, 1986.

Sorosky, Marlene. *Entertaining on the Run.* New York: William Morrow, 1994.

Stewart, Martha. *Weddings.* New York: Clarkson Potter, 1987.

———*Entertaining.* New York: Clarkson Potter, 1982.

Thuries, Yves. *Le Livre de Recettes d'un Compagnon du tour de France, La Nouvelle Patissier, Les Pieces Montees, Le Travail du Sucre.* Société Editar, Cordes-sur-Ciel, 1979.

Walter, Carole. *Great Cakes.* New York: Ballantine Books, 1991.

Welch, Adrienne. *Sweet Seduction.* New York: Harper Colophon, 1984.

INDEX

Acorns, Marzipan, 74
Albert Uster Imports, Inc., 186
Allergies, food, 11
Almond(s)
    Banana Cake, 73
        with Amaretto
            Buttercream and
            Marzipan Leaves, 73
    Chocolate, Torte with Sugared
        Nuts, 21
    to peel, 147
Amaretto Buttercream, 140
    Almond Banana Cake with
        Marzipan Leaves, 73
Apple Cheesecake, Sour Cream,
    113, 114
Apricot
    Filling, Marzipan Chocolate
        Cake with Cognac and, 83
    Lekvar, 121
    Roses, 119
    White Chocolate Satin, Cake
        with White Chocolate
        Flowers and Grapes, 121

Baked Alaska Wedding Cake,
    Flaming, 39
Baking, planning, 10, 13
Baking core, 178
Baking pans. See Pans
Baking soda, measuring, 4
Baking times, 5
Banana Cake, Almond, 73
    with Amaretto Buttercream
        and Marzipan Leaves, 73
Bases, cake, 178

Bellini Cake with Champagne
    Flutes, 55
Bench scraper, 178
Beranbaum, Rose Levy, 93, 113
Bergamot essential oil, 51
Beryl's Cake Decorating
    Equipment, 186
Bilheux, Roland, 173
Bittersweet Chocolate
    Ganache, 23, 145
    Sauce, 127
Blackberry Curd, 142
    Buttercream, 142
    White Cake with Lemon Curd,
        Pressed Flowers, and, 37
Blue Magic, 178
Bottles, plastic squeeze, 183
Braker, Flo, 178
Bridge Co., The, 186
Broadway Panhandler, 186
Budget, 11
Butter, clarified, 4
Buttercream
    Amaretto, 140
        Almond Banana Cake
            with Marzipan Leaves
            and, 73
    amounts of, 8
    Blackberry Curd, 142
    Caramel, 33
    Coconut, 141
    covering a cake with, 154–56
    Cranberry, 25
    Dark Chocolate, 141
    Egg Yolk, 142
    Espresso, 141

Grand Marnier, Poppyseed
    Cake with Orange
    Marmalade Filling and, 63
    Honey or Maple Syrup, 143
    Italian Meringue, 139
        freezing, 6
        to reconstitute, 140
    Kahlúa, 140
    Lemon Curd, 141
    Liqueur-Accented, 140
    Marmalade, 141
    Raspberry, 141
    Vanilla, 140
        Buttermilk Spice Cake
            with Marzipan Sweets
            and, 87
    White Chocolate, 141
Buttermilk
    Lemon, Cake, 107
        White Chocolate , with
            Sea Shells, 105
    Spice Cake, 87
        with Vanilla Buttercream
            and Marzipan Sweets, 87

Cake(s). See also Cheesecake
    Almond Banana, 73
        with Amaretto
            Buttercream and
            Marzipan Leaves, 73
    Bellini, with Champagne
        Flutes, 55
    Buttermilk Spice, 87
        with Vanilla Buttercream
            and Marzipan Sweets, 87
    Chocolate

Almond Torte with
    Sugared Nuts, 21
    Raspberry, 29
Chocolate Raspberry Truffle,
    93, 95
Coffee, Ginger Peach Pecan, 47
Croquembouche, 101
Dacquoise, 135
Double Espresso Wedding, 43
Earl Grey Chocolate Mousse,
    51
Flaming Baked Alaska
    Wedding, 39
Fruitcake, English-Style, with
    a Twist, 79
Gâteau Opéra, 109
Génoise, 131
    Nut, 132
Gianduja Truffle, 75
Hazelnut Dacquoise and
    Hazelnut Génoise Wedding,
    91
Honey Lavender, 97
Honey Maple Carrot, with
    Pecans and Raisins, 19
Lemon Buttermilk, 107
Marzipan Chocolate, 85
    with Apricot Filling and
        Cognac, 83
Poppyseed, 63
    with Orange Marmalade
        Filling and Grand
        Marnier Buttercream, 63
Pound, 130
Pound, Tahitian Vanilla Bean, 69
    with Orchids and Fruit, 69

Pumpkin, with Crystallized
Ginger, Walnuts, and Dried
Cranberries, 25
Sachertorte, 117, 119
Savory Smoked Salmon
Cheesecake Wedding, 31
Sour Cream Chocolate Cake,
134
Tropical Passion Coconut,
with Macadamias, 67
Vanilla Sponge, 60
with Raspberry Mousse
Filling, Italian
Meringue, and
Crystallized Flowers, 59
White, 136
with Lemon Curd,
Blackberry Curd, and
Pressed Flowers, 37
White Chocolate, 137
Lemon Buttermilk, with
Sugar Sea Shells, 105
Satin Apricot, with White
Chocolate Flowers and
Grapes, 121
Cake bases, 178
Cake comb, 178
Cake drums, 152, 181
Cake leveler, 178
Cake pans. *See* Pans
Calyx, 172
Caramel, 103
Buttercream, 33
Rum Cake with Caramelized
Walnuts, 33
Caramelized Coral Fans, 108
Caramelized Nuts, 149–50
Sliced, 149
Whole, 150
Caramelized Walnuts, Caramel
Rum Cake with, 33
Cardboard rounds, 152, 178
Carrot Cake with Pecans and
Raisins, Honey Maple, 19
Champagne, Peach Filling, 55
Chandré, 186
Chantilly Cream, 126
Cheesecake
Savory Smoked Salmon,
Wedding Cake, 31
Sour Cream Apple, 113, 114
Chef's Catalog, The, 186
Cherubs, Golden Sugar-Molded, 33
Chocolate
Almond Torte with Sugared
Nuts, 21
Bittersweet
Ganache, 23, 145
Sauce, 127
Curls, 29, 166–68
-Dipped Spoons, 40
Earl Grey, Cake, 52
Mousse, 51

Earl Grey, Mousse, 53
filigree, 166–67, 169
flowers, 169
Ganache. *See* Ganache
initials, 128
leaves, 166–69
Marzipan, Cake, 85
with Apricot Filling and
Cognac, 83
melting, 6–7
molding, 166
Plastic, 148–49
grapes, 170
Raspberry Cake, 29
Raspberry Truffle Cake, 93, 95
Sour Cream, Cake, 134
tempering, 165–66
White. *See* White Chocolate
working with, 165–66
Chocolate Gallery, The/N.Y. Cake
and Baking Distributors, 187
Chocolate thermometer, 166, 184
Clarified butter, 4
Cocoa Piping Gel, 53
Coconut
Buttercream, 141
Cake with Macadamias,
Tropical Passion, 67
essence, 67
Coffee. *See* Espresso
Coffee Cake, Ginger Peach Pecan,
47
Cognac
Marzipan Chocolate Cake
with Apricot Filling and, 83
Truffle Filling, 109
Coloring marzipan, 173–74
Combing tool, 178
Cookie cutters, 179
Cookie sheets, 183–84
Cooking spray, 4
Cooling a cake, 5
Cooling racks, 179
Coral Fans, Caramelized Sugar, 108
Corn syrup, measuring, 4
Coulis, Raspberry, 127
Country Kitchen, 187
Cranberry(-ies)
Buttercream, 25
Dried, Pumpkin Cake with
Crystallized Ginger, Walnuts,
and, 25
Purée, 25
Cream
about, 126
Chantilly, 126
Cream Cheese Frosting, White
Chocolate, 144
Creativity (creative process), 10,
12, 13
Crème Anglaise, 126
Croquembouche, 101
serving, 104

Crystallized Flowers, 163–64
Vanilla Sponge Cake with
Raspberry Mousse Filling,
Italian Meringue, and, 59
Crystallized fruit, 165
Cuisine, La, 188
Curd
Blackberry, 142
Lemon, 142
Cutters
cookie, 179
gum paste, 179
Cutting and serving tiered cakes,
175–76
Dacquoise, 135
Hazelnut, and Hazelnut
Génoise Wedding Cake, 91
Daisies, 172
Date of the wedding, 10
Decorating, planning, 10, 13
Decorating tips, 179
Decorating turntable, 179
Decorations, seaside, 105
Decorator's comb, 178
Dessert
buffet, 2, 3
cake as, 3
Dessert sauces and creams
Bittersweet Chocolate Sauce,
127
Chantilly Cream, 126
Crème Anglaise, 126
plating techniques, 128
Dill Toasts, 32
"Dip and sweep" method of mea-
suring, 4
Doneness, testing for, 5
Double Espresso Wedding Cake, 43
Dredger, 179
Drying flowers, 164
Duffy, Elizabeth, 74
Dusting bag, 179
Earl Grey
Cake, 52
Chocolate Mousse, 51
Chocolate Mousse, 53
Syrup, 51
Easy-Leaf, 187
Egg Yolk Buttercream, 142
English-Style Fruitcake with a
Twist, 79
Equipment, list of, 10
Escoffier, Alain, 173
Espresso
Buttercream, 141
Double, Wedding Cake, 43
Génoise, 44
Soaking Syrup, 43
Filling
amounts of, 8

Apricot, Marzipan Chocolate
Cake with Cognac and, 83
Champagne Peach, 55
Cognac Truffle, 109
Orange Marmalade, Poppyseed
Cake with Grand Marnier
Buttercream and, 63
techniques, 154
Finishing touches, 13
Fisher, M. F. K., 79
Flame tamer, 180
Flaming Baked Alaska Wedding
Cake, 39
Flavors, couple's favorite, 11
Flour, measuring, 4
Flowers, 162–65
arranging, 165
chocolate plastic or marzipan,
169–73
Crystallized, 163–64
Vanilla Sponge Cake with
Raspberry Mousse
Filling, Italian
Meringue, and, 59
drying, 164
edible, 162, 163
Pressed, 164
White Cake with Lemon
Curd, Blackberry Curd,
and, 37
purchasing, 164–65
White Chocolate Grapes and,
White Chocolate Satin
Apricot Cake with, 121
wrapping and wiring stems
and flower spikes, 164
Flower spikes, 164
Food allergies, 11
Food processor, 180
Freezing
cake components, 6
cakes, 14
Frosting
Italian Meringue, 61
White Chocolate Cream
Cheese, 144
Fruit
crystallized, 165
fresh, about, 128
Layer, Fresh, 71
Fruitcake, 80
English-Style, with a Twist, 79
Ganache
Bittersweet Chocolate, 23, 145
glazing with, 156–57
Whipped, 145
Gâteau Opéra, 109
Génoise, 131
Espresso, 44
Hazelnut, Hazelnut Dacquoise
and, Wedding Cake, 91
Nut, 132

Square, 134
Gianduja Truffle Cake, 75
Ginger
    Crystallized, Pumpkin Cake
        with Walnuts, Dried
        Cranberries, and, 25
    Peach Pecan Coffee Cake, 47
Glaze
    Quince, 115
    Vanilla Icing, 49
Glazing with Ganache, 156–57
Godiva chocolate shells, seahorses,
    and starfish, 105
Golden Sugar-Molded Cherubs, 33
Gold leaf, 96, 174–75
Gold powder, 128, 175
Gold skewings, 174, 175
Grand Marnier
    Buttercream, Poppyseed Cake
        with Orange Marmalade
        Filling and, 63
    Pastry Cream, 146
Grapes
    chocolate plastic, 170
    White Chocolate Flowers and,
        White Chocolate Satin
        Apricot Cake, 121
Greenery, purchasing and arrang-
    ing, 164–65
Green Valley Growers, 187
Guests, number of, 10–11
Gum paste cutters, 179

Hazelnut(s)
    Dacquoise, and Hazelnut
        Génoise Wedding Cake, 91
    Génoise, Hazelnut Dacquoise
        and, Wedding Cake, 91
    to peel, 147
    to toast, 148
Honey
    Buttercream, 143
    Lavender Cake, 97
    Maple Carrot Cake with
        Pecans and Raisins, 19
    measuring, 4

I. C. E. S. (International Cake
    Exploration Society), 185
Icing
    Glaze, Vanilla, 49
    Royal, 81, 144
        Monogram, 97
Icing spatula, 180–81
Ingredient and equipment lists, 10,
    12–13
Initial planning stage, 10–11
Initials, chocolate, 128
Italian Meringue
    Buttercream, 139
        freezing, 6
        to reconstitute, 140

for Flaming Baked Alaska
    Wedding Cake, 39
    Frosting, 61
    Vanilla Sponge Cake with
        Raspberry Mousse Filling,
        Crystallized Flowers, and, 59

J.B. Prince Co., 187

Kahlúa Buttercream, 140
King Arthur Flour Baker's Catalog,
    187
Knife, slicing, 184

La Cuisine, 188
Lavender
    Cake, Honey, 97
    Syrup, 99
Layers
    defined, 2
    splitting into, 153–54
Leaf cutters, 172
Leaf forms, metal, 173
Leaf veiners, 172, 181
Leaves
    Chocolate, 172
    Crystallized, 163
    Marzipan, 74, 172
        Almond Banana Cake
            with Amaretto
            Buttercream and, 73
Lekvar, Apricot, 121
Lemon
    Buttermilk Cake, 107
        White Chocolate, with
            Sugar Sea Shells, 105
    Curd, 142
        Buttercream, 141
        White Cake with
            Blackberry Curd,
            Pressed Flowers, and, 37
    leaves, for Chocolate Almond
        Torte with Sugared Nuts, 23
    oil, 105
Leveler, cake, 178
Leveling cakes, 152–53
Light Raspberry Mousse, 59
Liqueur
    -Accented Buttercream, 140
    Crème Anglaise with, 127
    -Flavored Syrup, 147
    passion fruit, 67
Liquids, measuring, 4
Lists, ingredient and equipment,
    10, 12–13
Lo Manto, Suzanne, 87
Luce Corporation, 188

Macadamias
    about, 67, 148
    Tropical Passion Coconut
        Cake with, 67
McNamara, Mary, 25

Magi-Cake Strips, 5, 47, 181
Mail-order companies, 185–89
Malgieri, Nick, 117
Maple
    Honey, Carrot Cake with
        Pecans and Raisins, 19
    Syrup Buttercream, 143
Marmalade
    Buttercream, 141
    Orange, Filling, Poppyseed
        Cake with Grand Marnier
        Buttercream and, 63
Marzipan, 148
    Chocolate Cake, 85
        with Apricot Filling and
            Cognac, 83
    Coloring, 173–74
    covering a cake with, 157–59
    flowers, 169–73
    Leaves, Almond Banana Cake
        with Amaretto Buttercream
        and, 73
    Leaves and Acorns, 74
    Sweets, 89, 173
        Buttermilk Spice Cake
            with Vanilla Buttercream
            and, 87
Masonite boards, 152, 181
Matfer Kitchen and Bakery
    Equipment, 188
Maxi Flowers à la Carte, 188
Meadowsweets, 188
Measuring cups and spoons, 181
Measuring ingredients, 3–4
Melting chocolate, 6–7
Meringue, Italian. *See* Italian
    Meringue
Microwave oven, 181–82
    melting chocolate in, 6
Mixers, 180
Molding
    sugar, 173
    chocolate, 166
Molds with sea themes, 105
Monogram, 97
Mousse
    Earl Grey Chocolate, 53
        Cake, 51
    Raspberry
        Filling, Italian Meringue,
            and Crystallized
            Flowers, Vanilla Sponge
            Cake with, 59
        Light, 59

Nonreactive saucepans, 182
Nougatine, 102
    second and third batches of, 103
Nut(s)
    Caramelized, 149–50
    for Dacquoise, 135
    Génoise, 132
    Square, 134

to peel, 147–48
Sliced Sugared, 149
Sugared, Chocolate Almond
    Torte with, 21
to toast, 148
N.Y. Cake and Baking Distributors,
    187

Orange Marmalade Filling and
    Grand Marnier Buttercream,
    Poppyseed Cake with, 63
Orchids, vanda, 45
Outdoor weddings, refrigeration of
    cakes for, 14
Oven racks, 5
Ovens, 182
Oven temperature, 5
Oven thermometers, 182

PAM, 4
Pans, 182
    preparation of, 4
    removing cakes from, 5–6
    sheet, 183–84
    sizes, 183
    volumes of, 2, 3
Parchment paper, 182
    cones, making, 7–8
Parrish's Cake Decorating
    Supplies, Inc., 188
Passion Coconut Cake with
    Macadamias, Tropical, 67
Passion fruit
    liqueur, 67
    syrup, 67
Pastry bags, 7, 182
Pastry Cream, Vanilla, 146
Pâte à Choux, 101
Peach
    Filling, Champagne, 55
    Ginger, Pecan Coffee Cake, 47
Pecan(s)
    Ginger Peach, Coffee Cake, 47
    Honey Maple Carrot Cake
        with Raisins and, 19
    to toast, 148
Pillars, assembling cakes with,
    159–62
Piping Gel, Cocoa, 53
Planning stages, 10–15
    baking and decorating, 10, 13
    creative process, 10, 12
    initial planning stage, 10–11
    serving the cake, 10, 15
    storage and transportation, 10,
        14–15
    time schedule and ingredient
        and equipment lists, 10
Plating techniques, 127–28
Poppyseed Cake, 63
    with Orange Marmalade
        Filling and Grand Marnier
        Buttercream, 63

Pound Cake, 130
Pressed flowers, 164
Pumpkin Cake, 26
    with Crystallized Ginger,
        Walnuts, and Dried
        Cranberries, 25

Quince Glaze, 115

Racks, cooling, 179
Raisins, Honey Maple Carrot
    Cake with Pecans and, 19
Raspberry(-ies)
    Buttercream, 141
    Chocolate, Cake, 29
    Chocolate, Truffle Cake, 93, 95
    Coulis, 127
    for Decoration, 96
    Mousse
        Filling, Italian Meringue,
            and Crystallized
            Flowers, Vanilla Sponge
            Cake with, 59
        Light, 59
Reception
    degree of formality of, 11
    time of, 11, 12
Refrigeration. *See also* Storing
    of cakes, 6, 14
Releasing cakes, 182
Resources, 185–89
Rosbottom, Betty, 117
Roses
    Apricot, 119
    for Chocolate Almond Torte
        with Sugared Nuts, 23
    sculpting, 170–71
Royal Icing, 81, 144
    Monogram, 97
    rubber spatula for, 183
Rubber spatulas, 183
Rum, Caramel, Cake with
    Caramelized Walnuts, 33

Sachertorte, 117, 119
Salmon Cheesecake Wedding
    Cake, Savory Smoked, 31
Saturating cakes (with sherry), 81
Saucepans, nonreactive, 182
Sauces and creams.
    See Dessert sauces and creams
Savory Smoked Salmon
    Cheesecake Wedding Cake, 31
Scale, 4
Schedule, 10, 12–13
Scraper, triangular, 184

Seaside decorations, 105
Serving cakes, 10, 15, 175–76
Servings, sizes and number of, 2–3
Sheet pans, 183–84
Sherry, Saturating cakes with, 81
Sifting, 4
Silver leaf, 174–75
Silver powder, 128, 175
Silver skewings, 175
Sliced Sugared Nuts, 149
Slicing knife, 184
Smoked Salmon Cheesecake
    Wedding Cake, Savory, 31
Sorbet, for Flaming Baked Alaska
    Wedding Cake, 39
Sour Cream
    Apple Cheesecake, 113, 114
    Chocolate Cake, 134
Spatulas
    icing, 180–81
    rubber, 183
Spice Cake, Buttermilk, 87
    with Vanilla Buttercream and
        Marzipan Sweets, 87
Sponge Cake, Vanilla, 60
    with Raspberry Mousse
        Filling, Italian Meringue, and
        Crystallized Flowers, 59
Spoons, Chocolate-Dipped, 40
Spun Sugar, 103
Square Nut Génoise, 134
Squeeze bottles, plastic, 183
Stacked cakes, cutting and serving,
    175–76
Stacking cake tiers, 159
Stems, wrapping and wiring, 164
Stephanotis-like blossoms, 171–72
Stewart, Martha, 113
Storing
    cake components, 6
    of cake components, 10, 14–15
    clarified butter, 4
    dry ingredients, 3–4
    pastry bags, 7
Strainer, 184
Sugar
    Molding, 173
        Golden Sugar-Molded
            Cherubs, 33
    Sea Shells, White Chocolate
        Lemon Buttermilk Cake
        with, 105
    Spun, 103
    Syrup, 147
        adding to a cake, 154
Super Elasticlay, 105
Sur La Table, 188

Sweet Celebrations/Maid of
    Scandinavia, 189
Syrup
    amounts of, 8
    Earl Grey, 51
    Espresso Soaking, 43
    Lavender, 99
    Liqueur-Flavored, 147
    passion fruit, 67
    Sugar, 147
        adding to a cake, 154
    Vanilla, 147

Tabletop decorations, 175
Tahitian Vanilla Bean
    about, 69
    Pound Cake, 69
        with Orchids and Fruit, 69
Tamis, 184
Techniques
    baking, 5
    plating, 127–28
Testing for doneness, 5
Thermometers, 184
    chocolate, 166, 184
    oven, 182
Tiers
    defined, 2
    freezing, 6
    making extra, 2
    on pillars, assembling, 159–62
    stacking, 159
    top, saving for first anniver-
        sary, 3, 10–11
Times, baking, 5
Time schedule, 10, 12–13
Tips, decorating, 179
Tip Saver, 184
Toasts, Dill, 32
Torte
    Chocolate Almond, with
        Sugared Nuts, 21
    Sachertorte, 117, 119
Torting, 153–54
Transportation of cake, 10, 14–15
Triangular scraper, 184
Tropical Passion Coconut Cake
    with Macadamias, 67
Truffle
    Chocolate Raspberry, Cake,
        93, 95
    Filling, Cognac, 109
Turntable, decorating, 179

Vanda orchids, 45
Vanilla
    Bean, Tahitian

about, 69
    Pound Cake, 69
    Pound Cake with Orchids
        and Fruit, 69
Buttercream, 140
    Buttermilk Spice Cake
        with Marzipan Sweets
        and, 87
custard sauce (Crème
    Anglaise), 126
Icing Glaze, 49
Pastry Cream, 146
Sponge Cake, 60
    with Raspberry Mousse
        Filling, Italian Meringue,
        and Crystallized Flowers,
        59
Syrup, 147
Vegetable oil-based cooking spray, 4
Veiners, leaf, 181
Veining mats, 172
Vermont Country Store, 189

Walnuts
    Caramelized, Caramel Rum
        Cake with, 33
    Pumpkin Cake with
        Crystallized Ginger, Dried
        Cranberries, and, 25
    to toast, 148
Walter, Carole, 132
Weighing ingredients, 4
Whipped Ganache, 145
Whisks, 184
White Cake, 136
    with Lemon Curd, Blackberry
        Curd, and Pressed Flowers, 37
White Chocolate
    about, 105
    Buttercream, 141
    Cake, 137
    Cream Cheese Frosting, 144
    flowers, 169
    Flowers and Grapes, White
        Chocolate Satin Apricot
        Cake with, 121
    Lemon Buttermilk Cake with
        Sugar Sea Shells, 105
    plastic, 148, 149
    Satin Apricot Cake with
        White Chocolate Flowers
        and Grapes, 121
Williams-Sonoma, 189
Wilton Industries, 189
Wrapping a cake, 6